Barbara Naylor's

The Basic Ingredient

The Becomer's Balanced Diet & Complete Weight Loss Program

HAROLD SHAW PUBLISHERS
WHEATON, ILLINOIS

Naylor, Barbara, 1922–
The Basic Ingredient.

Bibliography: p. 270
1. Reducing diets–Recipes.
2. Reducing–moral and religious aspects.
I. Title
RM222.2.N38   641.5'635   78-12404

ISBN 0-87788-057-3

To all who recognize our common need for the power to become lean and effective. Ginny found it in THE BASIC INGREDIENT, and so can you.

CONTENTS

INTRODUCTION

Did you ever wonder why your diet doesn't work? Are you disappointed with diet pills, candy vitamins, and two-dimension diets? Do liquid diets and crash diets leave you limp? Are you utterly confused with carbohydrate and calorie counting? Have you found that exercise alone is a time consuming treadmill for burning calories that continue to pile up because you can't stop eating? Are you disgusted because amphetamines keep you awake and offer only temporary weight loss, leaving habits unchanged and producing risky side-effects?

There is no shortcut to losing weight and keeping it off. If you've tried them all, you may be ready now to try *the real thing*. A safe, medically proven, balanced diet and exercise program is absolutely necessary. But the key to successful dieting and satisfying lifetime maintenance is *motivation*. If a doctor's prodding, fear of health hazards, even ridicule or pressure from family and friends still leave you apathetic and unmotivated, hang on. There is a more dependable key to unlock your potential! The more you use it, the more dependable it becomes. The priceless key, the basic ingredient for a successful diet regime is supportive love to build up your own self-respect. That's how I have learned to cope, to eat well, and to hold a high self-image, maintaining my thirty-pound weight-loss for seven years.

A group can motivate with the therapy of contagious enthusiasm and concern. However, not everyone can afford to join a diet club in these inflationary times. If that is your case, you're not alone. Overweight is a typical American predicament.

Do you have a friend who also feels desperate for real help with a weight problem? Where two or more are gathered together with love to motivate worthy desire and purpose, the Lord has promised to instruct: magnifying and supporting your good intentions. Instead of wasting time with wishful thinking or undermining your confidence with unstable human will-power, how would you like to avail yourself of the support of an automatic programmed Instructor within? Deep in the human soul is a power potential which can be sparked, fanned, and fueled to change eating behavior. Love is the beginning and the long term generator of successful dieting and normal lifetime eating habits.

Don't underestimate the power of love. It's the mysterious power behind the universe. Man will never discover a power greater than the Almighty to hold the vast galaxies in place. The intricate pattern and functions of human life are His marvelous design—His highest creation. God, Himself, is Love. We've heard that it's Love that makes the world go around. Through population growth, Love stimulates housing, banking, business, industry, and education. Good will is a basis for credit, through faith—one of the remarkable facets of Love. Even the Dow Jones Industrial Averages depend on the confidence apparent in business. All success and confidence are ultimately derived from Divine Love.

Love is the power and purpose of creation. The most amazing thing about Divine Love is that it is also personal. It is at the point of greatest need that Love is strongest. With a bit of faith, Love can move mounds of pounds! Look to the Creator of your body, mind, and spirit: the Author and Finisher of your faith. In His hand is health: the regulation of every body process, assimilation, digestion, peristalsis, breathing, circulation, metabolism, growth, and healing. Even our decisions, appetites and emotions can be subject to His control if we are ready for constructive help. He not only created us, but came in the flesh to fulfill His work and save us from ourselves by His internal control: a vivid demonstration of the power of Love to change lives. Love guaranteed your beautiful machine, even gave you many duplicate parts.

Give your tired body, mind, and spirit back to the Manufacturer. Stand for Something, or you'll fall for anything! With His help and the help of a friend, you can discover how easy it is to follow a nutritionally balanced diet and exercise program. You can become the unique child of God He created you to be: controlled from within; effective in work, recreation, rest, and personal relationships. You can be an integrated whole person with a life directed to larger purposes that fulfill. By an act of your own will you can choose to lose weight. Do you see that need but feel that something is missing in the way of motivation?

It's not a sin to be fat. Overweight is a symptom of dissatisfaction, boredom, or unhappiness, each, perhaps, unrecognized. *The real sin is blindness: the refusal to admit to personal helplessness.* Don't limit yourself. Look in a full-length mirror and believe what you see. If you can face reality, you can be guided by faith and Love to do something about your condition. Love can free you from the slavery of insidious habits. Love can motivate and steady you in a true pattern for living. Let Love dissolve your resentments and pounds day by day. Discouragement and apathy disappear as the new perspective and confidence shape your life style. Values, motives, and weight are lifted together by caring. Love is the oil in the beautiful machine.

This volume is not merely a collection of kitchen-tested diet recipes. It presents proven methods and reasonable goals for sensible, permanent weight reduction. The basic ingredient is Love, the writer's motive to stimulate your own faith in your Creator and in yourself, His masterpiece. The human body is His temple. With our consent He can clean house without pills, promotions, or paperwork.

Both Jews and Christians affirm the great Commandment of our common heritage: "You shall love the Lord your God with all your heart, and with all your soul, and with all your mind. . . . you shall love your neighbor as yourself." (Matthew 22:37b, 39b, KJV) When the Old Testament prophet exhorted people to "fear" the Lord, he inferred respect and love. As we learn to respect and love ourselves as well as our Maker, we discover and attain our true self-image. Only then can we develop purposeful eating habits with satisfaction.

Originally, dietary laws were set down in the Old Testament Book of Leviticus. Fish, fowl, bread, and milk were recommended in safe combinations and portions for the needs of those days without refrigeration. Manna was supplied with instructions for one day's use at a time. From the beginning, God has provided for our real needs. He has been concerned about what we eat and has endorsed His own provisions. He gave us the power of choice, to follow His directions or suffer the consequences.

In the miraculous New Testament story of the loaves and fishes, Love was the multiplying factor. Enough bread and fish were passed to all because Love motivated the willing heart of a little boy to share. His example was contagious. It was Love that satisfied the hungry thousands: a lesson in group therapy. In the homes of our affluent nation we are more hungry for love and understanding than we are for bread. Even the failure of our Foreign Aid program can be traced to our calculating political motives which are void of love and real understanding. Whatever mistakes we've made as a nation or as individuals, we don't have to wallow in despair.

God's not dead, He's bread! When you think of home-made bread, associate the kneading with discipline, the growing yeast with faith and the baking aroma with the winsomeness of Love. The breaking and eating of bread symbolize fellowship and sacrifice. Since we're made in God's image, we need more than bread as food. When Jesus was tempted with food at the point of real hunger, he said, "Man shall not live by bread alone, but by every word that proceeds out of the mouth of God." (Matthew 4:4b)

Whatever our faith or denomination, we are all one body. We have one God, the Father of us all. Scientists are more and more awed as they unlock the secrets of the earth and discover God's marvelous provisions for His children. Everyone ever born has the capacity to believe and become a child of God. With the facing of your need and the provision God has made in His Son, you can change your physical appearance and your inner attitudes.

HOW TO BEGIN
You and a friend may help yourselves to happiness together, trusting

the Creator and using the Becomers' Balanced Diet and the exercises recommended in Chapter 11. Keep a record to show your progress week by week. If you slip, remember, you're still human. But your overall success will encourage you to grab the lifeline and start again immediately. Weigh each other at the same time each week with the same clothing, in stockinged feet. You do need a human friend to weigh you regularly; otherwise it's too easy to rationalize at the scale, or, worse, to avoid it completely. You can lose twenty pounds in ten weeks if you have the desire and the Love to lean on. Chart your course (See Appendix A). You won't get in any trouble if you take the Lord in one hand and the diet in the other. You won't even need to feel hungry!

Intelligent shopping for your Becomer's Balanced Diet foods will be less expensive and faster than in past days when you used to stand pondering over the cookies and potato chips. In our program, we don't use convenience foods. Prepared salad dressings, for example, have unknown quantities of eggs and starches which are not on our program, although labeling is improving as the computer checkout system develops. It's much easier to keep track of what we're eating by starting from scratch; planning the portion with appreciation; using only one gourmet dish at a time to simplify calculations. Remember, store packages labeled "diet" may be planned with other kinds of diets in mind, such as low sodium. It is worth the effort to make and follow your own diet recipes. They taste better cooked with Love!

Preparing our recipes is faster and easier than making cakes and pie crust. You will need Teflon pans, a lecithin spray such as Pam or Mazola No Stick, a blender, and some postal scales to weigh protein portions. The fare will tempt any family, or please the ladies at luncheon. You may eat simply, according to the menu, with 150 foods to choose from, or you may try some of the easy, exciting gourmet combinations described in the latter half of this book. To be right up-to-date, we have also included both standard and metric measurements throughout the book. The menu is planned not only for low calorie content and weight loss, but for variety and optimum nutrition. The calories have already been counted. Sensory appeal is achieved with color, texture, flavor and temperature contrasts. Attractive service puts it over with the family.

In one week the scales should indicate approximately a five pound weight loss. If you can let Love help you for a day—then for a week—you have it made for a lifetime. Praise the Lord and pass the French string beans!

Do you really want self-control? The Lord wants to be your Instructor within. He is your health and strength, your life and breath,; your one last hope. Give Him a chance to direct your efforts. Put your hand [and your life] in His hand. He'll train your mind, guide your shopping, and recondition your taste buds. He'll give you peace of mind, releasing you from all those horrible compulsions. He will equip you with joy and satisfaction day by day. For the dieter, self-control is the ultimate fruit of the Spirit. It grows out of the parent virtue, Love. He cares for you. Accept His Love. How else can we accept an overfat condition without self-hate? "We love Him, because He first loved us." (I John 4:19) Together the load gets lighter, the mind gets brighter, and the heart gets right with God and with people. Make each day count with this prayer of commitment:

Teach us to number our days and recognize how few they are; help us to spend them as we should . . . and let the Lord our God favor us and give us success. (Psalm 90:12, 17 TLB)

PART ONE

1
MOTIVATION

FACING REALITY: A NEED

An overweight lady was looking at herself, undressed, in her full-length bedroom mirror when, from the corner of her eye, reflected in the mirror, she saw a man's face looking in the window at her. Horrified, she ran screaming to her husband for protection. His reassurance was, "Don't worry, Dear, he won't be back." Do you dare identify with her? Are you ready for honest self-appraisal?

Perhaps you don't have a full-length mirror. Most overweight people don't realize how grotesque their full-length profiles actually appear. If you've jammed a zipper or popped a button lately, did you wonder why sizes aren't what they used to be? Each new season presents the dilemma of choosing a larger size or squeezing into the classic wardrobe in the closet. We married people forget that we represent our spouses with our appearance. Weight is a touchy subject when one partner becomes over-sensitive. Barriers don't solve the problem. Overweight has to be faced by the individual before motivation can begin.

CHANGING PERSPECTIVE: A DESIRE
If you have looked in a full-length mirror at yourself and you don't like what you see, the perspective can be changed. Imagine what it would do for your family life to have the children proud of their parent's good looks. Dare to dream that your spouse may appreciate you in a new shape: the size you were on your wedding day. Self-pity is destructive if you give in to it. There is a normal, satisfying way to eat and live—instead of living to eat. You can reduce safely and steadily. You can maintain goal weight successfully for the rest of your life. Your dignity, well-being, and your health are at stake. You must care enough about yourself to accept the truth about your overweight condition and grab the lifeline before it's too late. No one has to be fat. Do you choose slow deterioration, or life with love and fulfillment?

Certainly you love your family and would do anything for them. You can be much more valuable to them by improving your own health and vitality, your self-esteem and your appearance. No one can do it for you. Inside you is the slim person you may have forgotten about: the girl who wore that size ten wedding dress. Did insidious habits pile on pounds and hide the bride? Like alcoholism, compulsive eating is a sick habit. The cure is basically the same as for an alcoholic. Start by recognizing your need for moral support. Someone does care about your success. Wouldn't you like to cope with life by learning intelligent, selective eating habits? Cultivate friends who've done it. Deepen your faith and desire for help through friendship. We know how to reset your "appestat" in the hypothalamus gland deep inside your brain. A certain quality of love will change the attitude, the habits, the selectivity, and the satisfactions of eating. I believe it is love that takes away the insatiable desire for fats and carbohydrates and sets the mind at peace with control. Someone has said that wisdom is love plus knowledge. If you're desperate enough, open your heart and mind. Appropriate your birthright. The Becomers' Balanced Diet provides a satisfying life style—a proven plan.

HOW DIETS WORK
There are all kinds of diets on the market today which claim to help people lose weight. All of them, if they're to work, depend upon cer-

tain basic principles which deal with calories and energy. A calorie is a basic unit measure of energy. When this energy is assimilated into the body in the form of food and is not used, either through exercise or other body functions, it is stored in the form of fat. 3500 calories of stored energy forms one pound of body fat.

If you continue to take in more energy in food (that is calories) than you put out in exercise and body functions, your body must store that potential energy as fat and you will *gain weight*. On the other hand, if you take in less energy in food than you expend, you will use up the energy the body has stored and so you will *lose weight*. This is a basic law of nature. You cannot evade it or take a short cut. To lose weight, *the amount of calories you take in from your daily diet must be less than the amount of calories you get rid of in exercise and body functions.* Thus, for you to lose one pound a week (that is, 3500 calories of stored energy) you must average a weekly intake of *3500 calories less than the calories you use up each week in physical activity.* (That means 500 calories less than the amount of calories you use up in *daily* activity.)

The principle behind any effective weight loss program, then, is to *limit intake of calories* and *increase energy output* so that the first is less than the second. The Becomer's Balanced Diet helps you by calculating the calories in various food portions *for you*! If you stick to the diet, carefully measuring and weighing your food portions, you won't need to count calories, but you will be taking in only about 1200 calories a day, or 1500 if you're a growing teenager or adult male. Combined with vigorous exercise, this diet assures that your calorie intake is less than your output and therefore you will lose weight—a dramatic demonstration of the First Law of Thermodynamics.

Once you have achieved your goal weight, you may maintain it by *balancing* your calorie input with your energy output.

YOUR POTENTIAL

You can acquire a taste for real food instead of junk. Health and vitality are better than life insurance. It doesn't cost anything to have good eating habits, and no one can take them away from you. As you make consistently wiser food selections, your hair and skin will improve in texture. You can learn to enjoy vigorous exercise each day. The more calories you can burn up through jogging, tennis, swimming, or calisthenics, the faster your weight-loss program will progress. You'll have a new profile, better posture, a fresh mental outlook. Weight-losers on this program discover a sense of well-being and agree that resentments melt away with the pounds. As you gain self-control and self-respect, despair will lose its grip on you. *Proper foods eaten in the correct quantities will sustain you from one meal to the next without uncontrolled snacking.* You will not be hungry. You will appreciate every beautiful bite, planned and digested with Love.

WHY THE BECOMERS' BALANCED DIET?

With the Becomers' Balanced Diet the dieter is well nourished. Proteins and carbohydrates are balanced, with low fat. Bread, milk, and fruit have their place along with cheese, eggs, and certain of the less starchy vegetables in limited amounts.

Recent studies are indicating that lack of bulk may be a contributing cause in cancer of the colon. The roughage factor is being discussed widely by the press, almost like the vitamin craze. Our Becomers' Balanced Diet calls for a sane use of vegetables and whole grain cereals which supply needed bulk and provide valuable vitamins for good health and to protect us from hunger, constipation, and boredom.

The Becomers' Balanced Diet is adapted from The Prudent Diet developed by Dr. Norman Jolliffe of the New York City Health Clinic.[1] The same diet is used with adaptations by the diet clubs rated highest by *Consumer Guide* in a recent book by Theodore Berland, *Rating the Diets*.[2] The basic diet is also featured in magazine articles by Dr. Morton B. Glenn, Past President of The American College of Nutrition and Chief of the Obesity Clinic at Knickerbocker Hospital in New York City. Dr. Glenn has written two splendid books on dieting: *How to Get Thinner Once and for All*[3] and *But I Don't Eat That Much*.[4] Each uses a special adaptation of the original Prudent Diet with examples from clinical experience in the author's own private practice.

A safe diet is essential and the Becomers' Balanced Diet *is safe*. Confirm this with your doctor. Have him give you a thorough physical and set a personal weight goal for you. He knows your medical history and the great value of preventive medicine.

A better life style is ready for you to discover! Consider the joy of better fitting clothes; better family relationships; better attitudes about work, rest, and exercise. Proper nutrition will make a difference. Food actually tastes better when your taste buds get reconditioned. You may even find yourself more resistant to infections. A whole new world of shopping, cooking, and eating is yours. Making new friends will be exciting. And to top it all off, you can have that slim figure you've always dreamed of!

POWER TO CHOOSE
The Oriental proverb says: "A long journey begins with the first step." The power to choose proper food is yours. Wake, live, sleep with commitment. Only you have the privilege of selecting each mouthful. The moral support comes from a group or a friend and God your Creator, your unseen Physician-Instructor within. You think that's "way out?" Would you rather try hypnotism? Would you risk the side-effects and the dangerous results and disappointments of diet pills? Can you, alone, escape the depressing cycle of apathy, failure, and rationalization? If your eating is out of control like a car careening downhill without brakes, what do you have to lose by dieting?

WHAT DO WE HAVE TO LOSE?
1. If we feel unbalanced and awkward, we'll always be getting into clumsy and dangerous situations.
2. If we lack identity, our special personality, we may even be mistaken for another overweight person!
3. If we lack a sense of purpose and a drive to work, play, and exercise, we'll feel fearful, lazy, depressed.
4. If we lack self-esteem, authority, recognition, that loss will show up profoundly at home where confidence is essential for control and self-respect.
5. If we lack that valuable sense of approval which everyone needs for meaningful existence, we will deliberately avoid social encounters. We will stay at home and eat, longing for fellowship, but seeking solace in food.

6. If we lack the comfortable feeling of acceptance and belonging, boredom, guilt, and irritability will increase our feelings of rejection.
7. If we are not experiencing the joy of giving, self-indulgence and self-pity will accompany our compulsive eating. We will eat on the sly. How lonely and demoralizing!
8. If we lack a sense of responsibility, even for our own health and grooming, we will tend to despise ourselves all the more.
9. If we lack a regular meal schedule, we'll be eating constantly, unconsciously compensating for loss of emotional satisfaction—our real need.
10. If our bodies degenerate as overweight compounds all the major diseases, stress will be felt on the heart, lungs, joints, and muscles, even on the bones.

If all these are true, what do we have to lose by committing ourselves to be Becomers? When I say "we," I mean that I myself have personally experienced these problems. I know that they are very real indeed. But I realized that by dieting I had nothing to lose but fat, clumsiness, rejection, loneliness, self-pity and poor health, and everything to gain! Since I have found a way back, you can, too.

GET OFF THE TREADMILL INTO THE SUCCESS CYCLE
How do you get off this treadmill when your life seems futile, and you can't budge an ounce? How do you become secure, healthy, radiant with confidence? There are many ways to lose weight, but *how do you keep it off permanently?* This is the proof of real success. Why do so few succeed on any diet? Why do so many drop out and fail, becoming more discouraged than ever? Figures 1 and 2 may lend insight: "The Cake That Flopped" and "The Success Pie."

FRIENDSHIP
A permanently successful diet life style must be supported by the motivation of love, through activity and involvement—knowing that others care. Maintainers need continuing emotional support from a group or a friend. Find someone with the same need and desire to lose weight or keep it off. Face facts together with a scale. Give your body a fair chance to respond to good treatment. In your sphere of influence, stand a little taller as you discriminate and eat correct quantities at appropriate times.

FIGURE 1.

THE CAKE THAT FLOPPED (A Depressing Syndrome)

FIGURE 2.

THE SUCCESS PIE (Love and Self-Respect the Basic Ingredients)

THE PURPOSE OF FOOD

Food is not meant to be a pacifier for disappointments and frustrations. Food is for building and sustaining life. This diet is a control to teach us what food we actually need in order to be fit. There is no hunger, only an increased inner reserve of strength, endurance, and resilience. It's great to wake up rested and expectant for breakfast; peppy enough by evening to enjoy activities with family and friends. With adequate physical stamina there is no need to take naps or go limp by the television every hour, every night.

THE SUCCESS PIE

Look at "The Cake That Flopped" in Figure 1. Do you recognize any part of that treadmill? If failure has been a bitter pill for you, taste "The Success Pie" in Figure 2. Here, the basic ingredients are love and self-respect. Each piece of "The Success Pie" is a chapter of this book. Help yourself to happiness. It's more fun than taking diet pills or feeling desperate. Diet! You'll like it! You won't believe you ate that whole Success Pie!

A SUITABLE GOAL FOR YOUR FRAME SIZE

When you doctor measures your height, ask him to set a realistic goal for your frame size. If he wishes to have you make that decision, use the desirable weight list in Table 1. You'll see a rather wide range. If your frame is on the small side, pick a goal at the low end of the range for your height (or the one directly above your height, if yours comes in between). Thus, if you are 61 inches high, (152.5 cm) you may use the range for 62 inches (155 cm). We do shrink in height as we mature, so if you don't choose a goal low enough, your proportions will be less than perfect. In women, the legs, thighs, and derriere are the last to go. But they *will* go if you continue to a goal that is just right for you. Without a goal, undoubtedly you'll gain all the weight back, and more besides. A goal will help you when you're shopping or when you're tempted to nibble. Include your specific goal in your prayers, as you develop a stronger faith. Your own goal is your personal achievement: the prerequisite to lifetime maintenance.

PLANNING

If you're motivated, you'll plan ahead. Planning eliminates many decisions about what to buy and what to eat. With 150 items to choose from, it's easy! Stick to the plain foods, since convenience foods confuse the issue of how many eggs or how much starch is involved. Eat simply and you will know just what you're having: a correct portion. That's why I recommend that you cook only one gourmet recipe at a time.

When you do make a recipe, plan your portion precisely, dividing the largest ingredient by the allowance for that food at the meal. Add sensory appeal to your plate with spices and garnishes. Strive for contrast in color, texture, flavor, and temperature. Shop for only what you can have. You will be much more teachable when a binge threatens, and the next morning you'll be glad. Encourage the family to buy their own snacks away from home to help you avoid temptation. Keep those "emergency" vegetables ready for panic when you open the refrigerator. That's legal snacking. Fail to plan, and you plan to fail.

TABLE 1
DESIRABLE WEIGHTS FOR HEALTH AND LONGEVITY

	Height (without shoes)		Weight (without clothes)	
	Inches	Centimeters	Pounds	Kilograms
Women:	60	152	100-118	45.4-53.6
	62	157	106-124	48.1-56.3
	64	163	112-132	50.9-60.0
	66	168	119-139	54.0-63.1
	68	173	126-146	57.2-66.3
	70	178	133-155	60.4-70.4
Men:	64	163	122-144	55.4-65.4
	66	168	130-154	59.0-70.0
	68	173	137-165	62.2-75.0
	70	178	145-173	65.9-78.6
	72	183	152-182	69.0-82.7
	74	188	160-190	72.7-86.3

SOURCE: U.S. Department of Agriculture Home and Garden Bulletin No. 153, published 1972. Metrics added.

RELIEF AT LAST

It's a taste of well being when you feel relief from backache associated with overweight and poor muscle tone. No more gas from overeating. No more bulky water retention, or sleepless nights and jumpy nerves from taking diet pills. No more physical, mental, and psychological fatigue from carrying extra pounds.

Self control becomes habitual: the sheer joy of a normal life. Think of the comfort you'll enjoy in hot weather. Whatever your age, you can skip again, take two steps of stairs at a time, run to the mailbox, ski, play golf, or even take up tennis. Your own agility and energy level will amaze you. Wait until you see what happens to your disposition! The family is going to find you more understanding of their shortcomings. You'll be overcoming in yourself a destructive pattern of escaping frustrations and boredom by eating the wrong foods. You'll be rewarding yourself with a more attractive size in clothing. You'll begin to love yourself and feel worthwhile. At last people will know that you're doing something positive about your weight. They'll admire you for being consistent. You'll be a joy to live with and work with. It's not what you are, but what you can become.

Can you see why the cake in Figure 1 flopped? "The Success Pie" in Figure 2 may help you see that you can turn in a new direction. Steady success is motivation. Are you ready for a little love and a plan?

THE BECOMERS' BALANCED DIET

Instructions:

1. Secure your doctor's permission by showing him the plan.

2. Find a friend or a group to check your weight weekly at the same time of day, in the same clothes, without shoes, on an accurate scale. Monitor your progress and potential using Appendix A (p. 267).

3. Buy a postal scale with both ounces and grams to weigh proteins and bread portions. For less than $5.00 you can buy a slide table showing metric conversions,[5] or see Tables 5-7, pp. 141, 144 and Figures 12 and 13, pp. 142, 143.

4. Choose three fruits a day, but no cherries, watermelon, dried fruits, or grapes (which are too sweet and too hard to count). Do include one citrus fruit.

5. Drink two glasses (500 ml) of skimmed milk or buttermilk a day, or substitute 6 ounces (188 ml) of plain, unflavored yogurt for 8 ounces (250 ml) of skimmed milk. Teenagers should drink twice the regular portion.

6. Meat, fish, and poultry should be boiled, broiled, baked, or roasted without added fat or oil. Remove all visible fat, including the skin of poultry, before eating.

7. Fish, shellfish, chicken, and low-fat cottage cheese are recommended over beef, lamb, ham or pork.

8. Limit eggs to four a week to guard against excess cholesterol. Middle-aged or older men with high serum cholesterol levels should use even fewer eggs. Hard cheese: 1 ounce daily.

9. Limit salt at the stove, the counter, and the table. Although salt is non-caloric, it holds water and causes bloating. Experts recognize that excessive salt tends to contribute to hypertension, or high blood pressure, because of its high sodium content. The body needs some salt, but plenty is supplied in canned foods, bouillon, in the natural state of meat, fish, fowl, cheese, and even in celery tops. Successful fat reducing diets avoid the use of salt. It's an acquired taste you can learn to limit. In his book *Human Nutrition* Dr. Jean Mayer cautions, "Do not use a salt substitute unless your physician recommends it."[7] The salt substitutes are made with potassium instead of sodium.

10. Set your goal with your actual frame size in mind, according to your height without shoes. (See Table 1, p. 11.) Remember that small, medium, or large frame may be further indicated by shoe, glove, and hat sizes.

11. Begin the whole new adventure with your own prayer of commitment. That will cost you nothing in dollars and cents, but everything in personal discipline. It's a contract between you and your Creator. No one else can do it for you. Be receptive. Be decisive. Make an effort.

THE BECOMERS' BALANCED DIET MENU

BREAKFAST:
4 ounces (125 ml) citrus fruit or ½ cup (125 ml) juice (orange, grapefruit, tomato). Fruit may be saved for a snack.

1 egg, or 2 to 4 ounces (57-113 g) cottage cheese, or 2 ounces (57 g) cooked fish, or 1 ounce (28 g) hard cheese (hard enough to slice.)
1 ounce (28 g) whole grain or enriched bread, or 1 ounce (28 g) cold plain unsweetened, whole grain cereal, or ½ cup (125 ml) whole grain cooked cereal. (Double for men and teenagers.)
Beverage: Coffee, tea, skimmed milk or buttermilk (double the milk for teens)

LUNCH:
3 ounces (85 g) Preferred or Alternate Protein, or 2 eggs, or 6 ounces (170 g) cottage cheese, or 2 ounces (57 g) hard cheese
1 ounce (28 g) whole grain bread (2 ounces) [57 g] for men and teenagers)
Unrestricted "Vegies"
Fruit for dessert or later for a snack
Beverage: Coffee, tea, skimmed milk or buttermilk (double the milk for teens)

SUGGESTED SNACK:
Hot or cold Chocolate Alba, or a milkshake (see recipe section)
Bouillon
Diet soda
Tea, coffee, skimmed milk, buttermilk
Fruit

DINNER:
6 ounces (170 g) cooked fish, fowl or occasionally meat (8 ounces [227 g] for men)
½ cup (125 ml) Restricted Starchy Vegetables
Unrestricted "Vegies"
Fruit for dessert or later for a snack
Beverage: Coffee, tea, skimmed milk or buttermilk

FINAL SNACK:
Whatever milk or fruit completes the day's allowance

FRUIT PORTIONS: Three a day for women, four for teenagers and
   men
Apple, orange, tangelo, or pear, 1 medium
Banana, small, 3 times a week
Berries, ½ cup (125 ml) any kind (about 16 strawberries)
Cranberries, 1 cup (125 ml)
Grapefruit, ½
Fruit, ½ cup (125 ml) waterpacked, or low calorie (canned in light
   syrup)
Juice, 4 ounces (125 ml) unsweetened
Melon, 2 inch (5 cm) wedge of honeydew, or ½ cantaloupe
Papaya, 4 x 5 inch (10 x 12.5 cm) piece
Pineapple, fresh, 1 cup
Pumpkin, canned, ½ cup (125 ml)
Plums, 2
Tomato, 1 medium
(Each of these allowances is 100 calories or less.) Juices are not as
satisfying as fruits whose texture gratifies your sense of touch.
Tangle with a grapefruit, and you'll remember you've had it.

BONUS FOODS:
Bouillon (Beef, Vegetable, Chicken, Tomato, Onion)
Clear Soup (Remove fat from drippings after refrigerating)
Diet Gelatine Desserts and Plain Gelatine (unflavored)
Diet Salad Dressing, used sparingly, diluted with Vinegar, Water,
   and enhanced with Sweetener
Diet Soda (Fruit Flavors, Chocolate, Club Soda, Cola, etc.)
Herbs and Spices
Horseradish
Lemon and Lime
Mustard
Soy Sauce (use very sparingly, it's salty)
Tea, Coffee
Tomato Juice, 12 ounces (375 ml) (or cooked down to equal 6
   ounces [188 ml] Tomato Sauce)
Water!

UNRESTRICTED "VEGIES": Especially for lunch and dinner, but whenever that intolerable urge to snack attacks you, turn to these "emergency rations" rather than to candy, cookies, chips or ice cream. By their very nature, they'll satisfy you without gorging. Ever try to "binge" on radishes? Protect yourself with vegetables four ways:

1. *Eat* vitamins instead of pill popping.

2. Guard against constipation with fiber, since a high protein diet offers little fat for lubrication of the bowel.

3. Prevent boredom with 28 different unlimited vegetables.

4. Portions of your favorite "Vegies" control hunger.

Alfalfa Sprouts	Endive	Romaine Lettuce
Asparagus	Escarole	Radishes
Bean Sprouts	Green Onion Tops	Rhubarb
Broccoli	Kale	Sauerkraut
Cabbage	Lettuce	Spinach
Cauliflower	Mushrooms	Summer Squash
Celery	Mustard Greens	Spaghetti Squash
Chinese Cabbage	Onions, Raw	String Beans,
Chinese Pea Pods	Spanish	French (young
Chives	Parsley	beans)
Collard Greens	Peppers, Red and	Swiss Chard
Cucumber	Green	Turnip Greens
Dandelion Greens	Pickles, Dill	Watercress
Danish Garden Cress	Pimentos	Zucchini

RESTRICTED STARCHY VEGETABLES: Take the place of bread for dinner in carbohydrate content.

Artichokes	Okra	Buttercup, and
Bamboo Shoots	Onions (cooked)	Hubbard)
Beets	Parsnips	String beans
Beet Greens	Peas	(mature)
Brussel Sprouts	Pumpkin	Tomatoes
Carrots	Rutabagas	Tomato Sauce,
Eggplant	Scallions	2 Ounces (62 ml)
Kohlrabi	Squash (Winter,	Turnips
Leeks	Acorn, Butternut,	Water Chestnuts

THE PROTEIN ALLOWANCE: Protein foods are our largest calorie item, because they contain fat as well as protein. Preferred Protein Choices are 300 calories (1255 kJ) or less. Alternate Protein Choices are approximately 400 (1674 kJ), while Occasional Protein Choices are up to 700 calories (2929 kJ)! For that reason, use Occasional Protein Choices only once or twice a week, at most. The calories (kiloJoules) have already been counted for 6-ounce (170 g) portions. Weigh the protein *after* cooking. For the most efficient weight loss, halve your Occasional Protein Choice (3 oz. or 85 g) and complete your menu with an equal portion of fish or fowl from the Preferred or Alternate lists. This will also help keep down the amount of saturated fats which contribute to high cholesterol levels. The daily total calorie count of the plan is about 1200, or 1400 calories for teenagers and 1500 calories for adult males.

PREFERRED PROTEIN CHOICES:

Abalone
Bluefish
Chicken Breast
   (without skin)
Chicken (legs
   and thighs)
Clams
Cod
Cornish Game Hen
Cottage Cheese
   (Low-fat—use
   double the weight
   allowance)
Crab
Egg Whites
Finnan Haddie

Frog Legs
Haddock
Halibut
Heart (Chicken)
Liver (Chicken)
Lobster
Mussels
Oysters
Partridge Breast
   (if you're lucky)
Pheasant
Pike
Salmon (Canned, Pink;
   Chum; Coho; Fresh)
Scallops
Shrimp and Crayfish

Sole
Squab
Squirrel
Sturgeon
Sweetbreads
   (Calf and Lamb)
Swordfish
Tongue (Calf)
Trout (Brook
   and Rainbow)
Tuna (light meat,
   rinsed or water-
   packed)
Turbot
Venison

*See Appendix B p. 268 for sample calorie breakdown of typical daily menu for the Becomer.

ALTERNATE PROTEIN CHOICES:

Bass

Bonito

Butterfish

Egg, Whole (one a
   day)

Flounder

Ham (lean and trimmed)

Heart (Veal and Beef)

Herring

Lamb (lean and
   trimmed)

Liver (Beef)

Mackerel (Canned
   Pacific)

Rabbit

Salmon (Canned
   Atlantic and
   Smoked)

Sardines (with Tomato
   Sauce or Mustard
   or water-packed)

Shad and Shad Roe

Trout (Lake)

Tima (dark meat,
   rinsed or water-
   packed or
   in bouillon)

Turkey (light and
   dark meat)

Veal (Round with
   rump)

Whitefish

OCCASIONAL PROTEIN CHOICES: (Recommended for only once or twice a week, to be divided equally with Preferred or Alternate Protein Choices.)

Beef (lean and
   trimmed)

Cheese, hard enough
   to slice (Use half
   the weight allow-

ance in substituting
   for other protein.
   Four ounces a
   week recommended.)

Egg Yolk (four a week)

Kidney

Liver (Calf)

Perch

Pork (lean and
   trimmed)

SPLITTING PROTEIN:

Substitute only when splitting your protein allowance to furnish variety and to reduce calories. There is no need to split the breakfast protein, since it is the smallest meal. You'll have variety from day to day as you select from the four items on the Becomers' Diet Menu.

   Breakfast: 2 to 4 ounces (57-113 g) low-fat Cottage Cheese, or

   1 ounce (28 g) Hard Cheese, or

   1 Egg, or

   3 ounces (85 g) Cooked Fish (Add lemon juice
         and dash of Soy Sauce to leftover fish.)

   Reviewing the menu, you will see that the lunch protein is twice the amount of the breakfast protein, except for low-fat cottage cheese. Don't gag on six ounces (170 g). Divide it and make the diet livable! Half the cottage cheese with half the egg or tuna allowance suggests a delightful sandwich spread without mayonnaise. Mix it thoroughly, and you'll hardly know the difference.

Lunch: 1 Egg and 3 ounces (85 g) Cottage Cheese with chives

Or,   1½ ounces (42 g) Tuna and 3 ounces (85 g) Cottage Cheese with horseradish, if you wish.

Since hard cheese is limited to four ounces (113 g) a week, that is a good item to split for lunch.

Lunch: 1½ ounces (42 g) Tuna and 1 ounce (28 g) Hard Cheese with Tomato Sauce for a Tuna Pizza, using toast.

At dinner, you may use your low-fat cottage cheese for part of the six-ounce (170 g) portion required, since that is a large portion of meat. It fits the family pattern of normal meat servings. Here's the trick. For every ounce (gram) of cottage cheese you substitute for meat, double the cottage cheese.

Dinner: 5 ounces (142 g) Lamb and 2 ounces (57 g) Cottage Cheese

If you need an egg in a recipe, allow for it, too.

Dinner: 3 ounces (85 g) Beef, 4 ounces (113 g) Cottage Cheese and 1 Egg

A smart way to split dinner protein when the family is having an Occasional Protein Choice is to halve your portion (3 ounces or 85 g) and add the same amount in a choice from the Preferred or Alternate Choice protein lists.

Dinner: 2 ounces (57 g) Fresh Salmon (Occasional Choice) and 2 ounces (57 g) Shrimp and 2 ounces (57 g) Minced Clams

Or,   2 ounces (57 g) Pork, Center Cut, or Lean Ham, and 4 ounces (113 g) Tuna in a salad.

Be cautious with hard cheese. In substituting it for meat protein at night, use half as much, especially when it is grated Parmesan cheese which is partly dehydrated. Cheese makes an interesting topping for casseroles, but beware! It is not just a protein. It is fat and salty. One ounce (28 g) of cheese replaces two (57 g) of meat.

Dinner: 4 ounces (113 g) Beef and 1 ounce (28 g) Hard Cheese

Men need eight ounces (227 g) of protein at night instead of the six (170 g), for women, on this diet. It is a huge serving, but men lose well when they comply. Men have more opportunity to try combinations, since they have more protein to split. They may enjoy soups, salads, and sandwiches at business luncheons by keeping track.

WEIGH, WEIGH, WEIGH, ALL THE WAY HOME TO GOAL
When you establish the food-weighing habit, you can expect both a transformation of the body and a very satisfied appetite. The point of weighing food is to make sure you are within correct calorie limits. Weighing is a discipline, but it gets faster results than trusting your own judgment. I made a brief survey in which four maintainers and twenty dieters were asked to participate. Not one person could accurately guess the weight of common diet portions without a postal scale. The more you use the food scale, the more you'll like what the bathroom or doctor's office scale tells you. Pray, weigh, and stay with the menu: mind over platter.

AVOID THESE FOODS
If you're motivated but want a few privileges, heed this caution: do not substitute a cookie, a brownie, or even a saltine for bread or limited vegetable. Eat only as directed for good nutrition and weight loss. You can live meal to meal, day to day, week to week. When sweets or starches tempt you, choose fruit, diet soda, unrestricted "vegies," or perhaps half-strength bouillon.

Avoid conscientiously the following foods until you reach goal. One taste will revive their memory, so beware! You will have plenty to eat without these snares. You won't die without them. You're going to live more fully.

Alcoholic Beverages	Condensed Milk	French Fried Foods
Avocado	(sweetened)	Gravy
Bacon and Sausage	Cookies	Honey
Butter and Margarine	Crackers	Ice Cream (even Ice
Cake	Cream	Milk)
Candy	Creamed or Scalloped	Jams and Jellies
Chocolate	Foods	Jelled desserts con-
Coconut	Donuts, Fried Cakes	taining Sugar

Ketchup
Marmalade
Mayonnaise
Nuts
Oil (in any form)
Olives
Pancakes
Pastries
Peanut Butter
Pie

Popcorn
Potatoes of any
kind
Pretzels
Puddings
Salad Dressings
with Oil and
Sugar
Salt in excess

Soft Drinks with
Sugar
Sugar
Syrups
Sherbet
Swiss Style Yogurt
(sugar and/or
fruit added)
Waffles
Wheat Germ

LOVE MOTIVATES

Go forward in faith with self-control. Select, this day, the correct foods and amounts to accomplish your goal. No one else can do it for you. As soon as you start in the new direction, help is on the way. You don't have to shape "this old house" alone. Love will accompany you and modify your behavior in private as well as in public. Love can transform an ordinary person into somebody special. Discover your real self. Be humble enough to learn a better "weigh." Submit.

You can deliberately cultivate new attitudes to form valuable habits for dieting. The next chapter will show you how. Perhaps it's not just food you're craving. Are you ready to find out?

2
ATTITUDES FORM HABITS

SELF-IMAGE

Like the question about the chicken and the egg, which came first, destructive eating habits or low self-esteem? A low image of yourself can bind you into a "holding pattern" of constant despair, but an improved self-image can release you toward a worthwhile goal. Everyone wants to be charming, but we are all so self-centered—so very human—that we lose sight of the values and ideals that make us attractive. Someone has said that ideals are like tuning forks. We should sound them often to bring life up to standard pitch. A desirable self-image must be habitual.

Visualize yourself in a job you would like. Imagine yourself in an improved relationship with a neighbor, relative, friend, or spouse. If you have tension, frustration, or anxiety in your marriage relationship, stir your home with this witty truth from the late, famous philosopher-in-verse, Ogden Nash: "I believe a little incompatability is the spice of life, particularly if he has income and she is pattable."[6]

Enjoy a safe and satisfying diet while you become pattable. A good trick to reinforce your self-image is to buy a dress one size smaller than your present size. Then grow smaller to fit it. As you think, you will become. That is the thought in the Book of Proverbs, Chapter 23, Verse 7: "As he thinks in his heart, so is he"—behavior modification 2500 years ago. Prove it for yourself. Set a suitable goal for yourself according to the chart. Confirm it in your heart. You've taken the first step toward a new self-image.

We're fearfully and wonderfully made in the image of God. As we believe in Him, we become his joyful children with power to become even more like him. (See John 1:12). Can you put your hand in His? His love can make you charming.

CHARM

Charm isn't pretense or affectation. Charm is confidence that we are loved. Feeling worthwhile helps our self-control. There's no need to eat for compensation or amusement. Our worth and abilities enrich every relationship. Whatever our age or circumstances, we can concentrate on positive conversation, expressing warmth and empathy. Stand tall, think thin, and listen creatively. A minister summarized charm this way:

For lips—truth, kind words and a smile,
For eyes—friendliness, interest and sympathetic understanding,
For ears—courteous attention and wholesome listening,
For hands—honest work and thoughtful deeds,
For figure—active helpfulness and right living,
For voice—prayer, praise and the lilt of joy,
For heart—love for God, for life and for others.

How charming are the loved and the loving! St. Paul's message in I Corinthians, Chapter 13, puts it well.

Love is very patient and kind, never jealous or envious, never boastful or proud, never haughty or selfish or rude. Love does not demand its own way. It is not irritable or touchy. It does not hold grudges and will hardly even notice when others do it wrong. It is never glad about injustice, but rejoices whenever truth wins out. If you love someone you will be loyal to him no matter what the cost. You will always believe in him, always expect the best of him, and always stand your ground in defending him. (I Corinthians 13:4-7 TLB)

CHOICE OF FRIENDS

Cultivating slim friends is like playing golf with a stiff competitor. You'll try harder. Fat friends, on the other hand, are friendly foes. Prepare yourself to handle them with poise and understanding. Show your stand with a positive smile and a succinct comment about your increased vitality. They think that they mean well by tempting you, but subconsciously, they may be jealous of your success. They want to share their excuses and failures. They actually wish that they could try, as you are, to do something constructive about their weight problem. A negative, complaining person is out of tune with the universe, multiplying his own problems and spreading gloom. Don't wallow in self-pity along with such friends. Don't listen to their rationalizations. Find some new friends who have goals similar to yours.

SMILE POWER

A simple exercise you can do while dieting is to smile. Even if it's raining for the twenty-eighth day of the month, show a little faith and confidence in tomorrow with a smile. Accept today and its opportunities. Praise God for what you have. Smiling is contagious. You can set the tone of your home or office, even bridge the generation gap, with a smile. A teenager said wisely that a smile is a curve that straightens out many things. A smile lifts the face and the heart —it charms. It's a mark of self-confidence—a universal language. Our Lord spoke of the fasting countenance in the Sermon on the Mount.

> When you fast, declining your food for a spiritual purpose, don't do it publicly, as the hypocrites do, who try to look wan and disheveled so people will feel sorry for them. Truly, that is the only reward they will ever get. But when you fast, put on festive clothing, so that no one will suspect you are hungry, except your Father who knows every secret. And he will reward you. (Matt. 6:16-18 TLB)

Smile, then! You're on God's Candid Camera! When He rewards you openly, others will feel the warmth and power of His love in your smile.

GROOMING

Careful grooming is a must at any stage of dieting. Neither long eyelashes nor an expensive hairdo will make you look skinny, but tidiness shows confidence.

Today's makeup is natural and fresh looking. Pancake makeup can only partly cover blemishes, but good nutrition speeds the healing to smooth and clear those pimples. Night cream, moisturizer, and cleanser have their place, of course, but overweight teenagers with acne have noticed a marked skin improvement when they eat more protein and vegetables and omit sweets.

Hair can always be attractively styled to frame the face. The effect of adequate protein can be appreciated in stronger, healthier hair and nails. Trim fingernails show that you care about yourself. Don't apologize for hands that work; just use more hand lotion!

Overweight people tend to perspire more than thin people, so daily bathing is important for grooming, especially to control foot odors.

A valuable grooming aid for women is support panty hose. You can discard that rolling, binding girdle when you get near your goal weight. In all brands of support panty hose the weight chart on the package helps you select your size for proper fit and long wear. You'll feel like a skin diver. No more garters, pinches, bulges, or unsightly bumps of rearranged fat to embarrass you. Feel the support gently but firmly all the way to your toes. Be free to wear shorter skirts or fashionable slacks. Look trim and sleek like an airline stewardess. Learn to control your own stomach muscles—your own built-in girdle—instead of perspiring under the pressure of nylon and rubber, and you'll be free to enjoy an active summer. Support panty hose don't bind or constrict but gently remind the tummy. Goodbye to leg fatigue; hello to full-length glass and mirror reflections!

While you are losing weight you can choose clothes to your advantage. Dark colors and a minimum of patterns are the least conspicuous. When you near your goal you can wear any size stripe, pattern, or color. Make this your desire in clothes: to graduate from dark colors to pastels and prints.

A BALANCED DIET VERSUS SHORTCUTS

We must admit that our eating habits have been slipshod. The American people are misled by the colossal advertising of junk foods and fad diets. It has been said that the average American consumes 100 pounds (45.3 kg) of sugar a year, in the name of quick energy. The energy from these unneeded sweets is stored in the body as fat if it isn't burned up during activity. All those empty calories are not compensated for, nor is hunger appeased by vitamin supplements.

Convenience foods, even those labelled "diet", are not really shortcuts. They cost more, and for the most part, offer less actual nutrition than the fresh foods prepared with love at home.

Diet pills are another disappointing shortcut to losing weight. Irritability, nervousness, fatigue, and low resistance show up eventually with your weight loss. There may be a psychological dependence as well. No one can be happy with a shortcut that leaves them enslaved and jumpy. The public has been warned of the dangerous side-effects of diet pills. The obese, often so hopelessly smitten with low morale, discomfort, and illness compounded by weight, are the victims of many fads and fallacies.

By contrast, the Becomers' Balanced Diet is safe and easy to follow. With a successful water loss at the beginning, good morale starts to function. Standing tall, a touch of self-respect suggests your new self-image. Improved posture makes you appear ten pounds slimmer. Vigorous exercise restores your muscle tone while burning up excess calories. Use a tape measure to record inches lost in strategic places. That will encourage you when the inevitable plateaus occur. The full-length mirror will confirm the good news of your new shape. Also, plot your course with the graph in Appendix A.

NUTRITION AND WELL-BEING

On this program you won't need a vitamin chart or a bottle of pills. Physical attractiveness and glowing health are achieved through nutrients derived from the variety of foods on the menu. We could give a complex nutritional analysis of the foods in the diet, but for the layman it is enough to say that Vitamin A (for healthy eyes, skin, and hair) is found in egg yolk, cheese, colorful vegetables, and liver; the B vitamins aid digestion, calm nerves, boost morale and alertness; they are available in whole grains, vegetables, and meat. Citrus fruits, melons, dark green vegetables, cabbage, and tomatoes supply Vitamin C for regulating body processes; Vitamin D protects us as we enjoy eggs, fortified milk, and fish. In this diet our carbohydrate comes primarily from enriched or whole grain breads and cereals, fruit and limited starchy vegetables. These furnish necessary heat and energy. Correct amounts of carbohydrates are important to team with protein for balanced nutrition. Together with vitamins and minerals, the high quality proteins found in meat, fish, fowl, cheese and milk form the building blocks and repair system of the body. Muscles, tissues, inner organs, digestive juices, and hormones all function together automatically to make a regular turnover of the body's protein. Don't neglect your protein intake.

One look at the world crisis in food proves that good nutrition is basic to well-being. We in America are privileged to have every resource for health. Let's begin to take a personal responsibility for our abundance.

APPRECIATION

We take for granted the miracle of modern cold storage. In May we have both apple blossoms and crunchy apples. Today, marketing techniques provide us with fresh and varied produce in and out of season from all over the world. At the same time, half of the world is hungry. As Americans, we should be better stewards as we shop, serve, and eat. If you think it's greed that makes the farmers hold back supplies to boost prices, consider the greed at our own tables. We regulate the supply and demand as consumers. We affect prices by our buying and eating habits. We who overindulge are as much to blame as the cattlemen who slaughtered their beef rather than market it. At least they had a reason.

Particularly in the maintenance diet, you may use more cereal grains and less animal protein. As you learn to eat more slowly, assessing your portions, you will come to appreciate the taste, texture, color, and variety of your food. An appreciation of proper nutrition also helps establish your attitudes and habits.

THANKSGIVING

Thankfulness is a success-making attitude in any endeavor. It opens doors of understanding and opportunity. You can almost guarantee persistence with thankfulness. We don't have to be inconsistent, bored, frustrated, depressed. We don't have to be fat! We can count our blessings. We have a free country, free will—the power of choice —with every shopping convenience and attractive packaging as well. Unit pricing and nutritional labeling challenge us to shop wisely instead of appeasing gluttony.

Fat is a result of apathy. You can succeed at dieting if you will just remain aware of the privileges, the safeguards, the responsibilities, and the benefits of your program. How you feel about food affects your looks and your behavior as well as your rate of weight loss. Your outlook, ambition, and performance determine your measurements, your skin and hair texture, your general posture.

The diet is only a tool. A thankful attitude is the oil in your beautiful machine. You can learn to eat more slowly by being thankful. You'll eat less and be more satisfied. Create a pleasant atmosphere with some quiet music, a candle, a pretty place-mat, some stimulating conversation. Chew thoroughly, savoring the individual flavors, enjoying the combinations of different textures and temperatures.

It takes ten minutes for your food to "hit home" and give a sense of satiety after it passes your lips. Fast eaters eat at least ten minutes too long, and then they have indigestion. So *savor each bite and chew it longer.* Learn to be thankful for your generous portion, beautifully served. When you've finished, say, "I've had a complete meal, and I'm completely satisfied." That's appreciation. Clean your teeth and say it to the bathroom mirror, if you must. Find something useful to do for that ten minutes, such as vacuuming, or handwork, or relaxing and reading the paper. You'll recognize that feeling of satiety if you anticipate it, by eating slowly and thankfully.

A table grace is a family habit that reinforces one of our precious early American values. Norman Rockwell painted a picture for a *Saturday Evening Post* cover showing a grandmother and a little boy bowing their heads in a restaurant amid awed glances. Formal manners may seem stuffy and the blessing stilted from memorized repetition, but a thankful attitude naturally stimulates good manners at the table. Thanksgiving may be expressed in listening, passing to others, eating slowly. Which is better for digestion: the tension of speed and greed at the table, or a peaceful simple supper, eaten slowly with thanksgiving? No wonder my Aunt Frances said you'd get a stomach ache if you ate before the blessing!

IS IT A MORAL ISSUE?
Catholics regard gluttony as a sin. Mohammed defined sin as "deviation." I myself have been a compulsive eater. It wasn't someone's judgment of me that caused me to face it. A loving friend provided an example by losing twenty pounds. I noticed and admired her, but I couldn't face that weight control group alone. She *took* me to the meeting. After that, love motivated me to lose weight.

One time a lawyer stepped on the scale and confessed, "I've been bad." It sounded strange for a professional man to speak that way. No one is "bad" for having gained weight. It's just that sometimes we make poor selections or we eat thoughtlessly. As long as friends and family make allowances for us, we refuse to face the fact of our overweight. The momentary thrill of eating pleasure makes our lives less effective. Eventually, continued overindulgence and over-rich selections cause us misery. There is a wider vision of misery, however. Compare your discomfort, or even the resulting ill-health, with the hopelessness of starving millions. Then decide for yourself if it is a moral issue.

THE BASIC INGREDIENT
Facing the scale with an understanding friend will help you *look forward to success*, not backward to failure. Accepting kind discipline restores our physical and mental health. Positive attitudes reinforce habits which really do pay off. Life becomes more dependable. Remember, the Creator who made you has plans for you. He loves everything He has made, especially you. Were you tense, tired, lonely, anxious, or just bored? Learn to cope, with Love and self-respect. Love modifies behavior automatically. Love makes you stand tall and reach out. Emotional growth and insight are the priceless results. If you are sure that you are loved, you can forget your fears. You can forget your resentments, your anger, your suspicions, your disappointments. Stress and pressure are relieved by Love and confidence. Why worry, hurry or compensate by stuffing? The joy of achievement is exhilarating—nothing like the depression you may have known in diet failure. Love is a voluntary attitude: it's not forced. Let it become a reflex action, a habit. Are you desperate?

Then this is your teachable moment. Let the gentle Spirit of Love curb your willful compulsions.

Love is constant, always available, never giving up. Nothing outlasts love, not even Linus' blanket. Love perfects, building confidence with faithful, positive habits. Consistency at last! Love will help you to be patient for results. Patience is a mark of maturity, a fruit of the Spirit. Learn to be patient with yourself. If you're humble enough to step on the scale and face facts, you can learn these new attitudes. Self-control is the virtue you acquire when you stop feeling sorry for yourself and start realizing that you are a loved person, important to others and important to your Maker. All these successful attitudes stem from love. Let God love you. Love yourself.

For God loved the world so much that he gave his only Son, so that anyone who believes in him shall not perish but have eternal life. (John 3:16 TLB)

Hope is helpful, and faith is free, but Love is the basic attitude which can heal destructive eating behavior patterns at the inner level of the heart and soul. Love activates the will: it modifies. Love restores sane eating.

LOVE'S FRUIT

The Fruits of the Spirit are analyzed for the dieter in the following poem:

Joy is Love serving.
Peace is Love trusting.
Longsuffering is Love persevering.
Gentleness is Love's sensitivity.
Goodness is Love's sufficiency.
Faithfulness is Love's obedience.
Meekness is Love's willing sacrifice.
Self control is Love's mastery.

A MENTAL VEGETABLE GARDEN

We'd like to be known by our fruit, but we're so fallible. Total commitment must be mental as well as spiritual. How about planting a mental vegetable garden? Here are some seeds for your fertile mind. Let the "Son-shine" warm the good soil (that's you, all enthusiastic and ready). You'll need some water. The Word of God is living water . . .

> *As the rain and snow come down from heaven and stay upon the ground to water the earth, and cause the grain to grow and to produce seed for the farmer and bread for the hungry, so also is my Word. I send it out and it always produces fruit. It shall accomplish all I want it to, and prosper everywhere I send it.* (Isaiah 55:10, 11 TLB)

SEED PACKETS FOR YOUR MENTAL VEGETABLE GARDEN

First, plant twelve rows of peas:

1. Planning
2. Preparation
3. Perseverance
4. Practice
5. Possibilities
6. Potential
7. Power
8. Perfection
9. Persistence
10. Prayer
11. Positive Conversation
12. Personal Goals

In the next row plant five hills of squash:

1. Squash apathy with caring.
2. Squash boredom with meaningful activity.
3. Squash gossip with good news.
4. Squash criticism with a good example.
5. Squash resentments with confidence.

Then plant eight rows of lettuce:

1. Lettuce split protein for variety.
2. Lettuce weigh in weekly.
3. Lettuce share responsibility.
4. Lettuce weigh protein and bread allowances.
5. Lettuce love one another, lending encouragement.
6. Lettuce take a giant step past potato chips, cookies, mayonnaise and cake mixes.
7. Lettuce serve fruit instead of sweets for dessert.
8. Lettuce keep a slim self-image.

Don't forget to plant four rows of turnips:

1. Turnip for your buddy's weigh-in.
2. Turnip for salad smorgasbords and turkey dinners.
3. Turnip with a good weight loss yourself.
4. Turnip with a smile no matter what happens this week.

Every garden needs a few rows of carrots:

1. Carrot home.

2. Carrot school or the office.
3. Carrot your Mother-in-Law's!
4. Carrot night when no one is looking.
5. Do you carrot all?

Round off your garden with four rows of beets:
1. Beet bulges.
2. Beet depression.
3. Beet that low self-image.
4. Beet defeat!

THE CULTIVATOR

Reading the Old Testament scrolls as a teenager, Our Lord saw Himself: His purpose, His priorities, His relationships, His responsibilities. Would you dare appropriate one of these Old Testament passages for yourself? It could be an efficacious rototiller for your mental vegetable garden. Permit the mind of Christ to cultivate the good seeds you have just planted in neat rows. You can count on Him to weed out temptations and let your good resolutions grow strong and productive. How else can you root out compulsive eating, slavery to fats, sweets, and starches, rationalized tidbits in social situations? Weeding is too discouraging to do alone. Charge up the rototiller! Isaiah 58, verses 6, 8 and 11 are pertinent for dieting.

> The kind of fast I want is that you stop oppressing those who work for you and treat them fairly and give them what they earn ... If you do these things God will shed his own glorious light upon you. He will heal you; your godliness will lead you forward, and goodness will be a shield before you, and the glory of the Lord will protect you from behind ... And the Lord will guide you continually, and satisfy you with all good things, and keep you healthy too; and you will be like a well-watered garden, like an everflowing spring. (Isaiah 58:6, 8, 11 TLB)

THE POSTURE TEST

Your habitual posture reveals your attitude: whether you're confident or discouraged. Concentrate and care. You can improve. Poor posture aggravates joints, as well as back and foot problems, especially for the overweight. Try squatting like a model instead of stooping. A slipped disc is frequently triggered by poor posture along with a lack of muscle tone from lack of exercise. You can work and lift more safely with good posture. Make it a habit to sit, walk, stand, and run with your back straight and your head up, as if being held like a puppet by the head. Don't do it just when you're trying on a new garment and looking in the dressing room mirror. If you stand correctly, you'll tire less and be more effective in every motion. Breathing will be deeper with good posture, increasing alertness and endurance. Correct posture will even make you look ten pounds thinner. Prove that for yourself by looking at your side view in the mirror, first slouching, then standing tall. Start where you are by facing your present posture in the full-length mirror. Nobody's perfect. Pull yourself together. Show some hope and courage in your stance! You have what it takes to succeed. Believe it! Stand tall and be convincing. Correct posture is a reminder to eat correctly. Believe and become.

How's your self-image now? It's not what you see, looking down, depressed. It's what you *will* see, living at your best. (See Figure 3.)

FIGURE 3.

HOW'S YOUR SELF-IMAGE?
It's not what you see looking down, depressed . . .

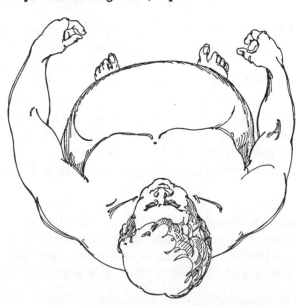

Your individual prescription for new contact lenses—the Christ-correction vision of yourself—is available to you in the Scriptures. Get a picture of yourself through the eyes of your Creator. He was there. God said, "Let us make man in our image." (Genesis 1:26) He knew what we would do with that power of choice. He provided personal power for restoration and perfection. See what your Internal Instructor has to teach you about yourself.

1. I Corinthians 15:57
2. I Peter 5:5, 6
3. Psalm 24:7
4. John 3:16
5. Matthew 5:14
6. Proverbs 3:12
7. Hebrews 12:6
8. Revelation 3:10
9. James 4:10
10. Philippians 2:5-13
11. John 1:12
12. Hebrews 12:1-13
13. I Peter 4:1-3
14. Luke 21:34-36 AV
15. II Corinthians 5:10, 17-21
16. Luke 4:3-4
17. Matthew 11:28-30
18. II Corinthians 4:5-17
19. Proverbs 3:5, 6
20. I John 5:5
21. Colossians 1:27

DIGESTING LOVE

Are you almost persuaded? Only Love can help you accept discipline. Put your heart into your habits. Your new perspective, the fruit of the Spirit, will be growing and reproducing in lives around you. You'll notice your own harvest of mental values: a new awareness. You won't be slovenly or preoccupied with self-pity any more. You'll look and feel happy, glowing with physical, mental, and spiritual health. Start by *caring*. Establish your self-respect. You have discovered the basic requirement for success in any endeavor.

A scribe once asked Jesus which is the first commandment of all. *Jesus replied, "The one that says, 'Hear, O Israel! The Lord our God is the one and only God. And you must love him with all your heart and soul and mind and strength.' The second is: 'You must love others as much as yourself.' No other commandments are greater than these."* (Mark 12:29, 30 TLB)

You'll never be able to really love yourself properly until you accept God's unconditional love for you. Swallow that, and Love can shape your attitude about eating. Love can form your new eating habits and make you slim again. Christ in you is your one sure hope.

FIGURE 4.

But what you *will* see living at your best!

FIGURE 5.

Believers are perfected. "Till we all come in the unity of the faith, and of the knowledge of the Son of God, unto a perfect man, unto the measure of the stature of the fulness of Christ." (Ephesians 4:13)

If you can't swallow that whole, let me break it into pieces for you to chew on.

The mystery of God's love for us becomes clearer as we recognize His care through a sane eating regime. As in any part of our Christian life, *discipline* is required. A just and perfect God requires obedience, but He knows it's futile to regiment our human nature. Being a God of love, he gave us the power of choice. Better, still, He gave us His Son to die for us all, to satisfy His justice, and fulfill our longing for obedience and perfection and acceptance. As you believe the mystery and lean on Jesus, you reflect His perfection. Then you are enabled to love yourself. Obedience becomes a joyful response to God's love. The Power of the Universe *is* personal. It's available moment by moment. Love perfects people. But there is nothing to fear or to be embarrassed about. It's a private contract. Love covers every situation, protecting your morale, establishing your true identity, guiding you into the main stream of effective living. If that's what you want, invite Him to the table now. See how His love affects attitudes and habits. (Come, Lord Jesus, be our guest; may this reader Love digest.)

When you are convinced that you are a loved person, you have an open mind. You are ready for Chapter 3, "Acquiring New Tastes." There's joy in discovery through the sense of taste. You can program your preferences and reset your "appestat," aware of your inner security. You can re-educate your taste buds. You may even develop an *aversion* to fats and sweets. Only Love can teach you to care with regular self-discipline. Love is more than just an attitude. Love is a Person: Jesus Christ, who cared enough to obey for us. If Love can change death to life, darkness to light, slavery to freedom, then Love can surely change slipshod fattening habits to an orderly, healthful routine.

3
ACQUIRED TASTES

VARIETY IS DIET INSURANCE

Are you suspicious of new foods and combinations? Do you wonder why you should try foods you've never liked before? Someone has said, "The only difference between being in a rut and being in a grave is the depth." Do you want to eat yourself to death?

Perhaps you think that all diets are boring. Then adventure out of your old ruts into some new tastes, using the Becomers' Balanced Diet. You can acquire a taste for a great variety of safe foods. There are probably many low calorie foods you haven't tasted since childhood: foods that could protect you, add enjoyment to your menu, and keep you from cheating.

The Becomers' Balanced Diet Menu offers about 150 items to choose from. As you work through the list of recommended foods, keep trying the ones which at first are new to you. Patiently persist. You can begin to enjoy new flavors and textures in delicious contrasting combinations, all within this safe, sensible plan. You'll be having about 1200 calories a day (5022 kiloJoules), staying within your calorie limits by weighing your portions. If you're not using all that is offered, you are wasting precious research. Trying to improve the diet by skipping something just doesn't work. Besides, you risk the boredom of the same old fare. Then sweets tempt. Without well-being and satisfaction, the old treadmill of failure and frustration becomes a threatening possibility. Consider the great selection of Unrestricted "Vegies." They protect you not only from monotony but from constipation, hunger and vitamin deficiencies. I can truthfully say I haven't been ill in the seven years I've been eating properly!

Dividing your protein allowance adds interest to your meal. Acquaint yourself with a new food by combining it with a familiar one you already like. Then try the new food solo. Tell yourself "How distinctive this is!" Venturesome tasting can be fun. Wide choices insure your steady progress and keep you content while you lose weight.

WHAT IS METABOLISM?
One of the most valuable parts of our body chemistry is the process called *metabolism*, which can be defined as either one of two functions: *anabolism*—the building up of body tissue; or *catabolism*—the breaking down of body tissue. The rate of building up or breaking down is called the metabolic rate. It depends on food intake and exercise. In an efficient weight loss diet, catabolism works like a fire, figuratively speaking, to burn the stored fat, and the excreted wastes are the ashes.

THE SPARK OF FAITH
Do you need a spark to ignite your metabolic fire? Your very own desire can be that essential spark. Look at your decision to be a Becomer as an act of faith. Then strike that match and begin. It shouldn't be hard. We already practice faith in numerous ways as part of our daily lives: in traffic as we drive; in business, giving and receiving credit; and in organizations, as people work together.

To spark your body, mind, and spirit, have faith in the Almighty God, your Creator. "Without faith it is impossible to please him: for he who comes to God must believe that he is, and that he is a rewarder of those who diligently seek him." (Hebrews 11:6) He planned those marvelous automatic functions of your beautiful machine, the human body. He even sent His Son in the flesh to demonstrate life and faith, to prove that Love is personal. You don't have to learn endocrinology or psychology to lose weight. You don't even have to count calories if you weigh pre-calculated foods on your scale. Just taste everything on the balanced menu with faith in your Heavenly Father, your Provider. A few accurate facts about nutrition plus your growing faith will pave your road to success straight through every obstacle. St. Paul said, "Faith is the substance of things hoped for, the evidence of things not seen." (Hebrews 11:1) With faith in God's help you can see your new size ten coat, your sustained high energy, your peace of mind, your health and longevity.

Faith is free, so be your own ignition. Turn over your engine to the Source of Power. He is the generator of your self-esteem, the battery of your determination. Make contact with Him. Better still, make a covenant connection with Him. Depend on Him to hold you strong. He can drain off the fat for you and reveal your true body, in His own image, beautifully proportioned muscle and bone, gold tried in the fire of unwise social and private eating in affluent America.

At a church convocation an eminent theologian was asked this question: "What is the one most profound statement of faith in Christianity?" His simple answer: "Jesus loves me, this I know."

FELLOWSHIP

As you taste new foods, you will probably find that your tastes will change and mature. It's delightful to try new foods with like-minded friends. If you could eat all those cookies in the name of fellowship as I did, you can try new foods surrounded and supported by friends who think thin. Acquiring new tastes takes a receptive attitude, though. Taste and see. In the absence of sweets, fats, and excessive starches, correct food tastes delicious. For instance, cabbage is sweet if you're hungry, but who would want cabbage after eating chocolate? Everyone has the capacity to acquire new tastes, and among friends, taste training can be a very pleasant experience. Give yourself a chance. If you don't like something, try it again another day when you're more hungry, or more ready, with dieting friends. The supportive love of fellowship helps to recondition the taste buds for the basic foods.

BASIC FOODS

One of the first foods you should learn to like is *nonfat dry milk*. Regular milk contains 3 percent fat and skimmed milk 1 percent fat, so bottled skim milk doesn't help much when you drink a pint (500 ml) a day. But nonfat dry milk is entirely fat free, and half as expensive as the bottled variety. It is versatile, too. You can use it both dry and reconstituted. Be sure it is fortified with Vitamins A and D. Also, the taste has been improved. All brand names compete for the most fresh tasting flavor for just pennies a glass. Measure it right, usually one-third of a cup (83 ml) per glass, and chill it well. Not bad! I like the taste so well that I even use it double strength to pour on my cereal, like cream. If it took you three weeks to learn to like your coffee black, surely you can try more than once or twice to appreciate the taste of nonfat dry milk. It is so very available in dry form, easy to carry home and store in a twenty-quart box; and it never turns sour! At our house one boy, one cat, one English Setter, and I use one twenty-quart (18.9 l) box a week.

You can make a soda for in between meals by using one-third of a cup of nonfat dry milk with a can of any fruit flavored diet soda and six ice cubes in the blender. It is thick and fresh-tasting, surprisingly delicious. Chocolate Alba nonfat dry milk is another pleasant product you can use for your milk allowance. Combine one-third cup with a chocolate diet soda and six ice cubes. Faygo, Shasta, and Cott all have the chocolate flavored soda. "Chocolaholics" love this frothy soda. (Some diet products substitute carob for chocolate.) Plain chocolate skim milk is made with the Chocolate Alba and cold water, or use hot water and make cocoa, stirring well. Do you like mocha? Add a tablespoon of Chocolate Alba to your coffee. With plain gelatine such as Knox, these nonfat dry milks can become rich and zesty puddings. You can even make cookies with nonfat dry skim milk. Or banana or blueberry muffins, if you wish. Or cranberry bread, carrot, or pumpkin bread. Until you acquire a taste for it as a drink, this can be a happy introduction to nonfat dry milk, using it as a "flour." See the recipe section to learn how to do this.

Reconstituted, nonfat dry milk is useful in any way that you previously used whole milk. The only nutrient missing is fat, which you replace with love, as you stir. A delicious pumpkin pie can be made with skim milk, eggs, sweetener, and no crust. Custards are easy and taste very much like your normal custard made with whole milk. Your family will also be getting all the benefits of milk without fat as you sneak it into the general cooking. Some people stretch their milk dollar by combining whole milk and skim milk for the family. This is one way you can help them acquire a taste for skim milk gradually. Butter and cream with its saturated fat is not for us; beside containing cholesterol it is high in calories so the more we eat of it (unless our energy output is greater) the more it goes straight to storage in the places where we don't want it.

Since all adults need two glasses of skim milk a day, and teen-agers need four, do give this basic food a place in your plan. Every-one has heard that milk is a nearly perfect food, but you may have forgotten about drinking milk in your middle or later years. If you want clear skin and strong bones, as well as weight loss, remember this most valuable high protein food, skim milk. While it is low in iron, copper and manganese, it is high in calcium.

Another way of enjoying milk is to drink buttermilk. Ugh? Don't knock it until you tried some of these beautiful ways with butter-milk. Consider this equation: buttermilk is to milk as wine is to grape juice. It has fullness, body, and sparkle. A mere sprinkle of salt (1 ml) stirred in may remind you of the good flavor of cottage cheese. It makes a change from milk. Some people tell themselves it's more "adult" to drink buttermilk instead of milk! It adds variety, contrast, and harmony to other delicious foods. Buttermilk can be a tenderizer in baking meats or poultry. A little buttermilk poured over a fish fillet keeps the fish from drying out, and it makes an attractive background for a paprika and parsley garnish on top. The oven heat separates the buttermilk into curds and whey, so it comes out cheesy on top with a "legal" clear sauce. How do you like that, Miss Muffet?

People have been fooled into trying buttermilk when it is served in combination with pineapple juice and a little sweetener. You can call it an egg nog holiday drink or a summer cooler. Or combine equal parts of chilled buttermilk and tomato juice with a dash of tabasco, a pinch of onion salt and a dash of Worcestershire sauce for a delicious cold soup on a hot day. One-fourth cup (62 ml) of butter-milk combined with one cup (453 g) of cottage cheese blends with two tablespoons of lemon juice to make a smooth "sour cream." This treat can be used as a dip for your unlimited "vegies" when flavored with onion, bouillon or blue cheese. A little more buttermilk and you have a gourmet salad dressing. For a fruit salad, try accenting the "sour cream" with a dash of grated orange peel, sweetener, and almond or coconut flavoring. Soon you'll be enjoying buttermilk as a beverage for variety, having acquired the taste gradually with the definite purpose of good nutrition.

You can learn to make your own buttermilk for half the cost of the cultured store product. Start with one cup (250 ml) of the regular store buttermilk and add three cups (750 ml) of warm skim milk reconstituted from the nonfat dry form. Pour it into a quart (or 1 liter) Thermos bottle and wait about four hours. Your mixture will have formed a soft, gentle curd. Give it a shake and a pinch of salt (1 ml) and refrigerate it in a glass bottle. When it is all used except for one cup (250 ml), repeat the process. This buttermilk will become fat free as you continue to make your own. You will save calories (kilo-Joules), money, shopping and carrying.

There are endless ways to spark up your cooking with buttermilk. When you like it well enough to make your own, you'll discover new ways all the time. Buttermilk blended with frozen fruit and sweetener makes a delicious instant sherbet. Combine buttermilk and hot tomato juice and you have a thick and justified tomato soup at just the right temperature to enjoy. Cold spiced buttermilk on your favorite cooked vegetables is something like hollandaise sauce, but it has fewer calories. You can be a creative cook. Take it from there with love and imagination.

Yogurt is another form of milk you will discover. I do not recommend the fruited Swiss type yogurt, because the commercial preparation has so much sugar added that the calories (kiloJoules) equal a scoop of ice cream! And don't be fooled by the 99 percent fat free label. The extra sugar would be converted to fat, unless you burn it off with hours of strenuous exercise. You can add your own fruit, either fresh, juice-packed, canned with low sugar, or frozen without sugar. Best of all is unsweetened crushed pineapple for the fruity touch. Another warning: be sure you buy plain yogurt without sugar, not vanilla yogurt, which includes sugar.

Yogurt can be sweetened artificially to use as a fruit salad dressing. Float some plain yogurt on your hot bouillon for contrast in color, texture, temperature, and flavor. Because it is thicker than milk, you need a spoon to eat your milk allowance in yogurt—a slower way to enjoy it. Yogurt is made with whole milk, so eat only six ounces (188 ml) to replace eight ounces (250 ml) of skim milk. You can learn to make your own yogurt with a yogurt maker using reconstituted nonfat dry milk, and then you can enjoy eight ounces instead of six. It's easy and quite inexpensive.

Try yogurt as a sundae with sliced peaches on top. Remember, anything you can eat more slowly and enjoy with more of your senses is to your advantage. Then it becomes an eating adventure. You'll remember that you've had one milk allowance so far today. And milk can be enjoyed at any time of the day or night, in the allotted amount, so a yogurt snack is perfect for in between meals or at bedtime.

The next important milk derivative is *low-fat cottage cheese*. If you haven't acquired a taste for it already, make friends right now. Introduce yourself to cottage cheese by combining it with diet peaches. You'll love this reasonable facsimile of a sundae. Cottage cheese is useful in a casserole such as diet lasagna or as a thickener for uncooked dressings, as we mentioned in the discussion of buttermilk. A good diet mayonnaise made from scratch is easy and delicious. It holds the water pack tuna together for a sandwich, or it makes a potato salad, with cauliflower substituted for potatoes. To make the mayonnaise, blend together a hard boiled egg, three ounces (85 g) of cottage cheese, two tablespoons (31 ml) of lemon juice, two tablespoons (31 ml) of vinegar, one-half teaspoon (25 ml) mustard, a pinch of salt (1 ml) and sweetener to taste. Another diet mayonnaise is made by using one envelope of plain gelatin such as Knox softened in two tablespoons (31 ml) of water. Add 2 tablespoons (31 ml) of vinegar and 2 tablespoons (31 ml) of lemon juice, and heat. Don't leave, Cinderella, or it may turn back into a horse's hoof. There's not much liquid for that amount of gelatine, and it must be dissolved gently with low heat. Add six ounces (170 g) of cottage cheese and three-fourths cup (188 ml) of yogurt with a whole raw egg in the blender. Add a little paprika, mustard, and Worcestershire Sauce. Pour into a pint (500 ml) container. This sets like gelatine, but it is spreadable and keeps well without separating.

A delightful cold hollandaise sauce can be made with low-fat cottage cheese, raw egg, and lemon juice in the blender. The hot vegetable contrasts in temperature, texture, color, and flavor. Cottage cheese combines well with clams for nutrition and flavor. Add a touch of horseradish and some tuna fish to cottage cheese and you have a tasty sandwich spread which is all protein and low in fat. The egg salad treatment is similar, splitting your protein allowance for lunch. Use a hot hard boiled egg, mash it, and marry it to three ounces (85 g) of cottage cheese. Seal the deal with a bit of dill weed or some chives. Presto! A safe protein lunch which can be prepared ahead if you're a brown-bagger.

A glamorous way with low-fat cottage cheese is to make jelled cheesecake. Make diet gelatine using pineapple juice for one-half cup (125 ml) of the liquid. When partly set, combine in the blender with cottage cheese. Save a little of the gelatine for a glaze. Vary the fruit flavors and add crushed pineapple if you wish, remembering that a half cup (125 ml) of fruit or juice is one fruit portion.

After you try using low-fat cottage cheese in combination with other foods, you'll begin to realize its distinctive value and flavor. Soon you'll be trying it plain and savoring its freshness and sparkle. Low-fat cottage cheese itself is made from skim milk. Cream is added in some form (sour cream, half-and-half, etc.). The amount and style of cream determines whether it is labeled low-fat or considered regular. You'll pay a little more for low-fat cottage cheese, but get fewer calories (kiloJoules).

You probably know, or have heard of, people who lost weight dramatically by eating cottage cheese and peaches exclusively. The problem is that when they are happy with their weight loss, they are tired of cottage cheese. Then they gain the weight back by reverting to their original, careless eating habits. I recommend low-fat cottage cheese for breakfast and/or lunch or in a recipe at dinner. Use it wisely, and you will cultivate a taste for cottage cheese. It's a fine protein buy for the money.

Bread is a basic food. It satisfies. It really is the staff of life. Most people already like it too well. While bread is not a consolation prize for life's disappointments, it has an important place. To enjoy the amount you need—and that amount only—choose bread that is tops in nutritional quality and flavor. Arnold Diet Slice Bread is such a loaf, as is Pepperidge Farm Very Thin. Two thin slices of whole grain or enriched weigh just an ounce (28 g), perfect for breakfast, and the same for lunch. (Double this, of course, for men and teenagers.) Psychologically, it is gratifying to have two pieces of toast, or two open-faced sandwiches, or a real sandwich, even if it is just thick enough to keep the mustard off your fingers. Dry thin toast is better than a cracker. The bread can be crumbled in the blender to use as flour for cheese sauce. This way you know exactly how much you're using. The bakers carefully include fine ingredients, kneading, raising, and baking the bread, then slicing it thin. Reduced to crumbs, it is still scientifically controlled. One warning: watch out for "homemade" bread, which is likely to have a buttered crust.

Make an ice cream cone or Roman Cannoli by using a thin slice rolled with a rolling pin, fastened with a tooth pick, and baked briefly. A sweetened cottage cheese, flavored and blended with orange rind and almond extract makes the filling. To make timbales, cut a two-inch wedge out of a slice of bread. Roll, moisten, and shape in muffin tins, baking to hold the shape. Turkey a la king doesn't sound like diet fare, does it? The recommended bread companies also offer rye and pumpernickel, but weigh these thin slices, which are larger.

Use bread for breakfast and lunch for your carbohydrate and B vitamins, but do not use it for dinner. The evening meal calls for a restricted vegetable instead of bread, providing more bulk and vitamins such as A, not so available in bread. Think of your kitchen as your laboratory. Prove to yourself that bread can be controlled with enjoyment and resulting weight loss, everything else being equal.

Tomato sauce is a boon to the dieter, regardless of cultural background or nationality. We are allowed twelve ounces (375 ml) of tomato juice daily as a bonus unrestricted "vegie." If you reduce this, by simmering, to six ounces (188 ml), you have tomato sauce. The same result is available in Hunt's Plain Tomato Sauce. You may add two more ounces (62 ml) of sauce (your limited dinner vegetable allowance), totaling eight ounces (250 ml), or one full cup.

There are several things you can do with tomato sauce. Add horseradish, lemon juice, and sweetener for a seafood sauce on lobster, crab, or shrimp. Seafood expensive? Try Poor Man's Lobster, which is haddock sauteed with equal parts of vinegar and water. Add oregano and sweetener to tomato sauce for a "spaghetti" sauce on rinsed bean sprouts, with five ounces (142 g) of cooked beef chuck and a grated cheese garnish (½ ounce, dehydrated = 28 g). Another clever use of tomato sauce for dieting is as barbecue sauce. It greatly enhances dry chicken breast, since we don't eat the chicken skin. It is easy to make with tomato sauce. Just add vinegar, brown sugar sweetener, cloves, mustard and allspice. Make it as zingy and tantalizing as you wish, maybe adding some chili powder and Worcestershire sauce. Also try it on franks or other meats.

Bouillon is another winner. Made not too strong, it will comfort you and taste hearty and filling. I dare you to drop your cottage cheese in it! Isn't it something like French Onion Soup with grated cheese, only better? You can vary the experience by using chicken, beef or vegetable flavors. Since it is rather salty, make two cups (500 ml) from one packet, or else use one-half packet for a cup (250 ml). Most of us know that salt retains water, but we forget how much we're using. Salt holds up to seventy times its weight in water! Remember, (if you were once pregnant), how you learned to appreciate the taste of real food without salt? A bit of bouillon flavor in powdered form is a good way to flavor vegetables without using additional salt. A mild bouillon poaches fish to perfection in your electric skillet. Chicken flavor is best for this since it doesn't overpower the fish in color or flavor. Add a little dehydrated parsley and paprika. The moisture in the covered pan makes the parsley come back to life, blending the mild flavors of the paprika and chicken bouillon into the fish. If you respect bouillon and use it creatively, it will help you introduce, tolerate, and enjoy new or strange foods in your menus.

Perhaps the easiest taste to acquire is *pineapple*. It's such a natural sweetener for the diet when you buy it fresh or packed in its own juice without added sugar. The Dole and Del Monte companies have both captured the fully ripe, naturally sweet, peak flavor. Pineapple juice tempers the saccharine taste of diet gelatine when you replace one-half cup (125 ml) of the water with it. Then the family will accept your gelatine. Have you tried crushed pineapple and cottage cheese together? Most people like it. Go one step further and add minced clams to the mixture. Then feature this trio on lettuce for a distinctive salad. Make a fast, delicious pineapple sherbet in your blender with frozen pineapple, buttermilk, and sweetener. Chicken livers, too, are greatly enhanced with pineapple. They offer contrasting flavors and textures, or blend harmoniously when baked together. Combine pineapple juice with tomato juice as a novel drink, or combine them in gelatine: a mysterious aspic. Pineapple makes everything palatable. We can forget about the forbidden desserts because pineapple in all its interesting forms—sliced, juiced, in chunks, and crushed—now becomes our "goodie."

Fish is beautiful! In fact, fish and seafood are valuable treasures from the seas and inland lakes—a tangible shining gift from the Creator to the dieter. Generally, fish has one-half the calories (kiloJoules) of beef, pork, or lamb, with just as much protein, plus essential minerals and vitamins. (Mackerel and salmon are the exceptions.) According to one calorie (kiloJoule) counter, clams are approximately 90 calories (377 kJ) for six ounces (170 g), while beef is about 720 (3013 kJ). Although calorie (kiloJoule) charts vary considerably, you get the message—fish is a calorie bargain.

Tuna fish is our most widely accepted fish staple. Most people already like it. Waterpacked tuna is best for you (being oil free) but it is the most expensive, especially the solid light tuna. You can safely save money by choosing flaked tuna packed in bouillon. The best bargain is tuna packed in oil. But do drain and rinse it with warm water to get rid of as much oil as possible. You can still have creamed tuna on toast, if you use half your bread allowance for the crumbs to thicken the skim milk gravy. Try tossing tuna in your salad, especially if it is at a meal when the family is having an Occasional Protein Choice. You can taste the "Occasional" category meat with them, and enjoy a huge salad besides! It lasts as long as the high calorie (kiloJoule) protein they're having, you have their fellowship, and you leave the table a secret winner. If fish is distasteful to you, try to learn to see its fantastic benefits, and learn to cook it attractively. If some predictions are correct we may all some day end up eating fish as a necessity.

Start with a mild fish like haddock, or sole, a fine-textured sweet fish. Then graduate to a new fish occasionally. There are a great many textures and flavors to choose from. And recipes can make a difference. Avoid breading and overcooking. If possible, find a good source of fresh fish. If you can only get frozen fish, try a little wine and ginger to freshen it as the expert Chinese cooks do. Open your mind and heart. Care a little. Try a little. Be a receptive person. You're the one who benefits. It beats eating turkey or chicken every meal, when beef is out of the question.

Believe it or not, fish tastes better slightly undercooked than overcooked. Fine restaurants and hotels serve shrimp almost limp. It shrinks less than when cooked to toughness. Lobster behaves the same way. Did you know that the fish flavor gets stronger with overcooking? Watch for an opaque look in testing doneness.

Cultivate a love of all those "vegies." Speak of them affectionately. Buy them regularly, fresh, canned, and frozen. Or grow your own garden for real appreciation and quantities, as well as savings for your pocketbook. "Vegies," served regularly, can literally save your life. Recent studies have indicated that some forms of cancer may be due to a lack of roughage,[9] or too much fat. Keep vegetables prepared for nibbling in moments of panic. They protect you in several ways. They provide vitamin protection. They make you more resistant to the common cold and other infections. It's more fun to eat vegetables than to take vitamin pills, and much more satisfying. You have teeth to chew with and a tongue that needs to taste and masticate. Pity the dieter with wired jaws! Is that changing habits? One taste of freedom, and where's the stability of normal eating patterns?

You also need vegetables for bulk to prevent constipation. Your high protein diet needs water and roughage, or you may tend to be dehydrated and constipated. There is very little fat for lubrication in the digestive track with this program. After all, you are trying to eat your way out of the fat you have stored. Psychologically, it's great to have the generous quantities and interesting textures of unrestricted "vegies" to pacify your compulsions. Try all these vegetables every way you can think of. The more you try and enjoy, the more you will succeed.

French string beans are unrestricted because they are younger beans, while the regular mature string beans, having more starch, are limited. Have you wondered why raw onions are unrestricted, while cooked onions are limited? Onions are starchy, but people aren't inclined to eat too many raw onions. They might overdo the cooked ones, though, since cooking makes them sweet. For a good cook a raw onion is a necessity. Cooked onions provide a change now and then. You can mix your vegetables attractively. Try pearl onions and peas with diced carrots for a colorful trio. How about those Chinese pea pods cooked with onion?

Of all the vegetables, cauliflower takes the prize for being the most versatile and helpful. You can eat it raw with white vinegar and freshly ground pepper and sweetener, or use it cooked, with hollandaise sauce. Make a potato salad with cooked cauliflower in place of potato. The spices and flavors will be the same as in the good old days, but the end results will surprise you. A thick cream sauce for dieters can be contrived by pureeing cooked cauliflower with nonfat dry milk in the blender. Spread it generously over fish. Melt some cheese on top. Spinach or broccoli around the edge lends a Florentine effect for a company dinner. Add chicken bouillon powder to this cream sauce, lace it with crabmeat, and you have an outstanding buffet casserole. This same sauce with less liquid is your "mashed potatoes," a trick worth trying. (You'll need a long narrow spatula to get the pureed cauliflower and powdered milk out of the blender.) The worst it can do to you is make you gassy, as do broccoli and cabbage, should you get carried away and eat the whole recipe yourself.

Horseradish is the greatest discovery since fire. You may not like it in quantity as a free food, just as you don't like your house afire. But use horseradish discreetly, and you'll find it a special friend. It actually turns sweet when baked with cheddar cheese on toast. It transforms hot tomato juice into an instant gourmet drink. It makes a zingy flavor touch for a sweet and sour beet perfection salad. Try it in your tomato aspic. Cottage cheese, tuna, and horseradish make an unusually tasty sandwich spread or salad. Horseradish with our mayonnaise and tomato sauce create a fantastic Russian dressing for lettuce wedges. Don't be without horseradish.

CLEVER PROTEIN CHOICES

Of all the 150 foods in the diet, the proteins are the most valuable for staving off hunger. Animal protein also has the most calories per ounce (kiloJoules per gram) because of its fat content, so it behooves us to choose from the Preferred Protein List.

If you choose your protein foods cleverly, you can be sure of fast results. I know of someone who lost 101½ pounds (45.6 kg) in twenty weeks! His consistent, speedy weight loss can be attributed to his careful choice of protein from the Preferred Protein category. He found it worth the effort to pay attention, no matter what the cost. He found a new self-image, and he found the food satisfying.

Maintainers can even enjoy the privilege of a piece of pie once in a while if they wisely choose often from the Preferred Protein category.

If you don't like fish, or if you get tired of chicken, you may want to acquire a taste for organ meats such as heart and sweetbreads to extend your protein choices. These are Alternate Protein Choices but will add variety to your diet. Calf's heart tastes like veal, tender and juicy. Bake it in a covered dish at 350°F (176°C). After cooking, remove the ventricles and fat. Slice heart so that the family won't recognize it as heart. Add cooked green pepper and pineapple chunks for garnish.

Sweetbreads are the thymus, thyroid, and pancreas. Those of the calf are most frequently used. Choicest of the three is the thymus gland, located near the heart. The thyroid is the throat gland. The pancreas, or stomach sweetbread, is used less often. Sweetbreads are so delicate and easily digested that they are served to invalids. Soak the sweetbreads in cold water for an hour. Simmer in salted water with a tablespoon (16 ml) of vinegar for twenty minutes. Plunge into cold water. Remove the fat and membranes. Divide them and sprinkle with butter salt. Broil four minutes until brown on each side.

Beef liver is the least expensive of the livers. Cook it with tomatoes and onions for a real treat.

Be aware of rather high cholesterol in heart, sweetbreads, liver and shellfish. Only your doctor can tell you how cautious you should be, since cholesterol levels in individuals vary.

Does your family fight over the poultry giblets? If not, where's your example of adventure and appreciation? The price is right.

ALL THE SENSES TO THE RESCUE
In acquiring tastes that are new and strange to you, enlist the help of your other senses.

Eye appeal is one way to introduce a new food. Color is a feast in itself. Make your plate an artist's palette, fresh with contrasting colors and textures. It takes only a second to garnish with paprika, parsley, pimento, or hard boiled egg. Even a radish or a tomato slice will do. Fuss a little. You deserve some beauty. Tempt your palate.

You might like to make a three dimensional butterfly garnish with a fat carrot. It's fun to do and it will remind you that someday you too will fly. Choose a carrot with a diameter of 1½ to 2 inches (3.75-5 cm) at the top. Cut off the very top straight and perpendicular to the length of the carrot. Cut a slice 3/16 of an inch (.468 cm) thick ¾ of the way through the diameter of the carrot. Then carefully slice all the way through 3/16 of an inch (.468 cm) beyond the partial slice, forming a split slice held together at the bottom. Lay it flat on the cutting board and cut a diagonal piece off the bottom at the exact angle in the diagram. Cut A-B and C-D. Hold A with left thumb and forefinger. Gently lift E with right thumb and forefinger in direction of B. Slide point E between the emerging wings of the butterfly. A little carving by the sword of the Spirit, and you can become a gorgeous winged thing. (See Figure 6.)

Texture not only looks interesting, but feels challenging to the tongue and teeth. Just before I started the diet, I ate a whole can of nuts. That's how much I hated to give up texture. Now I get more crunch to the bunch with celery, cucumbers, carrots, cabbage, raw cauliflower, toast, and crisp, raw apples with tight skins. Finger foods are not just for preschoolers. They're also served at cocktail parties. Touching, chewing, and masticating satisfy the salivary glands, the teeth, and the tongue. A liquid diet doesn't satisfy, because it doesn't fulfill these marvelous functions of the mouth.

If you miss the texture of caramels, try freezing a peeled banana. First, cut it into bite-sized pieces, roll it in Chocolate Alba, then freeze. It's a county fair confection right in your home kitchen. If you miss the texture of nuts, try doing the same thing with pineapple chunks.

Did you ever look at your tongue in the mirror? Those craters and bumps are the papillae which house the taste buds. In each taste bud are cells which respond to sweet, sour, salty, and bitter flavors. Bitter taste is best sensed at the back of the tongue. Sour taste is more sensitive at the edges. Sweet and salty tastes are most easily recognized at the tip of the tongue.

Your sense of smell is a cue. It can turn you on to the wrong kind

FIGURE 6.

THREE DIMENSIONAL BUTTERFLY GARNISH FROM A FAT CARROT.

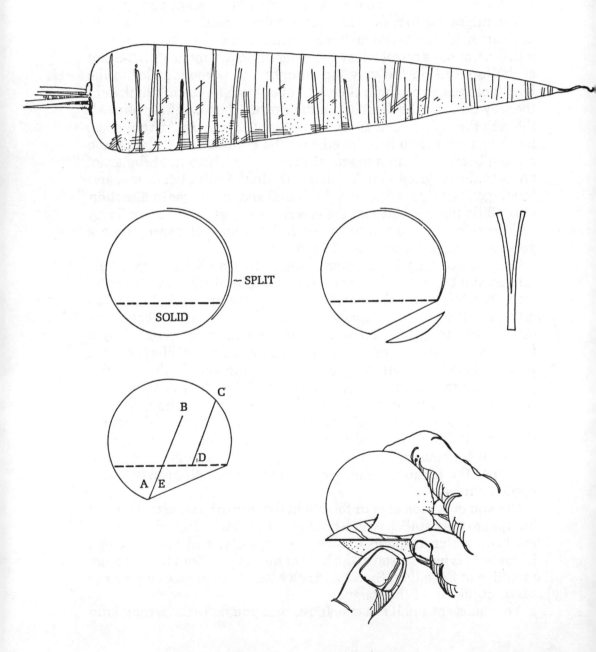

of food if you aren't prepared. Do you like to smell cinnamon or nutmeg baking? You can make apple pies and you can use spices, but omit flour and fat, and use a sugar substitute. (Bread is your thickener and crust.) Spices don't make us skinny but they help us appreciate what we *can* have.

Your sense of smell can help you shop for fresh fish. I heard a representative from the U.S. Marine Fisheries say that the public is entitled to pick up the product and examine it for odor and color. She handled raw fish so lovingly in her demonstration, it must have smelled fresh!

If your refrigerator smells foul from strong food odors, you can make an Odor Eater by putting baking soda in a jar with a picture of the Odor Eater colored and pasted on by your child. Write the Arm and Hammer Baking Soda people for the picture.[10] Of course you should keep your refrigerator clean. It's your main tool for the diet. You aren't going to live in it any more, or even stand there with the door open in the middle of the night, but when you panic, or open the door from habit, will the hydrator be stocked with bite-sized pieces of celery all cleaned and attractive? How much better to educate yourself with those remarkable senses than punish yourself for miseating with a padlock or guilt feelings.

PERSISTENCE

Is there a food on our list that you absolutely detest? Don't cross it out. Try it in the presence of friends. A dog and cat are natural enemies, but they respect each other in a home where there is love and trust. When a friend prepares something strange, with love, it is strangely acceptable, because of courtesy and friendship. If your taste still rebels, forget it temporarily, but come back to the strange food again later. Try again. It's like getting back on the bicycle or the horse after falling or getting thrown. Tastes mature. You can grow up in taste to enjoy more variety. It's a safety valve. Have you ever noticed how a child will try a food at a friend's house and find it good? A new situation with peers helped him dare, to be polite. His taste and receptiveness have matured since he last tried that same food with his dukes up under pressure at home. The same thing happens to adults in an atmosphere of understanding and acceptance. Since you belong, try what is offered. You're in for some happy discoveries with new foods.

Stay in the framework of the Becomers' Balanced Diet. Cultivate an appreciation of everything on the Menu. If you need help with a new food, add lemon, love, and sweetener. Give yourself a little time, and you can acquire a taste for all 150 items. It's worthwhile: a lifetime project to extend your happiness. You will find it true that variety is the spice of life. Longevity will be your reward.

TASTE AND SEE

Play a new game; taste and see how palatable all these foods are. When you're with friends who eat this way, you won't be misled by the dubious advice and bad examples of jealous fat friends. Give the whole diet a fair try. Give yourself a chance. Take time and make the effort to establish your quantity, texture, color, and balanced nutrition. And be thankful for variety. Every good gift comes from the Creator. Taste and see how good He is to us, providing such bounty. With discrimination, you'll be safe, happy, and successful. You can trust Him, following the Becomers' Balanced Diet. Jesus said that He is the Bread of Life. He satisfies our spirits as he wants our bodies to be satisfied. Since human life is at the top of the food chain, we are privileged to choose and be satisfied.

If you do truly want to be safe and satisfied as you lose weight, you will want to get your life structured. Chapter 4 gives practical methods of organizing your shopping, your serving, and your eating. Be part of an orderly universe!

4
A SATISFYING LIFE STYLE

DOCTORS, DIETITIANS OR LIKE-MINDED FRIENDS

A proper diet is not a cure-all, but most doctors agree that a life-style with good nutrition is effective preventive medicine. As the population increases, health education becomes a more widely recognized public need. By our 200th birthday, this nation had developed its food resources to the point of over-production and poor distribution, with rising costs and inflation threatening the economy. Individuals need to learn to make intelligent choices with their food dollars. Americans are surrounded by labor saving devices which require no human exercise. These days of increasing tension, pressure, and anxiety challenge our lifestyle. There *is* a practical way to be satisfied.

When someone tells me that he hasn't been feeling well and doesn't know whatever is the matter, I suggest that he see his doctor for a medical checkup. Even when you feel well, you should have an annual visit to keep in good shape. Overweight people tend to postpone medical checkups because they know that the doctor will suggest dieting, and they aren't ready to face the issue. In some cases, the patient seeks the doctor's help to find a cause for obesity. Then after exhaustive and expensive testing, the patient must accept the fact that the real cause of his obesity is unsatisfying, uncontrolled eating!

Dietitians working closely with doctors have recently been suspecting that one phase of a doctor's education may have been neglected: the important area of nutrition. Doctors are sending obese patients to reliable diet clubs for supervision, because they're too pressed with the immediate demands of critical illnesses and emergencies. An approved diet club can be fun as well as give you satisfying results.

On your own, it's too easy to put off dieting until tomorrow or next week. Your doctor may expect you to lose thirty pounds (13.6 kg), and then return in six months, but who will monitor your weight loss? A satisfying life-style can best be learned from someone who demonstrates it. Only with proper habits can you lose two pounds (a kilogram) a week steadily. Since obesity is usually a cumulative effect of neglect, it won't go away in a minute with a magic pill, or even a prayer. There must be a realistic approach: a sane method of *changing lifetime habits*. Your own sincere desire is the necessary motivation. A group or a like-minded friend can help you care.

Like-minded friends not only want to lose weight safely; they can admit their need for a strong instructor to guide and correct them. Christian friends have such an instructor in the Holy Spirit, "the divine presence in our lives whereby we are kept in perpetual remembrance of the truth of Christ, and find strength and help in time of need." (From the Methodist Creed) Although Christian friends are not perfect, you can discover them by the good fruit they are growing. Through knowing Christ, they have generally happy, well-adjusted children; they give service to church and community; they hold an improving self-image; and they love God in tactful concern for other persons. A positive vocabulary gives you another clue that Love is in control. It's Love that makes Christian friends like-minded, strong, and productive. The encouragement of these special friends makes the diet life-style satisfying.

READINESS
If you're ready, the Becomers' Balanced Diet is a safe, successful

method to help you find a satisfying life-style. A little faith and readiness on your part can grow into a deep reservoir to build up and support your whole person: body, mind, and spirit. This practical new life-style will support you indefinitely.

INTELLIGENT SHOPPING

Begin with intelligent shopping. Never buy what your diet says you can't have! Guard yourself against all those difficult decisions before you enter the store. Plan that giant step past the potato chips, mayonnaise, cake mixes, cookies, and sugar-flour combinations. Cancel your predictable cravings by preparing your mind beforehand. Plan your shopping list so that the decisions are automatic and painless at the store. Sometimes certain brand names are recommended for your list because they are measured and packaged to suit the purposes of dieters. Avoid convenience foods which are expensive, and which don't give you the exact amounts of every ingredient. For instance, commercial diet mayonnaise doesn't list how much egg, or even what kind of thickener is used. If it's cornstarch or flour, it doesn't fit your plan. Your shopping list includes basic foods from which you cook from scratch.

BECOMERS' SHOPPING LIST

Alfalfa Sprouts, fresh
Apples (fresh or canned without sugar)
Arrowroot
Artichokes
Artificial Flavorings (without sugar
Asparagus (fresh, frozen, canned)
Bamboo Shoots
Bananas (small)
Bass
Bean Sprouts fresh, canned)

Beef
Beef Franks
Beets
Berries (strawberries, raspberries, blackberries, etc., fresh, or frozen without sugar)
Bluefish
Bonito
Bouillon (beef, chicken, onion, tomato, vegetable)
Bread
Brussel Sprouts

Butterfish
Butter-flavored salt
Buttermilk
Cabbage
Cantaloupe (fresh or frozen without sugar)
Carrots
Cereal (hot or cold, unsweetened)
Cheese (hard enough to slice, or grated)
Chicken
Chinese Cabbage
Chinese Pea Pods

Chinese Vege-
tables (canned)
Chocolate Skim
Milk Powder
(such as Alba 66
or Alba 77)
Clams
Cod
Coffee
Cornish Game Hens
Cottage Cheese
(low-fat)
Crab
Cucumber
Eggplant
Endive
Escarole
Extracts (vanilla,
almond, etc.)
Finnan Haddie
Flounder
Game
Gelatine, plain
(such as Knox) or
diet desserts
(such as D-ZERTA)
Grapefruit (fresh or
diet-packed in
light syrup)
Haddock
Halibut
Ham
Heart
Herbs (all herbs)
Honeydew (fresh
or frozen with-
out sugar)
Horseradish

Juice (apple, cran-
berry, grapefruit,
orange, tomato,
etc., canned or
frozen concen-
trate)
Kale
Kohlrabi
Kidneys
Lamb
Leeks
Lemon Juice
Lemons
Lettuce
Limes
Liver (beef, chicken,
veal)
Lobster
Mackerel
Meat tenderizer
Milk (nonfat dry)
Mussels
Mustard (prepared,
yellow or Dijon,
stone ground
with horse-
radish, etc.)
Mushrooms
Mustard greens
Okra
Onions (raw only)
Oranges (fresh or
canned Man-
darin)
Oysters
Papaya
Parsley

Parsnips
Pears (fresh or
canned without
sugar, or in light
syrup)
Peas
Peppers
Pickles, dill
Pike
Pimentos
Pineapple (fresh or
packed in its
own juice with-
out sugar)
Pork
Pumpkin (fresh or
canned without
additives)
Radishes
Rhubarb
Rutabagas
Salad dressing
(diet)
Salmon
Sardines, in tomato
or mustard sauce,
water packed, or
in oil, if drained
and rinsed.
Scallions
Scallops
Seasoned Salts
Shad
Shad Roe
Shrimp
Soda (all flavors,
sugarless)

Sole
Soups (clear)
Spices (all spices)
Spinach
Sprouts, Mung and
   Alfalfa
Squash
String Beans
   (French and
   mature)
Sweetbreads
Sweetener (saccha-
   rine, granulated

sugar substitute,
   or liquid)
Swiss chard
Tea (including
   iced tea mixes
   without sugar)
Tomatoes (fresh or
   canned)
Tomato Sauce
Tongue
Trout (any kind)
Tuna
Turbot

Turnip Greens
Turnips
Veal
Vinegar (any kind)
Water Chestnuts
Watercress
Whitefish
Worcestershire
   Sauce
Yogurt (plain, un-
   flavored)
Zucchini

Be proud as you put the groceries away that you passed up the old goodies which would have been poison to your new program. *You have begun to become!* Being selective in your shopping won't kill you. You're starting to live a new way. You'll be surprisingly pleased with yourself.

CREATIVE COOKING

No doubt you are a fine cook. Learn now to be even more creative and resourceful. Out of the 150 items you can find some reasonable substitutes for butter, sugar, oil, and flour. I used to bake sweets for my family, tasting everything all day long. Now I use my time and talents on simple, delicious recipes made with basic foods. The more I learn about nutrition, the less time I spend in the kitchen pampering my family with empty calories (kiloJoules). The more I pray over my menu plans, the better the values come through: love, stirred in, baked in, digested easily without suspicion. My family is pleased with healthful fare, as yours will be. Our Tommy told his friend at lunch that no blessing was necessary. "Heck, no. My mother prays over the food when she cooks it." My husband, or whichever is the eldest son at home, approves the meal with, "What a cook!" That could mean anything, but with my improved self-image, I believe that they like my tricks. After seven years, they have forgotten to be suspicious. They don't miss rich desserts. Instead, they look for fruit in the drawer where the cookies used to be. Our dental records verify the results of our good nutrition without sugar.

PORTIONS

Weighing your protein and bread is worth the effort. Measure your one-half cup (125 ml) of limited vegetables for dinner. Count your three fruits, your two glasses of milk. Even modern math can't beat that precise little postal scale. Guessing portions accurately is impossible. You'll be surprised to find that by weighing, you will get more than you would have guessed.

Enjoy your protection from hunger with your large planned quantities of protein, the nutrient with sustenance. Did you know that cooked chicken is lighter in weight than cooked beef? Usually it takes two whole chicken breasts to provide six ounces (170 g) of dinner protein. Weighing plain, non-sugared cereal such as granola or grapenuts or oatmeal is important, too. The more you depend on your food scale for portions, the more you'll love your bathroom scale. Remember how you used to avoid the scale when you were gaining weight?

Any bread is permissible if it weighs one ounce (28 g): one slice (28 g) for breakfast and one (28 g) for lunch. Teenagers and men may have twice that. Weighing the food is your control for creative cooking and eating. There are many free and unrestricted foods to add which do not have to be weighed. Just learn to balance your calorie (kiloJoule) budget without counting calories. It's easy. Just pray, *weigh*, and stay with your portion.

SIGNIFICANCE OF THE TABLE

In a truly satisfying life-style, the table is significant. It's a place of fellowship, where joys and sorrows are shared, and plans are dreamed up. It's a place where discipline is practiced with Love.

Create some atmosphere by setting a pretty table. Give it an air of expectancy. Do simple, little things. A permanent-press tablecloth straight from the dryer needs no ironing, but indicates that something good is going to happen. Or a place mat could have the same gracious effect. Music, a candle, a pot-plant, even fresh flowers, a tidy kitchen, all set the stage for pleasant conversation and leisurely eating. That's what you pay for when you eat out. Why not enjoy it free when you eat in?

The Japanese with their very low table provide this gracious atmosphere of love and conversational exchange of ideas.

SERVING ATTRACTIVELY
When you serve a new food, packaging puts it over. Try scalloped sea shells to introduce a fish salad or clams casino. A little basket for fruit or bread makes all the difference in your presentation. Make serving a delight, not drudgery.

If you're eating alone, it's all the more important to sit down. Your conversation can be listening to a record, or reading a good book as you eat your planned portions *slowly*, savoring every bite.

Individual servings can be a personal safeguard. Use family style dishes only for unlimited foods.

New recipes break up old ruts. It takes a little planning and preparation, though. Why not invite a friend and make an effort to share correctly? Whether you're a hostess or a guest, practice your diet art with a regular eating pattern. Don't talk diet, just do it. If you're the guest, take along your diet dish as a gift, and make food selections tactfully. Decline forbidden foods with, "I've already had my share." If you are served something not on the diet, say, "Thank you," and stir or spread it around on the plate while you talk. Have your "vegies" at home later if necessary. When friends see your sincere determination, they'll admire you and try to help. Remember the encouraging words in the Twenty-Third Psalm, "Thou preparest a table before me in the presence of mine enemies: thou anointest my head with oil;" (That's love.) "My cup runneth over."

SIT DOWN, SLOW DOWN, SLIM DOWN
Sitting down to eat helps you see how very much food is allowed. If you pick and nibble standing up, you'll never know how many meals you've already had unconsciously. Conversation slows the eating process. But don't allow yourself to eat standing up, even with friends. Would you like a friend to add up all the calories (kilo-Joules) you taste at a cocktail party? Thirty-five hundred calories (14644 kJ) make a pound (453 g) of stored fat if you don't burn them

off exercising. Since you have made a commitment about your eating, Someone *is* watching and caring. Sitting, you're more conscious of your eating speed and portions. Try tying a bow on your fork to remind you to put it down between bites occasionally. It slows you down with a positive reminder. The family, too, will be reminded to help you.

REGULARITY
Regularity is one of the marks of an effective life-style. Eating Unrestricted "Vegies" for both lunch and dinner helps promote regular elimination after breakfast every day. Then your body is ready for the shocks and challenges of the day. Eating a good breakfast every morning starts the peristalsis and insures your metabolic action between breakfast and lunch. If you eat a balanced breakfast, you have a chance to lose weight early in the day and steadily through twenty-four hours.

Each proper meal is calculated to hold you and keep you satisfied until the next one. The days when you don't eat breakfast are inconsistent, with improper substitutions, neglect, and compensations. Those are the days when the evenings get out of hand. Overeating after dinner, late at night, naturally changes your desire for breakfast. If you treat your body well by eating regularly, it will respond automatically. You'll anticipate breakfast. A regular eating routine is fun, because it is pleasant and gets results. With a successful weight loss, you will feel more like having regular exercise, too.

RESTAURANTS
If eating out is part of your life-style, don't use it for an excuse to gain weight. Think of it this way: you like to look attractive when you're out, don't you? Enjoy the fact that you have your husband's undivided attention. That's more satisfying than sugar, gravy, or salad dressing. You don't need those extra side tracks to have an intimate dinner out. Enjoy the candlelight and the service. Ask for lemon wedges or vinegar for your salad. Carry a little pill box or a tiny bottle of a safe, delicious dressing in your purse. You care enough, don't you? Select unbreaded fish. Lobster or crabmeat is expensive to have at home, so now that you are being dined and choosing your menu, enjoy them. Either one makes a safe, delicious entree. Skip

the butter, of course, but remember that lemon brings out the flavor and texture. Crabmeat is the best value at our local classy restaurant. They broil it and toss it. You can do the same at home occasionally for half the price, but the idea of eating out is to make you feel special and festive. Preserve your good self-image by eating carefully when you're out for dinner at a restaurant.

VACATIONS
If you're going on a vacation or a long shopping trip, take a "care" package. I'd rather eat my planned lunch in the car than go beserk in a situation I can't control. Camping shouldn't be difficult if you plan ahead. Fresh, unlimited vegetables may not be easily available when you're camping, but remember, they also come in cans. Backpackers have their own dried foods to save weight, but weekend tenters can enjoy French green beans, bean sprouts, asparagus, and mushrooms, all from cans. Don't forget the can opener, low-cal soda, andned fish. What's easier or more delicious than tuna, minced clams, salmon, sardines, or even mackerel? Maybe you'll even catch a trout and have fresh fish. Most of our diet menu is just like the family's menu anyway. Just remember, you're going to be weighed in when you get home. A vacation is more fun if you can lean over, paddle, swim, and play tennis. You've come a long way, Baby. Don't spoil it now, on vacation.

SAFETY RULES
Specific suggestions make your new life-style satisfying. When you next look in the mirror, you'll know that you're becoming slim and happy. Some of those clothes in the closet will fit again. With controls, you'll have a good time each day. The results are deeply satisfying.
1. Never skip a meal.
2. Prepare ahead for safe snacks in moments of panic.
3. Enjoy an unlimited food with each lunch and dinner.
4. Eat slowly, sitting down, with genuine appreciation.
5. If you're going in the wrong direction, write down everything you eat for a week, prayerfully.
6. Use your tomato juice and tomato sauce creatively.

7. Experiment with spices to pep up the recipes. (Spice is the variety of life.)

8. Use fish, poultry, and seafood frequently for a faster weight loss.

9. Split your protein for variety, and to supplement your Occasional Protein choices.

10. Weigh all the way. Use your food scale for proteins and carbohydrates.

11. Meet regularly with friends who think slim. Contagious enthusiasm is needed. You must have someone weigh you who cares about you. Weighing yourself will not do the same for your attitude.

12. Drink more water. Use less salt.

13. Make only one gourmet recipe at a time, and eat only your measured, calculated portion.

14. Share your discoveries, recipes, and creative flavor contrasts.

15. Include proper amounts of milk and low-fat cottage cheese.

16. Consider fruits as a dessert. They are limited, and represent sugar in natural form.

17. Learn to use buttermilk, yogurt, and skim milk. Learn to make them, too.

18. When tempted to overindulge, get a visual picture of a size ten dress (metric size 38), or close your eyes and think of your own weight goal. Establish a good self-image in your conscious and unconscious mind.

19. Cultivate some new tastes to add zest to the diet.

20. Enjoy some form of regular exercise daily, bicycling, jogging, swimming, tennis, walking with a destination in mind. You'll feel more like it every successful day.

21. Be sure you get enough rest. Fatigue weakens resolve.

22. Strive for texture in your meal planning to satisfy that built-in desire to chew.

23. Include three bright colors on your plate to help make satisfying eye appeal for every meal.

24. Never shop on an empty stomach, or you'll fall for the wrong things.

25. Stand tall. You'll look ten pounds (4.5 kg) slimmer. Good posture helps you believe in yourself, shows you have a purpose. Be a walking advertisement of good nutrition and faith. You're becoming slim. Show that you know it.

26. Keep busy with some meaningful endeavor, a hobby or service to others. Develop new talents. Keep your heart and hands busy.
27. Face one day at a time, one meal at a time. If you can get through the first twenty-four hour period, you will find you didn't die. After a week, the scale will be down five pounds (2.27 kg), and you'll want to live this way till you reach goal, and then, for the rest of your life.

AWARENESS
As you find your new life-style satisfying you more and more, you will want to express your thanks. You'll feel like turning cartwheels. Satisfaction makes us aware. An unknown author has said it well:

> Let me be glad the kettle gently sings,
>   Let me be thankful just for little things;
> Thankful for simple food and supper spread,
>   Thankful for shelter and a warm clean bed;
> Thankful for friends who share my woe or mirth,
>   Glad for the warm sweet fragrance of the earth;
> For golden pools of sunshine on the floor;
>   For the love that sheds its peace about my door;
> For the little friendly days that slip away
>   With only meals and bed and work and play,
> A rocking chair and kindly firelight;
>   For little things let me be glad tonight.

OUR REAL NEEDS
Living in a controlled fashion, knowing our real needs, we come to realize that food is not just for kicks or for entertaining, although at times it may be that. The purpose of food is sustenance. Momentary thrills of wrong selections or over-indulgence will occur less frequently. We're on our way.

When we say, "Give us this day our daily bread," we will know just what that should be. Throughout the entire Bible, lamb, fish, and bread are symbolic. Fruit, too, is a biblical symbol. Food is our language, whatever our age or culture. The Bible has much to offer the dieter. Help yourself to strength; to courage and power in the Scriptures. The Spirit behind the author of each book in the Bible is the Creator of your beautiful machine. Open your heart and mind instead of your mouth. He'll dish out just what you need, because He cares about your success more than your spouse, or your parent, or your child. He cares more than you yourself care. Lean on Him for your real needs. It is really our Lord who satisfies us. "You constantly satisfy the hunger and thirst of every living thing." (Psalm 145:16 TLB) What is our desire, that He would feed our habitual greed or fill our real need with a closer walk with Him? You can run the race with the prize in your hand.

You can lose ten pounds (4.5 kg) in five weeks or less if you have the desire to follow this satisfying life-style. Then you will feel the undeniable surge of well-being. Chapter 5 describes that new state of mind, body, and spirit. May all your gains be in contentment and well-being!

5
WELL-BEING

THE NEW CREATION
Who can define well-being? How do we recognize it? People who
have lost ten pounds or more feel different physically, mentally,
and emotionally. They have a new sense of lightness and vigor, new
feelings of awareness and contentment. They sense the new creation, a state of sustained confidence in body, mind, and spirit—the
mark of a whole, integrated personality. Glowing health is preventive medicine. It fulfills our true nature. Until I reached my
weight goal, I never dreamed how good my new creation would feel.

PHYSICAL CHANGES
Physical well-being is obvious at goal weight; then your body functions normally. Weight loss relieves the stress on your heart, lungs,
and joints. No more complaints about headaches, backaches, and
fatigue due to burdensome pounds and their far-reaching effects.
Your well-being shines in your bright eyes and in your confident
upright posture. The texture of your skin improves. Your hair and
nails grow stronger due to high protein ingestion. Your sustained

high energy will amaze you. Women should beware of salt and sugar cravings at the onset of menstruation so that they will retain less water. The monthly cycle will adjust to this healthful regime.

Since the Becomers' Balanced Diet is low in fat, there is little lubrication and less bile flow than in a high-fat diet. Fiber and bulk are thus all the more necessary to prevent constipation. A temporary adjustment in bowel habits should not be construed as constipation, however. The planned eating pattern, with ample roughage, will soon help you to establish regular elimination.

Our culture is beginning to recognize the importance of fiber in the diet. In his recent book, *The Save Your Life Diet*,[11] Dr. David Ruben explains that a high-roughage diet takes longer to eat and is more satisfying. He indicates that fiber absorbs and expands gastric juices to increase your feeling of fullness, far more effectively than high-calorie, low-fiber foods. Furthermore, he contends that a high-fiber diet has faster transport through the intestines, removing fat with wastes instead of absorbing it. Carcinogens, too, are excreted quickly in a high roughage diet, lessening the possibility of cancer growth in the bacterial environment of the bowels. Dr. Ruben even suggests that a high-roughage diet induces tranquillity. Obviously, the greatest advantage of bulk and fiber in the diet is the prevention of constipation.

Lawrence Galton is the author of another recently published book, *The Truth About Fiber in Your Food*.[12] He points out that in the U.S., our fiber intake is one-tenth of what it was, while our disease incidence has shot up. He notes that Africans on unrefined diets may go hungry, but they rarely have the chronic diseases typical of our Western countries, such as cancer of the colon, heart disease, and diverticulosis. He explains that the constipation causes straining and outpouching of the intestine (diverticular disease); abdominal pressure may be the cause of hiatus hernia with its accompanying heartburn, varicose veins or hemorrhoids. He cites studies to show that people on high-fiber diets have lower blood cholesterol and less cholesterol deposits in coronary arteries feeding the heart.

Besides recommending the use of bran for fiber, Mr. Galton lists 20 fruits and vegetables found to be valuable for fiber content in the following order: carrots, apples, brussel sprouts, eggplant, spring cabbage, oranges, pears, green beans, lettuce, winter cabbage, peas, onions, celery, cucumbers, beans, tomatoes, cauliflower, bananas, rhubarb and turnips. You will note that eighteen of them are on the Becomers' Balanced Diet. Light cooking and the use of skins are recommended to keep the fiber content beneficial for digestion.

Watching for body changes, you may expect at some point to reach a plateau in your weight loss, even if you follow the program carefully. Be comforted with the knowledge that you may be losing inches as your body readjusts. Don't expect to lose the same amount each day, or each week, or exactly like any other person.

Be thankful for relief from gas discomfort. Look back and realize that you haven't caught a cold or picked up so many common infections recently. This will be true for you if you've been eating properly and having enough rest. Vitamins in the vegetables protect you. What better evidence of your physical well-being?

MENTAL SET
A positive, receptive attitude is a demonstration of mental well-being. Teachers recognize it in alert pupils. Good students are aware of their progress and hungry to learn more. You, too, are capable of accepting challenge. Your attitude becomes humble, then curious, then exuberant. As you marvel at the physical results of your bountiful diet, stop to realize that the motivation to follow it carefully is truly that basic ingredient, Love. Love clears your mind of doubts about dieting so that you are able to withstand temptations. Your behavior is reinforced by caring about yourself. Your mental determination is exhilarating. Nothing is impossible! At last you know in your own mind the dual secrets necessary for well-being: a safe diet, and Love to follow through. This diet has medical support, but Love is found in the counsel of the Holy Spirit. " . . . and his name shall be called Wonderful, Counsellor, the mighty God, the everlasting Father, the Prince of Peace." (Isaiah 9:6c) This kind of mental set shapes your will until wise choices are not only easy for you, but automatic.

Can you trust the menu and the Counsellor? Counting calories (kiloJoules) will probably only make you nervous, so give yourself a fair chance by simply using the calorie-controlled menu with a variety of foods. Make a ten-week commitment with a like-minded friend—one project to really finish. Together, take one day at a time.

Remember that you are a very important person. The exercise of seeing through your commitment with your friend will strengthen your four D's: your desire, your determination, your discrimination, and your ultimate discipline. Your Counsellor cares for you. Care about yourself and your mental well-being.

EMOTIONAL GROWTH
Emotional well-being is that sure feeling, at a deep level of the heart and soul, that life is good. The encouragement of your friends and family is supportive, helping you maintain your emotional stability. This in turn enables you to be satisfied with obeying the diet.

Your willing resolve and happy attitude can set the tone for the entire family. Acknowledge the improved relationships. Then, sure of your guidance, wait patiently for the inevitable results of well-directed dieting. The Creator, your Counsellor—your Internal Instructor—makes your life dependable. You feel held and protected in the everlasting arms. You know that you are lovable and teachable, that you deserve to be whole in body, mind, and spirit. Relaxed and inspired, you allow yourself more and more self-respect. Your Counsellor helps you to face your hidden anxieties. For your part, you learn to express anger briefly, without eating to soothe regrets. It's important for you to get enough rest and have a little casual fun and recreation each day. You'll find that your resentments melt away with your fat.

Every day that you overcome another insidious habit of over-indulgence, you become more of an authority in your own home, in the heart of the home, your kitchen. That's where Love is stirred in and dished out in unlimited portions, as needed. You'll find your previous need to eat for comfort or amusement will disappear. The more you lean on your Internal Instructor, the taller you'll feel. No longer will you be a jovial fat person hiding a lonely heart. Love heals human emotions just as surely as the warm sun promotes the growth and development of plants.

MEANING AND PURPOSE
If well-being involves body, mind, and spirit, how do you synchronize the tune-up? You've heard people say, "I'd give anything to lose ten pounds!" I'm here to tell you it takes a bigger commitment

than mere money. In America we have the habit of thinking that money will buy anything. Doctors send obese patients to reliable diet clubs for motivation. There, a dieter pays for someone to care. If you don't have the money, or don't want to spend it, the Becomers' Balanced Diet is a safe plan to use with one friend at home, or with a small group of friends. God's plan for you is free and priceless—the behavior modification of caring.

If you think it's quite a sacrifice to give up mayonnaise and butter, think of it as simply a significant way to surrender your own will. Cheer up! We who have maintained normal weight can testify that our cravings have been overhauled. Giving up sauces and gravies is hardly a sacrifice when new habits make you feel a hundred percent peppier. Foods actually taste better when eaten slowly, with appreciation, in an emotional climate of Love. It's a privilege to eat normally. Learn how. It's freedom to become the unique person you were created to be. What a security to be in control of your eating habits, to enjoy the good food you know you should have! You can learn to stop eating at the right moment. This perfect control comes only from Love. It's your opportunity for complete satisfaction and glowing health, mental and physical.

Clean our your cupboards so that you can stop nibbling junk foods. Begin to enjoy the flavor and texture of raw cauliflower, cabbage, mushrooms, cucumbers, green peppers, cooked broccoli, and asparagus. If you skip a meal, you'll be vulnerable to sweets and extra unmeasured carbohydrates. Develop the habit of eating at leisure, seated in a pleasant place. If you eat at the counter, standing, you'll surely forget how much you ate. It is love and self-respect that will teach you to be responsible. And remember to plan your plate attractively. You'll be surprised how the right amount of food will fill you up.

Do you know your bad habits? Are you a compulsive eater? Nighttime snacker? Taster? Nibbler? After-dinner raccoon? Garbage disposal for the whole family? Why? Is someone disappointing you or nagging you? Everyone in the whole world has problems, but there are certainly better ways to solve them than by eating. Try doing something for someone else. You'll find that your expansive concern for others will free you from yourself. Find something constructive to do to break the eating marathon. Surely you realize that continued eating and extra weight will only compound your ill-nesses and insecurities. Do you want to invite ridicule? How much more realistic it is to face life squarely and eat sensibly for the right reasons. *Let nourishment and well-being be your only eating motives.*

Once you succeed for a whole day, you'll have it made. Out of twenty-four hours, eight will be spent sleeping. If you ate a balanced dinner, your marvelous body will be losing weight as you sleep. The only thing you might have to do is get up in the night once to visit the bathroom. What could be easier? Only about five of the twenty-hour hours will be spent in food-related activities: shopping, pre-paring, serving, eating. Use the other nineteen hours for fun and fulfillment. Get out of the kitchen, away from the refrigerator. A hobby is much more rewarding than baking pies and tasting. Each new day will build on yesterday's success. If you really want well-being, take the initiative. Get off that treadmill of self-pity. Step out into the mainstream of life. While you live on the higher plane of the spirit, your body can enjoy a nutritionally balanced diet. Your faith can make you whole—beautiful!

SELF-CONTROL

Well-being depends on self-control, the final fruit of the Spirit, which grows out of the parent virtue, Love. Remember how the Bible describes the first tree—the tree that was created to encourage self-control?

> *But of the tree of the knowledge of good and evil, you shall not eat of it: for in the day that you eat it you shall surely die.* (Genesis 2:17)

According to David, the godly person will prosper like a tree near water.

> *But his delight is in the law of the Lord; and in his law he medi-tates day and night. And he shall be like a tree planted by rivers of water, that brings forth his fruit in his season; his leaf shall not wither; and whatever he does shall prosper.* (Psalm 1:2, 3)

Then read in John's description of the holy city the therapy to be gained from the tree of life.

> *And he shewed me . . . in the middle of its street, and on either side of the river was the tree of life, which bore twelve kinds of*

fruit, and yielded fruit every month: and the leaves of the tree were for the healing of the nations. (Revelation 22:1a, 2)

Blessed are those who do his commandments, that they may have right to the tree of life, and may enter in through the gates into the city. (Revelation 22:14)

Now notice one of Zechariah's prophetic references to Christ as the Branch.

... for, behold, I will bring forth my servant, the BRANCH. (Zechariah 3:8b)

Since Jesus is the living proof of God's love, think of the Branch as Love.

For God so loved the world, that he gave his only begotten son that whosoever believeth in him should not perish, but have everlasting life. (John 3:16)

All the Spirit's fruit grows from the Branch. Self-control is the fruit at the top of the tree of life. Grab the Branch, and you can reach the fruit. You've already tasted love, joy, peace, patience, gentleness, goodness, faith, and humility. In your diet group therapy, agape love will be felt; spiritual values will be caught. It is Love that nourishes the spirit and controls the emotions, making the mind fertile for the re-learning of habits and attitudes. When you know that someone cares about your success, know that you are accepted and that you belong, then you will start to care on your own. You'll be in charge of your own fork and spoon . . . and fingers . . . and life!

PREPARATIONS

One of the secrets of self-control is practical: plan and shop ahead. Obey your best intentions. What do you have prepared in the refrigerator when you open the door in a moment of panic? Be dependable. Vow to yourself today that there is a new authority in your home. You know that only you, under the guide of your Instructor, control the decision of what goes into your mouth. Decide immediately if nibbling and cheating are worth the risk of getting off the diet. Nibbles never satisfy. They only lead to more nibbles and feelings of hopelessness, despair, and abandonment, magnified over and over. Why live with these when you can hop on the opposite cycle that rewards, strengthens, and overcomes? Prepare! Try some new tastes now that your tongue is no longer numbed by sweets. Treat it as if it were a matter of life and death, because it is. Build some good habits for a lifetime. Careful preparations will help you lose extra weight and discover your well-being.

A NEW RELIANCE

You are not alone. David relied on the Lord, his Good Shepherd, for well-being. You can interpret Psalm 23 personally, for dieting, like this:

> The Lord is my shepherd (my Internal Instructor): I shall not want (be hungry). He makes me lie down in green pastures (to get enough rest): he leads me beside the still waters (makes me tranquil). He restores my soul; he leads me in the paths of righteousness for his name's sake (in the ways of self-control, depending on Him). Yes, though I walk through the valley of the shadow of death (self-destruction), I will fear no evil (temptation), for you are with me; your rod and your staff comfort me. You prepare a table before me in the presence of my enemies (friendly foe): You anoint my head with oil (my mind with loving obedience): my cup runs over (my body and spirit are satisfied). Surely goodness and mercy shall follow me all the days of my life: and I will live in the house of the Lord forever (I will consider my body His temple).

Relying on your Internal Instructor, you can make this great affirmation of well-being your own.

> Bless the Lord, O my soul: and all that is within me, bless his holy name. Bless the Lord, O my soul, and forget not all his benefits: Who forgives all your iniquities; Who heals all your diseases; Who redeems your life from destruction; Who crowns you with lovingkindness and tender mercies; Who satisfies your mouth with good things; so that your youth is renewed like the eagle's. (Psalm 103:1-5)

The next chapter will help you to find balance in your personal life-style. Make your own constructive evaluation.

6
TOTAL BALANCE

SHAPE UP, FAT AMERICA!
The Statue of Liberty stands balanced, slim, and poised in the New York Harbor, inscribed with Emma Lazarus' invitation to freedom:

Give me your tired, your poor,
Your huddled masses yearning to breathe free,
The wretched refuse of your teeming shore.
Send these, the homeless, tempest-tossed to me.
I lift my lamp beside the golden door.

We have become known as a melting pot, absorbing the cultural cuisine of many nations over these two-hundred years. Today, for instance, spaghetti is as American as it is Italian. What have we achieved with all this cultural heritage and the bounty of our "amber waves of grain," our "fruited plain"? Affluence? Yes, but with it, fat that endangers our "life, liberty, and the pursuit of happiness." To the starving millions of the world our fat is ugly. America's real freedom was built on responsibility. We grew strong with balanced values. Then, with material success, we began to grow repulsively condescending in our prowess. Fat is a symptom of our decline: a blemish on America the beautiful. God mend this very flaw.

To help us remember our nation's origin with pride, let's exercise our creative imaginations. Picture that majestic Statue of Liberty facing east toward the Atlantic. Suppose an act of God should turn it around to face America. A parody of the inscription might call us back to our God-given freedom of choice.

> Give me your rich, your poor,
> Your bloated populace, too stuffed to breathe free,
> The bored, indulgent, ill, from shore to shore.
> Turn these, the heavy, desperate ones, to me.
> Freely choose food, but gluttony abhor!

America is made up of states, cities, towns, neighborhoods, families, individuals. May God help us to see ourselves—and start with me. "Confirm my soul with self-control, make every gain divine."[13]

Does food make a slave of you? Do you deceive yourself that you can stop eating, though never get around to the right diet? Almost every family has at least one unhappy member trapped by the eating marathon. A more balanced life-style may be just what you need to lose weight safely and keep it off. So let's get going! Start by checking your life for balance in these five areas:

1. *Work.* Is yours meaningful? Do you enjoy your work role?
2. *Play.* Do you find time for stimulating exercise and recreation?
3. *Sleep.* Do you get enough refreshing rest?
4. *Belonging.* Are your family relationships fulfilling? Can you accept what can't be changed?
5. *Worship and Direction.* Are you committed to a cause or purpose greater than yourself?

If one area is weak, you may be trying to compensate by overeating. Do you realize what you're really doing to yourself? Besides the physical discomfort, which you know about, overfatness compounds most diseases and creates mental and spiritual stress. Stuffing and apathy are a vicious cycle. Break out of it, or you'll blow up out of control to a living death. Examine the five aspects of a balanced life. Perhaps you're neglecting or over-emphasizing some part of your life.

WORK PERSPECTIVE
Work is what God ordered after Adam ate the forbidden fruit. Some

folks go overboard on work. But remuneration isn't everything. Do-it-yourself families find that working together establishes a certain comradeship, communication, and intimacy. It's fulfilling to get a big job done together. Raking leaves, gardening, or painting the house can be fun when everyone pitches in. Sharing responsibilities relieves the drudgery. It makes the challenge exciting, and moves the work to completion sooner. We feel a common purpose and even enjoy a little healthy competition at the job. The joy of achievement can be celebrated with a swim or a bike ride together. The feeling of pride in a job well done is good for individual egos, and it boosts the rewarding feelings of togetherness and appreciation for one another, as well. In his story of the talents, Our Lord praised the good worker. " ... Well done, good and faithful servant: you have been faithful over a few things, I will make you ruler over many things: enter into the joy of your Lord." (Matthew 25:21b)

ROLES
Often, work loads are lightened by temporarily exchanging family roles. Today, many young husbands and wives are doing just that. They're finding new awareness of each other's needs and abilities. Try a new work role for yourself instead of a sweet roll.

After tasting the forbidden fruit, Eve's punishment was also a work assignment—to bring forth the children. Any mother knows that bringing forth and laboring last a lifetime. The work of motherhood is a great, sacred opportunity.

Now that I am eating sensibly, I notice my family is following my eating pattern more and more. I look back and see how my role of motherhood has changed. Once, I believed that the sign of a good mother was a full cooky jar; that the smell of baking bread was so homey. Fellowship was eating ... and eating ... and eating! Now, I'm learning a deeper fellowship. Eating has its place, but I try to practice discretion, discrimination, and self-control. You can do it, too.

Achievement and satisfaction are caught at the table through creative communication as we are sitting down together, not by gorging and grabbing. Work should be fulfilling. A parent's greatest fulfillment is to see the character developing in his children: the fruits of the Spirit—love, joy, peace, patience, kindness, goodness, humility, faithfulness, self-control. That is the spiritual food that satisfies. It nourishes life and grows in the family like yeast growing in bread, little by little, under the proper conditions. Strife, boredom, apathy, frustration, fatigue all result from false values. We hunger for permanent values grown from Love. The real work of motherhood, then, is providing supportive love to last a lifetime. For a balanced life you can't have too much of the right quality of love. If you didn't get enough from your mother to pass on to your children, God Himself can mother you.

> Sing O heavens; and be joyful, O earth; and break forth into singing, O mountains: for the Lord has comforted his people, and will have mercy on his afflicted. Can a woman forget her sucking child, that she should not have compassion on the son of her womb? Yes, she may forget, yet I will not forget you. (Isaiah 49:13, 15)

RECREATION

Exercise has been associated with losing weight, and rightly so, but the number of calories (kiloJoules) burned in exercise must exceed the calories (kiloJoules) consumed in food for you to actually lose weight. Consider how much easier it is to push back from the table than to do five hundred pushups. However, exercise is an important factor in the balanced life; it insures the proper functionin good body. Regular exercise improves muscle tone. It aids circulation and breathing, stimulates metabolism, affects peristalsis. Sound sleep is another benefit of exercise. Patients in nursing homes frequently suffer from constipation and insomnia because they lack exercise. One of the distinct benefits of exercise is that it's fun. You can feel the glow of circulation. The general relaxed feeling afterward helps you unwind and makes you ready for healing rest. Skin tone and color improve with exercise coupled with good nutrition. But be careful to increase your exercise gradually, so you don't suffer from overexertion or cramps.

Want a simple, safe, and beautifying exercise that can be practiced often for total balance? Laugh a little! In the midst of today's tension, a good laugh lifts the heart and exercises it beneficially, easing your nerves and muscles.

Exercise may formal and informal. You're exercising as you work and play and live your balanced life. But it is well to take time each day for a regular planned exercise period, whether it is aerobics, the Royal Canadian Exercise routine geared to your age and ability, an exercise class, a private workout with the recently popular ropes and pulleys gadget, or just a regular daily jaunt. Did you ever think how many miles Jesus must have walked?

Slow motion isotonic exercise is painless when it is a form of worship. For the regular tempo that encourages systematic exercise, play a favorite record—either sacred music or music which, by its beauty, directs your thoughts and actions Godward. (See Chapter 11 for a more detailed discussion of Exercise.)

Playing is a form of rest, since it gives even adults a new perspective. Doctors prescribe vacations just to give tired patients a change of scene; a rest from the pressures of heavy responsibilities. Make way for play. Could you take up horseback riding, skiing, swimming, tennis, walking, jogging, gardening? Maybe some of the quieter hobbies would appeal to you: macrame, crocheting, knitting, sewing, reading, painting, decoupage, or indoor gardening. As you grow slimmer, you'll feel more inclined to have regular exercise, recreation, and hobbies.

REST
Rest is your reward for work, exercise, and play. Most of us need eight hours of sleep to stay well and active. If you've had insomnia, you'll find it's a great feeling to sleep after exercising, without pills, to wake up rested, anticipating each new day with its fresh opportunities to succeed. You can function at top efficiency all day if you're rested and committed to the balanced life-style that satisfies your real needs.

Some people oversleep for an escape from problems they can't face, storing calories that could be burned with meaningful work or recreation. Well-regulated rest steadies your resolve to eat properly. No need for midday naps or snacks. Rest is also trust. A dieter must have trust and patience.

Trust in the Lord, and do good; so you shall dwell in the land, and truly you will be fed. Delight yourself also in the Lord; and he shall give you the desires of your heart. Commit your way unto the Lord; trust also in him; and he shall bring it to pass . . .

Rest in the Lord, and wait patiently for him:...(Psalm 37:3-7a)
   I have been young, and now am old; yet I have not seen the righteous forsaken, nor his child begging bread. (Psalm 37:25)
      The mouth of the righteous speaks wisdom, and his tongue talks with good judgment. The law of his God is in his heart; none of his steps shall slip. (Psalm 37:30, 31)

BELONGING

We hear constantly that in our modern society the family is becoming less stable. Men and women, unfulfilled, complain of loneliness and misunderstanding. Feelings of rejection, failure in family relationships, broken engagements: all these may contribute to compulsive behavior, whether it is over-eating, over-talking, or over-buying. Our destructive habits won't compensate us for our hurt, and they actually hurt the family unit. The divorce rate is alarmingly high and going higher, creating havoc in the lives of innocent children. Before it is too late, can you accept the possibility that overweight may be a signal that something vital is lacking in your life? We are created in families to belong together, intimately. The pattern of family life is perfect for the growth of all the individuals. Even as parents, we continue to grow in mental and emotional ways, long after attaining our physical prime. And we should be growing in responsibility, growing more and more sensitive to one another's needs. A happy family provides the acceptance, the contact, the vital belonging so necessary to us. Unconditional Love is the basic ingredient of an effective balanced life. We must belong or die. Do you recognize, now, that overeating is slow suicide? The family is our testing ground of Love.

St. Paul, a bachelor, had some sound advice on being content and steadfast:
   Prove all things; hold fast that which is good. (I Thessalonians 5:21)
      ...I have learned, in whatever state I am, to be content. I know both how to be abased, and how to abound: everywhere and in everything I am instructed both to be full and to be hungry, both to abound and to suffer need. I can do all things through Christ who strengthens me. (Philippians 4:11b-13)
      Godliness with contentment is great gain. (I Timothy 6:6)

Whatever your family situation, if you belong to Jesus, you will have contentment, and you will be steadfast. He holds the body, mind, and spirit together in total balance.

He is before all things, and in him all things hold together. He is the head of the body, the church; he is the beginning, the firstborn from the dead, that in everything he might be pre-eminent. For in him all the fulness of God was pleased to dwell, and through him to reconcile to himself all things, whether on earth or in heaven, making peace by the blood of his cross. And you, who once were estranged and hostile in mind, doing evil deeds, he has now reconciled in his body of flesh by his death, in order to present you holy and blameless and irreproachable before him, provided that you continue in the faith, stable and steadfast, not shifting from the hope of the gospel.... (Colossians 1:17-23 RSV)

Other groups in society develop from the pattern of family life. The worlds of business, finance, travel, and sports all depend on this basic unit of society, the family. That's where the habit and skill of love are ingrained, where consideration and teamwork are first taught and learned. Even our holidays are occasions of returning to the loved ones for belonging. If you don't have a family, find a church family, or become a volunteer for a worthy cause where you're needed. Man or woman, you need to relate to others in service and to be appreciated, for the sake of your own therapy and well-being. There is always someone who needs Love. Get busy and give what you can. You'll find that your own resources will be multiplied, and your own needs will be met. It's like using a siphon; you build your faith by expressing it.

You can grow to become a child of God with all the rights and privileges of the King's child. Do you see that there's a family pattern in the Christian faith? Jump into it with that bold leap of faith. Believe in Jesus Christ, God's own Son, His personal representative to you. He died not only for our salvation, but to teach us perfect obedience. That makes us brothers and overcomers with Christ. Can you be so believing and childlike? If you can, you will have the best help available to lose weight. You'll grow in spirit while your body comes back into proportion. Your life will come into sharp, stunning focus, totally balanced.

Broken relationships can be healed with His love. Whichever half you are, you can become the better half again. "But if we walk in the light, as he is in the light, we have fellowship with one another, and the blood of Jesus Christ his Son cleanses us from all sin." (I John 1:7) Food will have a more sane place in your life when you know you belong. The good news is that there is Love enough for all, and it's free. God proved that by giving His Son for us. He must have known what we would do with that freedom of choice. What if you hadn't believed in the fact of redemption? Think what you would have missed! The power to become a child of perfection; personal peace for now and all eternity. Wouldn't you rather experience belonging and peace than be huge with sweets, starches, and fats?

If the redemption is not yet a fact for you, maybe now is the time to make your personal commitment to Jesus. You need only ask Him for it. Tell Him you know you are a failure and helpless without Him. Ask Him to come into your life this moment as the center of it, as your Internal Instructor. Then you can accept as fact that His blood has cleansed you, and that His Holy Spirit will change your life forever—starting now!

WORSHIP AND DIRECTION

Devotion to a higher purpose completes life, giving it a whole new dimension of the spirit. When you have the Spirit, you have all the equipment you'll ever need for success in weight control or any other worthwhile venture. The Methodist Creed says:

> We believe in the Holy Spirit as the divine presence in our lives whereby we are kept in perpetual remembrance of the truth of Christ, and find help and strength in time of need.

In your mind and heart reach out for the resources of the Almighty. Jesus offers you a totally balanced life by re-establishing your priorities. You won't suffer hunger or lose out on anything that's good for you. Jesus liked parties Himself. He was there at the wedding, performing His first miracle. He can go with you anywhere, keep you safe, and put a sparkle into your eye; a new, positive posture into your walking, dancing, running, resting. It's common sense to have a balanced life. We desperately need it. *No one else can give it to us at any price.*

Alone, we get side-tracked. We've all tried it. You are His child.

Adore Him! Look to Him for your real needs. Hold His hand in the panic moments at the refrigerator. He'll see you through. He'll be there when everyone else has gone to bed—even when you fail yourself. He'll remind you of your resolve, comfort you, lead you, satisfy you with enough to eat. He'll give you the power of self-control. He'll do all this because He loves you. You belong to Him. Lean in His direction. He'll take away all your hangups and give you poise. He is worthy of your worship.

THREE BALANCED LIVES

Total balance is not achieved by a moment's quick decision. Look at the structured lifetime values of three great lives from history: Albert Schweitzer, Abraham Lincoln, and of course, our Lord, Jesus Christ. All were lean and strong. All three of them knew hard work, knew when it was time to relax. Each of them knew what it means to belong, even more than the significant belonging of family life. Albert Schweitzer felt "a kinship with all life." Abraham Lincoln "belonged to the ages." Jesus lived and died expressly to belong to the human race and to bring all men into the family of God.

View the deliberately structured life of Albert Schweitzer. After spending the first third of it in the study of medicine, he turned to playing Bach, and became an acclaimed virtuoso on the great pipe organs of Europe. His soul was so enriched that he decided to devote the rest of his life to service. He built the famous Lamborene Hospital in Africa while loving and serving God and man, trying to balance the evil he had seen in his childhood. Complete dedication!

Abe Lincoln, the log splitter, knew both physical and mental work. How we love the humorous stories he told; the nobility of his character shining through his humor. His study of Scripture blossomed into the Emancipation Proclamation. The towering, humble President of the United States knew suffering; knew obedience; knew self-control. His life was so structured, contained such balanced values, that he achieved freedom for slaves. Except for some Biblical characters, in my opinion only one other person in history was a better example of a balanced life.

Jesus, the Son of God, is also the supreme Son of Man. In His short thirty-three years He had it all together. We know that He was a studious, obedient child by His questions to the rabbis in the temple and His submission to His parents. We believe He worked hard with His hands in the carpenter shop. For a time He even shared the role of provider in an earthly home. We see that He knew the place of celebration by His performing that first miracle at the wedding feast, turning the water into wine. Jesus also practiced times of rest, renewal, and privacy for prayer. His life was powerful because He was always in touch with the Source of Power, instead of overworking His human skills. He knew close family relationships and extended the pattern of inclusive love to all who obey God.

> But he answered them . . . Who is my mother? and who are my brothers? For whoever does the will of my Father which is in heaven, he is my brother, and sister, and mother. (Matthew 12:48, 50)

To a dieter, one of the most helpful things to learn about Jesus' life is His sense of direction. He always looked up to God. He looked out on sinful people with love. We don't need self-pity; we need a goal. Having a direction establishes proportional values to live by. Jesus said:

> But the hour comes, and now is, when the true worshippers shall worship the Father in spirit and in truth: for the Father seeks such to worship him. God is a Spirit: and they who worship him must worship him in spirit and in truth. (John 4:23-24)

7
THE CHEATING GAME

PLATEAUS AND EXCUSES

The start of a diet is like a honeymoon, glamorous and exciting. Most people do well in the beginning, because they're desperate enough to follow instructions. Most dieters on the Becomers' Balanced Diet experience a dramatic water loss the first week. Then comes the nitty gritty. Sooner or later every dieter discovers that human will power runs out and human nature takes over. If you're at a standstill, or if you're gaining weight again, you're probably differing from the diet. Actual plateaus in weight loss do occur but after a brief rest of not more than two weeks, you should start to lose weight again. However, the result of unwise substitutions (such as a brownie for lunch) should not be considered a plateau!

Try not to substitute excuses for motivation. If you are tempted to blame your gain on water retention, remember that most overweight people have that condition. Have you excused your weight gain on the basis of the variation in your monthly cycle? That excuse may be good for one week only, but not three out of four. True, when your blood sugar is down, you are tempted by sweets, but there are alternatives. The most likely rationalization you will make is that your metabolism may be faulty. Remember: almost every dieter has considered this possibility.

WHAT THE DIET DOCTORS SAY ABOUT METABOLISM
In his latest book, *But I Don't Eat That Much*, Dr. Morton B. Glenn writes, "In my own experience of over 20 years in this field, I have found that less than .01 per cent of failures were for metabolic reasons, and even those cases were difficult to prove."[14]

Dr. Neil Solomon in his book, *The Truth About Weight Control*, uses the term "Yo-yo Syndrome," the cycle of gaining and losing weight. He explains that altered metabolism may be a result, but not a cause, of overweight due to inability to burn glucose properly.[15]

Weight gain is most often a result of indiscriminate eating. Subconsciously we know that, and we can save the tremendous expense of exhaustive testing by facing the facts.

INSIGHT
What happened to the effective life-style that worked for you in the beginning? Why are you cheating when you have planned, shopped, and served so carefully? Are you just careless, or are you loveless? Maybe a child rules your home, demanding sweets, and refusing to eat by a regular meal schedule, causing you to handle the wrong foods often, for his whims. Unexpected company can get you side-tracked. Time schedules and pressures can corner you into an apathetic attitude.

If excuses don't help, how will you ever get back on the diet even for one day or one meal? Dr. Glenn states that permanent weight loss requires both insight and the recognition that you will never be able to go back to your old eating habits. How can you stay motivated to follow through? He says, "It is essential to proper maintenance that you go all the way to reach your correct goal, and not quit a few pounds too early."[16]

Dr. Karl Menninger, in his book, *Whatever Became of Sin*, treats the subject of obesity in his sixth chapter, "Sin Into Symptom". He lists obesity as an emergency coping device—a psychological reaction to overstress—right along with headache, high blood pressure, depression, anxiety, the incorrigible impulsivity of child-beating, the distress and pain of stomach ulcers, and kleptomania. According to Dr. Menninger, other possible management reactions to tension include drug addiction and self-mutilation, check forging and convulsion.[17]

Dr. Isaac Ruben, the diet columnist, warns in his book, *Forever Thin*, "Obesity is a neurotic condition, an emotional sickness that, if uncontrolled, periodically produces overweight or fatness, a physical sickness. Obesity is a sickness of malignant magnitude in terms of destruction; emotionally—especially in terms of pain and suffering—socially, and functionally (all areas of function including the economic): physically (contributing to all degenerative diseases and destroying longevity); in terms of the deleterious effect on all areas of one's life."[18] This psychiatrist says that you must make the diagnosis yourself and help with your own cure by personal interest, involvement and understanding.

The medical experts seem to agree that something is missing in the psychology of motivation, in the dieter's ability to handle the inevitable crises of daily life. Insight is needed, and there is no pill for it. I have suggested that you take the diet itself in one hand and the Creator's hand in the other to remain steady. If you're slipping, did you let go with one hand and then the other? It's easy to be snared by the old nibbling habits when you're not guarded. Cheating is a fleeting pleasure which can only end in discouragement and guilt. Those destructive feelings are as heavy and as crippling as fat itself. Unchecked, cheating only leads to more and more unhappiness. Instead, hang on! Someone cares!

A LOOK AT CAUSES AND MOTIVES

If you are suffering from diet failure, you're not alone. All dieters cheat sooner or later. The real world has more distractions every day, especially with increased television advertising of junk foods. Prevalence of the overweight condition in America doesn't make it less miserable, however. You aren't giving up, or you wouldn't have read this far. Instead of wallowing in self-pity, why not learn something from failure?

You can forgive yourself and accept discipline. Permit your Internal Instructor to reveal your present attitudes and motives with these provocative questions. Since He loves you, He can help you understand yourself; help you to reverse your tendency to cheat. Submit to His kindly examination.

Does anyone really care or even notice if I cheat?

Does anyone else suffer from my indiscretion?

Is my depression a cause or a result of cheating?

Does fatigue send me looking into the refrigerator for a pick-me-up?

What does all this eating do for my loneliness?

Can I tranquilize tension and anxiety with sweets or fats or excessive starches?

When I express anger openly, I feel guilty afterward. Then I eat to soothe my feelings. What happens if I store up rage?

Do martyrs get fat? Are resentments related to pounds?

How can I accept disappointments without eating?

Can I anticipate frustrations?

How can I overcome the fear of failure?

Do I believe in myself?

Do I have a faith in any source other than the refrigerator for comfort and companionship?

Why do I eat unconsciously, on the run, in the car, watching television, or at the stove while cooking?

What's eating me, or who's eating me?

Am I or is my spouse threatened by my figure improvement or my changing role in the family?

Does one cookie or one potato chip satisfy me?

Am I aware that excess salt may be holding water? Do I use it at the stove and the table when I should not?

THE THERAPY OF PRAYER

The big question is: "What makes me a compulsive eater?" I can't believe I ate that whole thing!

After living with this last haunting question for a long time, I became desperate enough to pray about it. My Internal Instructor showed me that my compulsions were not just with food. When at last I listened, He revealed that I was a compulsive talker, monopolizing conversations wherever people were kind enough to listen. I recognized, too, that I was a compulsive buyer. These self-centered compulsions appeared to compensate for missing satisfactions in my life. As the Lord began to have His way with me, I felt more secure and strong, less prone to compulsive behavior. I can now wait more easily for my turn to talk, to buy, to eat. I am growing more emotionally mature because the Instructor within satisfies my cravings moment by moment. When you feel loved, you don't need to strive for attention, possessions, or food. The Instructor within is that very real, warm Presence, the Lord Himself, counseling, comforting, encouraging, loving His own highest creation, the human body, mind, and soul.

LIFETIME EQUIPMENT

The human body is truly miraculous in its lifetime equipment. It has an air filter—the nose; an oxygen and blood mixer—the lungs; sensory radar in the skin and olfactories; and a blood pump with miles of delivery channels to and from all parts of the body. Your mouth and stomach serve as a food blender with mechanical and automatic chemical controls. Don't make your blender a garbage disposal. You have a computer for programming good eating habits into the brain. Your body is guided, synchronized, and protected by an intricate electrical system of nerves connecting all the organs for smooth functioning. Your eyes are a stereo camera for selecting and appreciating food, and your ears are stereo receivers through which you learn from advertising, inspiration, and personal communication. Your voluntary motion apparatus of muscles, joints, and bones may be controlled at will. Involuntary muscles automatically take care of many body processes, leaving you free to think, choose and become a balanced organism; in fact, the highest form of life. For instance, breathing is effortless; so is the sorting and delivery of wastes, and the use of food and nutrients. Your body is also a chemical plant which produces enzymes and hormones with its glands, controlling your true appetite and well-being. Valves and duplicate parts in most of your organs stand by for emergencies. Whatever you eat beyond what you need for energy, your body will store as fat. Obesity is an abuse of God's temple, complicating all that beautiful equipment, and it's detrimental to your health and happiness.

THE SOLUTION TO THE DIET DILEMMA

Let your Internal Instructor take your picking fingers in His strong hand. In touch with Him, you'll discover all the treasures of wisdom and knowledge. You are completely adequate in Him. There is no temptation He has not known. Remember that even He was tempted to make stones into bread. He has overcome, and will provide a way of escape for you. (See I Corinthians 10:13.) Be faithful over each small decision: He will make you master over temptations. Receive His guidance once more, and be glad. Even if you should let go of His hand again, He will never let you go. He loves you unconditionally, everlastingly. He will restore your resolve. If He loves you enough to give His life for you in perfect loving obedience to His Father, then you can surely love yourself and begin again. Now His questions require your affirmation.

Do you want to be a better half in your marriage, improve your relationships, make your children proud of you?

Do you want to keep your job, or find a better one?

Would you feel more social if you wore a smaller size?

Does your doctor want you to lose weight for health reasons?

Do you want to stand up, slim, in a wedding party?

Could you participate in sports and dancing better if you lost weight?

Do you want to live ten years longer, play with your grandchildren?

Do you want to have an influence on family and friends and associates?

Are you ready for self-control?

Then lean on your Internal Instructor a little harder!

THE CHEAT CHART

Positive attitudes can help you cope with life. Your real hunger is for the nourishing aspects of love. Without them, you will continue to cheat. The Cheat Chart (Table 2) is a development of St. Paul's writing to the Galatians, the Fruits of the Spirit (Galatians 5:22, 23). These synonyms and antonyms will help you focus your attention on your particular deficiency. On one side of the chart are fulfillment resources to shoot for. You can't drum up these positive attitudes at will. But you can cultivate these deep virtues as you grow

TABLE 2. THE CHEAT CHART

Negative Results of Cheating	Positive Results of Caring
Self-deception, intro-spection, rationalization, defeatism	Love, devotion, brother-hood, benevolent concern, outgoing attitudes
Apathy, discouragement, despair, guilt, solace in food and drink, discomfort, misery	Joy, happiness, delight, pleasure, pride, direction, enthusiasm, motivation, achievement, appreciation
Frustration, slavery to poor habits, compensations, tension, hurry, worry, and work exhaustion	Peace, freedom from disorder, serenity, calm, tranquility, confidence, agreement, mental, physical, and spiritual well-being
Compulsive eating (licentiousness), crash dieting, anger at self and others, ill temper, temporary values	Patience, endurance, perseverance, good habits, ability to wait for results (emotional maturity)
Stubbornness, dissention, criticism, social withdrawal, tendency toward envy, jealousy, hopeless depression	Kindness, gentleness, good will, graciousness, affection, readiness, willingness to try
Gluttony, selfishness, over-indulgence, laziness	Goodness, generosity, excellence, desire to work, play, and exercise
Suspicion, distrust, unwise use of time and money, skepticism, inconsistency	Faithfulness, honesty, reliability, dependability, trust, belief, allegiance, resolution
Bullheadedness, unwilling-ness to face facts, reckless abandon with food, insistence, arrogance	Gentleness, humility, meekness, temperance, moderation
Self-hate, "martyrdom," increased devastating cheating, negativism, feelings of inferiority	Self-control, efficiency of body functions, increased awareness and alertness, contagious example, glowing health

in Love. There is a better way to live, a larger authority to depend on, a deep reservoir from which to draw stability. Love opens the mind for true evaluation, showing up futile habits for what they are. Love creates a climate for healing in body, mind, and spirit. The ultimate final blessing of Love is self-control: just the prescription for compulsive eaters and cheaters.

The most practical advice for a floundering dieter is this: Commit your whole life to Love, to the Lord as you know Him, and to a sound, balanced diet regime with friends who have a strong common desire—people who care. You will know these friends by their positive mental attitudes as they love and care for you. Friends will provide emotional support.

Naturally no group of persons is completely controlled. But when caring people meet regularly and share, the person needing help is surrounded with the happiness of other ordinary people who are overcoming the same hangups. In group therapy one can find encouragement, mental stimulation, safety, and achievement. The goal is not just to lose five pounds (2.27 kg). It's to maintain a goal weight for life with a style that satisfies. Faith, Love, and your own responsive effort will get you back on the track. As you think, you will become.

LOVE, THE BEHAVIOR MODIFIER
Proponents of behavior modification recommend writing down everything you eat, associating food only with the table, and eating slowly, at specific times. These are some of the worthwhile proven methods for people who are motivated. But sometimes even the fear of illness is not motivating enough. For instance, though someone has said, "The only difference between being in a rut and being in a grave is the depth," dieters smile in agreement at this, and continue to cheat. It is Love which has been motivating and modifying human behavior for 2000 years. If you know that Someone cares personally about your weight, you won't deliberately let Him down. The love of God in Christ demonstrates that personal concern. He has known across the centuries that we would need to be saved from ourselves.

In these trying days of unrest, shortages, and insecurity throughout the world, there is still one positive thing a frustrated dieter can do to keep sane: "Present your body a living sacrifice, holy and acceptable to God, a reasonable offering." What could be more motivating than to anticipate meeting your Maker? Will you measure up because of fear, or vanity, or because of Love? Shape up so you can ship out ship shape. Every resource for your fulfillment is within you, placed there by the Creator for response to Him and to all the rest of His good creation.

RENEWED COMMITMENT
If you dropped out of a diet group because of the expense, start looking for one friend (or more) who also needs and desires help. Where two or three are gathered together in the name of and for the purpose of Love, there is direction and power. For He will be there. Love can move mountains of fat. Agree on action. Shop selectively, cook wisely, serve attractively, eat slowly and thankfully again. You've heard all that before. But you've tried the alternatives, too, and found that it costs to cheat. If you can afford to be fat and depressed, you can afford even more to get help and be happy. In 1978 minimum daily hospital care costs over $200 a day! According to a recent television documentary, the cost of health care is rising faster than inflation. Who can afford to be sick? Since cheating makes you miserable and wastes your time and money, leaving you vulnerable to health hazards, why not try being obedient to the program again? Be true to yourself.

Jesus said, "I am the way, the truth, and the life." Commit yourself with humble obedience to your Creator who gave you that marvelous body with all its automatic functions uniquely wrapped with your own physique and personality. You are fearfully and wonderfully made. Don't hide your real self under a bushel of fat. He formed you with a mind and spirit to be nurtured—if and when you're ready. Invited, He can produce in you the fruit of the Spirit, the disciplined life, freedom from the tyranny of destructive eating habits. You can resemble Him, as a child resembles his father. That's His will for you here and now! You can live abundantly and have self control. Isn't that better than eating your cake and having it too, to carry around with you, tucking it in behind sliding zippers and squeezing it into too-short seat belts? "Taste and see; the Lord is good." He is our Father, and we are all one family. Accept His care and pruning with thanksgiving. Take as your own this verse from a birthday card I received from my Mother-in-Love:

Some family trees are full of nuts
And prunes and lemons, too.
It isn't every family tree
That grows a peach like you.

RECIPE FOR A HAPPY WEEK WITHOUT CHEATING

1 cup of friendly words with acceptance and belonging stirred in lightly
2 cups of understanding your own need, using a full-length mirror and a set of medical scales, if possible
3 heaping tablespoonfuls of care for shopping, preparation, and serving
3 appointed times to eat meals slowly each day
A pinch of warm personality, a like-minded friend with whom to share your victories and defeats
A dash of humor so that you don't take yourself too seriously
The Basic Ingredient—Infinite Love—to lift you and hold your days consistently
Mix well and serve regularly with unrestricted vegetables in generous portions. Garnish with exercise, recreation and rest.

8
THE JOY OF COMMITMENT

JOY IS BEING THIN
You can sing your happy commitment with this parody of "Joy Is Like The Rain" by Sister Miriam Therese Winter. Learn the lilting tune from the record album "Joy Is Like The Rain" by the Medical Mission Sisters on Avant Garde Records, Vanguard Music Corporation, 250 West 57th Street, New York, New York 10000.

Joy Is Being Thin
I saw butter on the table, more than just a whim;
Butter makes the fanny bulge, so I'd better not indulge;
Joy is being trim.

I saw tuna mixed with mayonnaise in a sandwich thick;
But I love my Melba Thin; water pack is really in.
What a nifty trick!

I saw gravy thick and greasy in a gravy boat;
To the salad I must go; in the mirror choices show;
Joy's a size ten coat!

I saw fruits at roadside markets, fruit from every tree.
They were ripe and very sweet, very tempting to repeat;
                    Joy is counting three.

I saw brownies made by daughter (I would not have dared),
I must pause and use my head, reach for cauliflower instead;
                    I will be prepared.

I had friends at last night's party tempting me to taste;
I have shopped all over town; on those goodies I must frown;
                    Calories go to waist.

I can smell those greasy French fries and potato chips.
Go away; throw them away, or they'll land upon my hips;
                    I will seal my lips.

I am feeling the commitment of a way to eat;
Knowing what I need each meal, proven by the way I feel;
                    Compliments are sweet.

I am growing slimmer, stronger; new tastes satisfy;
New morale is running high, much to do before I die;
                    I know what to buy.

I am changing all my habits, at the table sit,
Eat more slowly every day; steady does it all the way;
                    Joy is feeling fit.

Planned nutrition's most effective when I exercise;
Circulation gives me pep, tones my muscles step by step;
                    Confidence does rise.

Nonfat milk in cardboard boxes, all is surely skim;
Face grows smoother every day; sixteen ounces is the way;
                    Joy is feeling vim.

I like chicken, fish, and cheeses, so you now can see
Skin is velvet, hair is silk; I like vegetables and milk.
                    Joy is good for me.

COMMITMENT IS CARING

Do you know anyone who can stay on a diet or remain at goal by sheer will power? Being surrounded by high living and affluent entertainment makes slipping off the diet easy. Temptation is part of the real world. With the economic crunch, many families are turning more and more to day-old baked goods, sweets, the cheapest hamburger and excessive use of refined starches, such as pasta and white bread, thinking that they are cheaper than high quality protein, fruits, vegetables, whole grain cereals and bread, and milk. Shopping education and home gardening can help us all to be better stewards.

You may like the cute song to help you stay committed to your diet, but you will also need continuing insight. Commit your life with joy to the Person of Jesus Christ, the Basic Ingredient, your Internal Instructor, who brought you this far. "In all your ways acknowledge him and he will direct your paths." (Proverbs 3:6) Recognize your weakness and need. Not only is He sufficient; He is an ever increasing source of joy.

This kind of commitment will open your ears to conversation you need to hear. The caring and sharing process of a weight control group—either a nationally organized one or one of your own making—can be invaluable. The Lord knows you need recognition, like-minded, committed friends to encourage you with a sense of belonging, acceptance, and inspiration. Success is contagious, and it's fun. Committed to good nutrition, you're a credit to your Maker. He rewards you with well-being, energy, compliments, satisfaction: a balanced, happy life. His very words to you are, "For my yoke is easy, and my burden is light." (Matthew 11:30) Choose today which you will be, an undisciplined overweight person full of excuses and failures, or a slim, well-nourished person maturing in body, mind, and spirit, committed to caring.

THE JOY AND SAFETY OF OBEDIENCE

Who wouldn't be delighted to lose all that fat? Each new size is a joy. Remember the clothes in your closet? Those classic designs, all paid for? No one can take this joy away from you. All it costs is obedience. It's better than health insurance, social status, or fortune, because it's all of these—and more. Joy dawns when you trust and obey.

Look . . . "unto Jesus the author and finisher of our faith; who for the joy that was set before him, endured the cross, despising the shame, and is seated at the right hand of the throne of God." (Hebrews 12:2) Dr. Leslie Weatherhead, the famous English clergyman and psychiatrist, wrote a book, *The Resurrection of Christ*, in which he explains the manner of the resurrection in the light of science and psychical research, concluding that Jesus' great obedience, self-control, and trust made the resurrection possible.[19]

The Old Testament prophet Micah gives us a simple rule of life: " . . . what does the Lord require of you but to do justly, love mercy, and walk humbly with your God." (Micah 6:8b) That rule can be your joyful commitment, implying that you eat only what you need in a hungry world. Take the Becomers' Balanced Diet Menu in one hand and hold onto the Lord with the other. He'll be at your shoulder when you look in the refrigerator. He cares for you more than anyone. He can go shopping with you and advise you. He is your Counsellor. He knows your capacity, your weakness—peanut butter? The Koran says, "Speak to God and listen to Him, and He will tell you where you deviate." He wants you to be happy and safe.

SAGE MORSELS FOR BECOMERS
God's Word has nourishment for your soul. Your safe commitment depends on this daily bread. You can find it for yourself. To start with, share some hidden manna promised in Revelation 2:17.

Occasionally as a Maintainer you may be tempted by sweets, or even crave them. Then chew on this: "How sweet are your words to my taste! yes, sweeter than honey to my mouth." (Psalm 119:103)

When social eating threatens you, think quietly to yourself what Jesus said: "I have meat to eat that you do not know about." (John 4:32) From the Old Testament remember: "You prepare a table before me in the presence of my enemies: you anoint my head with oil; my cup runs over." (Psalm 23:5)

Are starchy foods your hangup? Eat your portion slowly, recalling Jesus' words, "I am the bread of life: he that comes to me will never hunger; and he that believes on me will never thirst." (John 6:35b) The Psalmist said, "Taste and see that the Lord is good: blessed is the man who trusts in him." (Psalm 34:8)

When you're distracted, concentrate on this: "I can do all things through Christ who strengthens me." (Philippians 4:13) The diet is easy when He reinforces your resolve.

Don't belittle yourself; " . . . your body is the temple of the Holy Ghost . . . ." (I Corinthians 6:19) You are made in God's own image.

When you want to remain steady, read the First Psalm. Be that person who associates with believers, who produces and prospers in the Lord's hand.

Should you feel estranged or lonely, recall that " . . . as many as received him, to them he gave power to become the sons of God . . . ." (John 1:12)

Even Maintainers have moods of exhaustion and weakness. Prepare yourself for these human moments with this passage:

> Haven't you known? haven't you heard, that the everlasting God, the Lord, the Creator of the ends of the earth, is never faint or weary? There is no searching of his understanding. He gives power to the faint; and to the weak he increases strength. Even youths shall faint and be weary, and young men shall utterly fall: But they who wait on the Lord shall renew their strength; they shall mount up with wings like eagles; they shall run, and not be weary; and they shall walk, and not faint. (Isaiah 40:28-31)

Then refer again to the 90th Psalm. This prayer of commitment is for every age and circumstance.

> So teach us to number our days, that we may apply our hearts to wisdom. O satisfy us early with your mercy; that we may rejoice and be glad all our days. Make us glad according to the days when you afflicted us, and the years of testing. Let your work appear unto your servants, and your glory unto their children. And let the beauty of the Lord our God be upon us: and establish the work of our hands; yes, the work of our hands, establish it. (Psalm 90:12, 14-17)

FULFILLMENT

At the end of the New Testament, St. John on Patmos has the final view of the new creation, and we're part of it! He saw us as we may become *if we choose*: the finished product of the Creator's hand, His masterpiece; you and me, our families, our community, our churches, our tired old world, changed because we let Him shape us where we need it today. "And I, John, saw the holy city coming down from God as a bride adorned for her husband." (Revelation 21:2) Could there be any greater joy of commitment than that beautiful vision of perfection? "You are worthy, O Lord, to receive glory and honor and power: for you have created all things, and for your pleasure they are and were created." (Revelation 4:11)

9
THE PRIDE OF ACCOMPLISHMENT

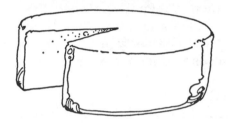

PRICELESS SHAPE AND MORALE

When one reaches goal weight, it's like winning an Olympic event. Admirers are inspired by the priceless new shape and the obviously high morale of the successful dieter. A unique personality has been uncovered, a new body and mind: attractive, agile, confident, alert, and supremely happy. Herbert Hoover once said, "Possibly the greatest source of human happiness is personal achievement." Because of the new life that has been won, the dieter is willing to show the "before" picture. With time, patience, and instruction, Love has wrought a miracle of change from degeneration to life, the miracle of re-birth! It's more awesome than anything man can do alone. It's the human body, mind, and spirit, attuned as a living instrument of God's glory.

SUCCESSFUL MAINTENANCE

Reaching goal doesn't guarantee permanent perfection, however. Temptations will come again. Under stress, or from boredom or fatigue, at an unguarded moment, a dieter who has previously been a compulsive eater may revert to unwise choices and quantities; old habits are hard to break.

But your like-minded friends will continue to care and watch for your recovery. As a Maintainer you protect your investment of time and effort by keeping in touch with your friends to share recipes, shopping tips, and emotional support. Being praised as a pioneer is one of your rewards for successful maintenance, and it's more heady than wine. You're both proud and vulnerable. As you continue to weigh in regularly you are living proof of successful maintenance. You in turn help others to believe in themselves. Think of it as part of your personal ministry. Remember, you will never dare be completely on your own. St. Paul reminded the Hebrews that God's promise to Joshua was for all of us: "I will not fail you nor forsake you." (Hebrews 13:5) Forever you will have the basic ingredient, Love, of which Jesus is the source and example.

OPPORTUNITIES
The pride of accomplishment is not ostentatious. The good proportions of your body and the lift in your step, even your confident posture, declare your success naturally, with hardly a word from you. You have a thankfulness resembling joy, thankfulness for new opportunities, jobs, friends, improved family relationships. Compliments are frequent. That's when you can begin to help others; they'll be eager to learn your secrets. You'll find it easier to handle the threats of jealous friends with poise when you're at goal weight. Exercise is no longer drudgery; it's fun. Your new sensible eating habits are satisfying. You can be slim and stay that way! Your body weight is one thing about your life that you can control. No one can take it away from you. All you need is continued motivation to stay in shape. It's a dream come true. As the new life-style evolves, you view food in its proper perspective.

Life doesn't just begin at forty. Life is not something just discovered in a test tube, or from hundreds of years of study of the stars, or from a little bit of dirt from Mars. Life is here and now, whatever your age; life is yours at goal weight. Jesus said, "I am the way, the truth, and the life." (John 14:6b)

Everything is provided here and now for your complete development. You have the pattern to follow, the menu, and the friends to make it work. You have all the potential for fulfilling human life, God's highest creation. With your open mind, your readiness to meet life head on, your life is good. Problems become only challenges. By overcoming the weight problem you have proven to yourself that you can overcome any obstacle. The strength is from within. The real pride of accomplishment is due to your Internal Instructor. He gives a Maintainer the judgment to make appropriate substitutions with foods. For instance, He may invite you to have a baked potato in place of a limited vegetable, but you will feel cautioned to eat it with yogurt instead of butter or sour cream. He gives His Maintainers eating opportunities with a practical sense of values.

CREDIT YOUR INSTRUCTOR WITHIN

Remember the girl in the first chapter who was looking in the mirror, reviewing the status quo? She noticed in the corner of the mirror a peeping Tom also making an appraisal. Were you like that girl, panicked by the real truth? Were you shocked into getting help? Look again, now. See what Love is doing for you.

> For now we see in a mirror dimly, but then face to face. Now I know in part; then I shall understand fully, even as I have been fully understood. So faith, hope, love abide, these three; but the greatest of these is love. (I Corinthians 13:12, 13)

Love is the power of success. The pride of achievement is never a smug judgment of others who need help. It's not thinking that you're perfect. Your boast is that you know the Source and value of self-control. You've formed satisfying lifetime habits depending on your Internal Instructor. You've proven that you can live this way. You are a living, breathing example of the miracle of change, accomplied by caring. Of course, the pride of accomplishment brings with it the risk of human vanity. To receive compliments graciously, we need to credit our Instructor within. Our new poise and authority actually reflect the orderly universe of a dependable Creator. Naturally, we need to be recognized and appreciated. But we also need to remember that no one can do it alone in this land of abundant sweets, fats, and starches. Our human will power is weak; it's Love that holds us steady.

The Instructor within who taught you to care is making your success contagious. Friends and family catch your positive attitudes

about food and about life. Do you see that you have more of an influence at goal weight? How true it is that "He's got the whole world in
His hand." There is enough food; there are enough commodities and
resources, enough Love to share.

Food is basic to our well being, but too much food spoils our true
contentment and health. Too much food unshared here in the U.S. is
surely cause for unrest in those large parts of the world where children go to bed hungry every night. God knows where your new self-
control will lead. Never in the history of the world have disciplined
leaders and citizens been more sorely needed. Can you believe that
the answer to the looming world food crisis can begin in your own
home? The family is the basic unit of society—what an effective
place to start! Family members will be inevitably affected by the
prudent pattern of eating that brought you to goal weight. The miraculous achievement of personal discipline, love, and self-respect are
appreciated most in the family—the daily testing ground. A healthy,
happy, long life to all of you! Thanks to your Internal Instructor
you're now in a position to love your neighbor as yourself.

MULTIPLY YOUR RESOURCES
As you digested the basic ingredient, Love, you learned to know
yourself and to be free of eating hangups. Although no one is perfect,
you and I enjoy the continuing adventure of becoming. As we
develop further in the spirit, maintaining our physical goal weight,
we are more motivated to express Love in even wider and more
meaningful activities. We gladly give ourselves in service and love
to friends and family, and we enter into community service. But now
that we're at goal weight, we may enlarge our horizons further with
our increased capacity to care. Perhaps we have something to offer
that is desperately needed—a token gift of our substance which
represents our successful life and work. You may already be par-
ticipating in a worthwhile mission or charity, and every mail brings
more pleas for money. You shouldn't have to give until it hurts; give
until it feels good. Each of us must decide which causes are most
beneficial to the recipients. The work of evangelists and the mis-
sions of church denominations, Care, and World Vision International are among the outreaches on God's priority list. While hunger
for God's Word is being recognized throughout the earth, world-

wide physical hunger is actually reaching famine proportions in our lifetime.

Now that you've reached maintenance and know the resource of Love, you have an opportunity to dish out the Basic Ingredient where it is most urgently needed. Would you like to be a shining light in a dark world of hunger because of the consumer education you've been learning? You saved money each time you took those giant steps in the grocery store past mayonnaise, cake mixes, potato chips, convenience foods, ice cream, cookies, candy, and sweet bakery products. After you've bought your new wardrobe and established your good self-image, you may be interested in a challenge which can make your good life even more productive and happy. I have a special attachment to a project which multiplies one's gift geometrically, because the living gift is an animal resource.

It is Heifer Project, Inc., a self-help, non-denominational charity which has served the world's hungry in over fifty nations for the past third of a century. The gifts are living pedigreed animals; cows, pigs, goats, rabbits, and baby chicks. They multiply rapidly, and each recipient must promise to give the first female offspring to someone else and teach him the agricultural skills learned from Heifer Project. The government agency, Aid for International Development, helps with transportation, and where it is feasible, the Peace Corps helps administer the program. Livestock is collected for distribution at The Fourche River Ranch, Heifer Project Headquarters, in Little Rock, Arkansas. Contributions may be sent to them at the Worthen Building, P. O. Box 808, Little Rock, Arkansas 72201. Such gifts are, of course, deductible for income tax purposes.

Involvement in Heifer Project is one example of a practical way to love your neighbor as yourself. A few cents a day saved from clever shopping and wise eating can mean life and hope to desperate families who are actually starving. The principle of caring helped you to lose weight. Now that you have achieved goal weight, and know how to eat well and care for yourself, you may actually desire to reach out and care, sharing in one solution to the worldwide hunger crisis. Imagine the joy of hungry children receiving the gift of a real live animal from you in America! A pet! A multiplying gift of protein food! To share expertise in animal husbandry and hold recipients responsible for teaching person to person is to bring hope and dignity to the gaunt faces of starvation. Read what our Internal Instructor says about feeding the hungry:

> Then the King will say to those at his right hand, "Come, O blessed of my Father, inherit the kingdom prepared for you ... for I was hungry and you gave me food, I was thirsty and you gave me drink, I was a stranger and you welcomed me, I was naked and you clothed me, I was sick and you visited me, I was in prison and you came to me." Then the righteous will answer him, "Lord, when did we see thee hungry and feed thee, or thirsty and give thee drink? And when did we see thee a stranger and welcome thee, or naked and clothe thee? And when did we see thee sick or in prison and visit thee?" And the King will answer them, "Truly, I say to you, as you did it to one of the least of these my brethren, you did it to me." (Matthew 25:34-40 RSV)

Why does it feel good to care for the hungry? They are God's children, our opportunity to give to Him. "We love him because he first loved us." (I John 4:19) We never could have reached goal weight without His loving care. The Christian who gives attention to God's priorities has another reason to feel good. Along with the giving comes God's response: He replaces and multiplies the resources, full measure, pressed down, and running over! Infinite Love pays off.

10
SHAPELY BREADS
FOR BECOMERS

A LOW-FAT, HIGH-PROTEIN LOAF

You may have heard of a dieter who made "diet bread" using bread crumbs for flour. Many of these recipes tell us we can eat half a loaf for breakfast or lunch. Wow! But did you know that sometimes this diet bread falls while baking, and doesn't stay in shape after it is taken out of the oven? How can the family be enthusiastic about a soggy loaf or muffins as hard as hockey pucks?

In the conscientious effort to follow a strict diet plan for one individual, many diet breads fail the test of light texture. Furthermore, a dieter who may eat half a loaf of bread for breakfast or lunch just because the recipe contains two eggs and two ounces (57 g) of bread crumbs is not restoring eating habits to normal. The reason this diet bread is so soggy is that two ounces (57 g) of finely crumbled bread are a heavy substitute for dry flour, and dry bread crumbs should not be measured as ounce (gram) portions because they have lost moisture.

That's why the Becomers' Balanced Diet bread recipes recommend a careful use of flour. Careful use of flour holds up a loaf, while cottage cheese and egg may replace the milk to boost the protein content. Doesn't it make more sense to bake a delicious, high-rising protein bread to enjoy one ounce at a time, as directed, for breakfast and lunch?

STRATEGIC USE OF FLOUR

The Becomers' bread recipes feature the least amount of flour necessary for good texture with about equal parts of nonfat dry milk. The strategic use of flour gives the bread shape and body texture even though it is nearly fat- and sugar-free. Used as a flour extender, nonfat dry milk adds protein. White refined flour is minimized because of its high calorie (kiloJoule) content and low nutritional value. Our loaf compares favorably in calorie (kiloJoule) count with conventional bread, ounce for ounce (gram for gram), and it is nutritionally superior. The following conversion table will help you calculate the flour before you use it in baking a diet loaf:

> 1 cup (250 ml) of flour (about 16 tablespoons) = 400 calories (1674 kJ)
>
> 1 ounce (31 ml) of flour (about 2 tablespoons) = 50 calories (209.2 kJ)
>
> A conventional 1-pound (453 g) loaf of bread (15 1-oz. [28 g] slices or 30 half-oz. [14 g] slices) contains approximately 2 cups (500 ml) of flour (about 32 tablespoons) and equals 800 calories (3348 kJ)
>
> 1 slice of thin bread (½ ounce or 14 g) = 40 calories (167 kJ)
>
> 2 slices of thin bread (1 ounce or 28 g) = 80 calories (334 kJ)

The calorie (kiloJoule) assessment in the conventional loaf is approximate, of course, since it contains other ingredients besides flour. Now you can readily see why gravy isn't worth the calories (kiloJoule) of the flour to a dieter, but a strategic amount of flour in baking will support a fine protein loaf of thirty calculated slices.

God meant for you to have bread. It's a vital link in our relationship with Him. It represents life and teamwork. Bread is both a universal language among people and a divine symbolic language. The baking and breaking of bread remind us of God's greatest gift to us: His Son, Jesus Christ—Love personified. Could it be that the great unrecognized hunger for this basic ingredient, Love, is what makes us overindulge in starchy breadstuffs? Be thankful for your special loaf.

> Back of the loaf is the snowy flour,
> And back of the flour the mill;
> And back of the mill is the wheat and the shower,
> And the sun and the Father's will.[20]

LEAVENING AGENTS

In baking diet breads, muffins, or cakes, obtaining that great shape requires suitable leavening agents to lift the dry ingredients. If wisely chosen, these leaveners (or combinations of them) help to produce light, even texture. Excessive baking powder causes a loaf to be too high and holey, like hot air in a pompous sermon. Too much soda for lifting action overpowers the various flavors of good breads. Even one extra egg can level a loaf, producing a sinking battleship which ends up in the garbage. Learn to understand the lifting power of leavening agents, and then you can develop your own good recipes with care and confidence.

Egg white is elastic; it holds air bubbles when beaten. But if you use the blender on egg whites when you're baking, you will cut the natural elastic strands, spoiling the power of the bubbles to lift your batter. Egg yolk helps to hold the batter in place until it coagulates during baking. Incidentally, the yolk adds a little precious fat to tenderize the loaf. You probably already know that egg whites won't beat stiffly if there is any yolk present in the bowl. That bit of fat is what cancels the stretching power of the egg white. That's why egg yolks and egg whites are sometimes added separately, after they have each been stabilized with other ingredients. During the baking, the right amount of gluten stretches to accommodate the air bubbles which you have carefully beaten into the egg whites.

Baking soda reacts especially well with acid liquids such as buttermilk or orange juice, releasing carbon dioxide gas bubbles to expand the batter in some recipes. When the moisture ingredient is bland and of basic chemical content, as in pumpkin or banana bread, the baking soda needs the acid of cream of tartar to create the lifting reaction. One-half teaspoon (2.5 ml) of cream of tartar reacts with one-fourth teaspoon (1 ml) of baking soda, and supplies the same lifting power as one teaspoon (5 ml) of baking powder.

Double-acting baking powder is a combination of two balanced reactions. One is caused by bicarbonate of soda with calcium acid phosphate activated by moisture. The second action comes about in the oven with heat from a third substance, aluminum sulfate.

Yeast is a more time-consuming method of raising bread, but using it can be very satisfying because you cannot escape getting creatively involved through your senses of touch, sight, and smell. When you make yeast bread you put yourself into an act of faith. Kneading can remind you of discipline, while seeing the bread rise in a warm room is a visual symbol of changing, becoming and maturing. You can feel the gentleness with which the living organism, yeast, grows and becomes part of the bread. Even the gentle touch of your fingerprint dents the rising dough. The smell of bread baking is almost like an irresistible prayer invoking Love, making the household eager. The family senses that when you bake bread you are taking time to mold the textures of love: joy, peace, patience, kindness, faith, meekness, and self-control. Such spiritual leavening agents can lift loads of depression due to fat. Yeast seems to have spiritual connotations, but beware of the yeast of the Pharisees, which speaks of growing spiritual pride!

Just as surely as the fragrant yeast grows, enlarging the bread under the right conditions of warmth and moisture, God's children grow strong and influential with regular portions of His Love. Bread is such a daily food—a constant reminder of humble daily submission to that supreme authority, The Bread of Life, the Lord Jesus Himself. Taste and see that He is good, more satisfying than any capricious momentary eating whim. "Humble yourself in His sight, and He will lift you up." (James 4:10) That's His own dependable promise. And so is this one: "And I, if I be lifted up from the earth, will draw all men unto me." (John 12:32) For that perfect, complete joy He kneads us—and we need Him. When you use God's reconciling Love in Jesus Christ as spiritual leavening, you can expect to see a reaction of joy and lightness in your family. Watch for it to increase mysteriously.

And now to summarize. When you convert your own recipes, to lift one cup (250 ml) of flour and one cup (250 ml) of nonfat dry milk (used as flour) in baking, use one of the following combinations:

1 egg and ½ teaspoon (2.5 ml) baking soda
1 teaspoon (5 ml) baking powder
¼ teaspoon (1.2 ml) baking soda and ½ teaspoon (2.5 ml) cream of tartar
½ teaspoon (2.5 ml) baking soda and 1 cup (250 ml) of buttermilk or tart juice
1 package dry yeast softened in warm water

BAKING

Baking time is an important consideration in making quick breads. Muffins take about twenty minutes, breads about forty-five minutes at 350°F (176°C). Glass pans heat higher than metal ones, cooking the bread about five minutes more quickly. Yeast rolls take about ten minutes to bake; yeast breads about thirty-five minutes. The dough must be cooked right through the loaf for successful slicing. Bake on the middle rack for even browning.

SLICING

Everyone adores warm bread. You can slice the high-protein low-fat loaf easily because it has a rigid crust. Do weigh your portion with the food scale, or you'll be carried away! If you let it cool and want to plan your slicing, thirty slices is about right, similar to the commercial loaf of thin-sliced bread. [Don't expect the diet loaf to be as high as the commercial ones, though.] You may safely enjoy two thin slices for breakfast, and two more for lunch.

THE BREAD OF LIFE

Every dieter needs a strong instructor. The Bread of Life is your Internal Instructor, always with you to correct and encourage you. He is to your resolve what texture is to your menu—satisfying. The more you chew on His Word, the more strong, sure, and controlled you will become. His Word is sweeter than honey, a light for every decision. You'll never be thirsty or hungry again; you'll never be hopeless, or left abandoned, or tempted beyond your ability. Recognize your greatest need—the Bread of Life. Appropriate the Staff of Life daily like manna. His very name can control your tongue.

At the name of Jesus every knee shall bow, of things in heaven, and things in earth, and things under the earth; and every tongue shall confess that Jesus Christ is Lord, to the glory of God the Father. (Philippians 2:10, 11)

If this strong Internal Instructor could take a compulsive eater like me and teach me to stay lean, steadfast, and satisfied for seven years (seven years of fulfillment, not famine), He can do the same for you. His instructions are dependable:

... Pray to your Father ... for your Father knows what things you need before you ask him. Therefore pray like this: Our Father in heaven, hallowed be your name. Your kingdom come. Your will be done on earth; as it is in heaven. Give us today our daily bread. (Matthew 6:6, 8b-11)

One of Jesus' three great temptations was to make bread from stones right at the moment of His greatest need and hunger. He resisted and replied to the tempter, "Man does not live by bread alone, but by every word that comes from God's mouth." That was the voice of the strong Internal Instructor who *is* the Word of God. Keep your eyes on Him.

For we do not preach ourselves, but Christ Jesus the Lord; and ourselves your servants for Jesus' sake. For God, who commanded the light to shine out of darkness, has shone in our hearts, to give the light of the knowledge of the glory of God in the face of Jesus Christ. (II Corinthians 4:5, 6)

You looked in the mirror to find your need in the first chapter. Now look at Jesus to realize your potential; not just to be at goal weight, but to be the recipient and the channel of God's nourishing Love and protection. You can be His powerful instrument, part of His plan. "If any man be in Christ, he is a new creature." (II Corinthians 5:17)

Do you see that He died so that you might live more abundantly now? Do you see now that He, as God's Son, is all-powerful over your compulsive eating? Where else can you go for permanent results? He is the basic ingredient of your faith, the personal Savior of your body, mind, and spirit. And you are the very substance of His new creation! Would you like to believe that? Then sign your name, and let this be true. That act of faith puts your life in His care. His strong mind is in your mind; He paid for your lean, whole body at the great price of His own broken body; and He guarantees your spiritual growth with His ever-present, victorious, renewing Spirit. The Word with its promise is within you now, eager to be nourished and watered. You are becoming His grain to be harvested, to be ground and milled, to be disciplined, to rise eternally moment by moment, to be re-formed into God's image, to glorify Him forever! Your future is in great shape, destined for perfection by the consuming fire of the Holy Spirit. Sign your release from the self-destructive weight of fat. Sign your commitment here and now to Jesus Christ, who is the Basic Ingredient, the only requirement for all eternity: simply Love.

_____

(Your Name)

Now you are a vital part of His recipe—a beautiful mini-loaf willing to be multiplied and shared by Love for the hungry waiting world. And look! You're skinny! And ready to meet Him face to face! Maranatha!

Even a mini-loaf has to be broken to be shared. If you want to be the best witness for Jesus, allow yourself now to be broken and molded by exercise, just as a filly has to be broken and trained to do the master's will. Chapter 11 combines simple exercises with worship for developing muscle tone, strength, and endurance. In these dark and fearful times, your habitually confident posture can be not only a bodily protection for you, but a winsome magnet for the Lord.

11
THE TUNE UP

WHO, ME?

Everyone knows that regular exercise is important, good for others of course, but we just haven't taken time to begin a regular program yet for ourselves.

Secretly, we hate to exercise even if we love the Lord, because we may be "a little overweight," slightly self conscious, and sooooo tired. Every day we procrastinate and think we work hard enough without exercise. What we need is a stimulating routine that's easy to follow in our own environment, something to catch the imagination and set us in motion, something inspiring to help us follow through. The same Internal Instructor who teaches us how to eat well, now calls our attention to the completeness of the Becomer's life style, which includes regular exercise. "Humble yourselves in the sight of the Lord, and he shall lift you up!" (James 4:10)

To be effective instruments in His hand we must *use* the marvelous bodies He has given us. Besides reinforcing the benefits of our good eating habits, regular, planned exercise tunes up all our body functions. Combined with worship, exercise may even become a means of grace! Not that you have to wear sack cloth and ashes; an old shirt and slacks will do. If you can submit to the diet, you can this too. And we know that "all things work together for good to those who love God." (Romans 8:28a) With our eyes on Him, our heads and hearts are lifted. Discouragements give way to creative energy. We can feel how worthy He is of our praise, and how unworthy are the magnified sorrows and resentments we accumulate.

THE BECOMER'S EXERCISE LITANY
For the pull of gravity which helps tone our muscles even when we
    aren't conscious of exercise, and
For our built in balance inside the inner ear,
                    thank you God, Our Good and Wise Creator.
For alertness of mind nourished by increased oxygen in the blood
    when we exert ourselves,
For new perspectives, fresh outlook, open minds, courage to defeat
    laziness,
For redirecting all our misguided habits with diet and exercise,
              we offer our wills, Strong Internal Instructor.
For cardiovascular equipment and its flexibility,
For life and breath,
For the love of God which is always seeking us, and directs us even
    more surely than the north star,
                        thank you, Holy Spirit.
For spiritual grace as well as physical stamina,
For opportunities to serve You more effectively,
                    we look to You, Lord Jesus.
For motivation, confidence, assurance, poise, and fulfillment,
          we seek your supportive Love, O God, Our Salvation.
For comprehension of the height, and depth, and length of God's
    love,
                  increase our insight, Lord Jesus.
For release from nervous tension, for the peace of believing, and
    sound refreshing sleep,
                  our praise and thanks, Lord Jesus.
For health and strength and daily food,
                  we praise thy Name, O Lord.[21]

PRAYER POSTURES

Two modern exercise terms describe our prayer postures, isometric and isotonic. Both are used here to convey equal muscle tension. If a firm handshake reveals sincerity, then strong muscular movements in slow motion doubly emphasize the prayer postures. Slow motion tension not only tones muscles, but develops coordination and equilibrium. Careful balance and concentration invite spiritual insights. Some of the simple exercises can be used at a secretary's desk. A sitting position is fine for hand and wrist, arm, ankle, head, neck, and facial movements. Invalids especially need to move at least some parts of the body to prevent weakness and atrophy. Whatever your circumstances, do what you can. Get started and feel the power and joy of the Holy Spirit to teach you worship through exercise. You can run the race for the prize.

God's correction is always right and for our best good, that we may share his holiness. Being punished isn't enjoyable while it is happening—it hurts! But afterwards we can see the result, a quiet growth in grace and character. So take a new grip with your tired hands, stand firm on your shaky legs, and mark out a straight, smooth path for your feet. (Hebrews 12:10b-13a TLB)

HANDS, FEET, AND ARMS

A simple hand exercise will get us started. With hands in front at waist, about a foot from the body, turn palms up with thumbs out. Stretch fingers as far as possible, then turn hand inward and clench the fist hard. Hold for a count of six. Repeat several times. Circle the hand from the wrists six times in toward the center, then six times outward. We'll be using hands to express deep needs and for receiving power to the whole body. Hands which sooth and serve need exercise as well as grooming.

Now for the feet. While you sit, extend both legs in front of you, knees straight. Imagine your ankles tied together. Hold them together tightly while you twist the toes and balls of the feet over and under each other. This strengthens both the front metatarsal arch and the main arch of your foot which helps distribute weight on the foot. This is an excellent exercise for flat feet. It also firms the lower leg. Strong feet will help you execute the prayer postures.

HEAD OF THE BODY

> *He is the Head of the body made up of his people–that is, his church–which he began.* (Colossians 1:18 TLB)

The head controls the body, so bow it reverently, close your eyes, unwind, and listen. Roll it loosely to the right, to the back, to the left, and around to the front again. Three times around. Reverse: to the left, to the back, to the right, to the front again. Three times around. Amen. Lift up your head. Rejoice! Open your eyes wide, squeeze them tightly. Six times. Now extend and retract your jaw out and back six times. Exhale and inhale deeply six times.

PRIVATELY PRONE

Lie down on the floor in the privacy or your own home to practice leg lifting. Swing one leg at a time from side to side at right angles to your prone body, slowly, six times each. Now lift one leg at a time slowly straight up, then down slowly, knee straight. Other leg. Six times each. Next hold your feet under a piece of low furniture and try a slow sit up, beginning with hands over head, raising first the arms, then the head, then the shoulders and last the back. Lower slowly. Do three times at first, then more as you feel able.

Figure 7.

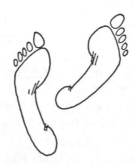

The Isotonic Genuflect is characterized by a restrained tempo. Proper footing frees you to make high, wide and deep movements with the entire body in absolute balance. A full-length mirror will help you learn. Arrange feet about one foot apart, pointing toes outward, the heel of the right foot angled toward the instep of the left, weight on left foot, legs straight. Ballet dancers have a name for this position. Weight lifters use it to achieve leg and back strength. This position enables you to be eloquent in body language. Why not remove your shoes, like Moses? As a Christian believer, you are always on holy ground! (See Figure 7.)

Sliding the right foot forward, toes still angled outward, bend both knees, gradually shifting the weight off the left and onto the right foot. Move as far forward as you can with your back straight. Hold while God blesses your feeble knees. Slowly return your weight back to the left foot by straightening the right leg. Tighten left buttock and bend left knee slightly, putting the weight completely on the left. In this position tense the left thigh, knee bent, and brace the back to steady you for a slow swing of the right leg back from the hip. It will help to push slightly on the floor with the toes and ball of that right foot. Remember that the weight is on the left, so this pushing is an effort. When your right foot is as far back as you can reach, you will feel the right buttock tight and your balance insured by the natural outward direction of your foot. By straightening the left knee while the weight is still on it with back rigid, the right foot simply drags back to its original position slightly in front of you. The exercise is reversed for the other foot, of course. When you become comfortable moving this way, you will be able to fill the place with steps of praise.

To use your right foot for a pivot take one giant step forward or backward with that right foot which is ready and waiting to go. Use the same simple technique of pivoting with the right foot and shifting weight to the left, as you slide the left foot forward, toes pointing out, hold, and swing to rear, dragging the free left foot forward again into starting position.

Practice this at your own pace until your rhythm is natural and habitual. The following diagram may help you to guide your footsteps with a simple foot path of the isotonic genuflect. (See Figure 8.)

Figure 8.

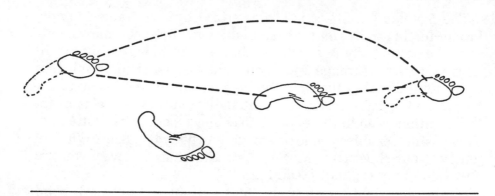

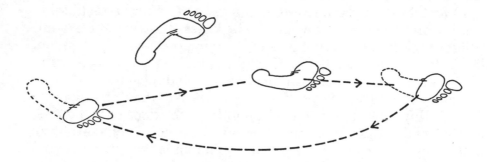

THE EVERLASTING ARMS ARE UNDERNEATH

If feet are made for walking, arms are meant for praising! Shoulders, hips, and knees will follow. (See Figure 9.) Using the original open stance with feet about a foot apart, pointing outward, combine the steps of the Isotonic Genuflect with your arms in movements of total worship. Begin with weight on your left foot, arms down at sides.

Position 1. As you slowly shift your weight forward to the right foot, raise both arms forward in a gesture of petition, palms up, pulling and reaching forward with the shoulders until your hands are directly in front of you, touching to form a bread basket. "Give us this day our daily bread." (Matthew 5:11) The isometric tug gives power to the symbolism, so stay firm as you reach. Stepping back slowly on the left foot, continue to raise your arms upward with your

FIGURE 9.

ISOTONIC GENUFLECT

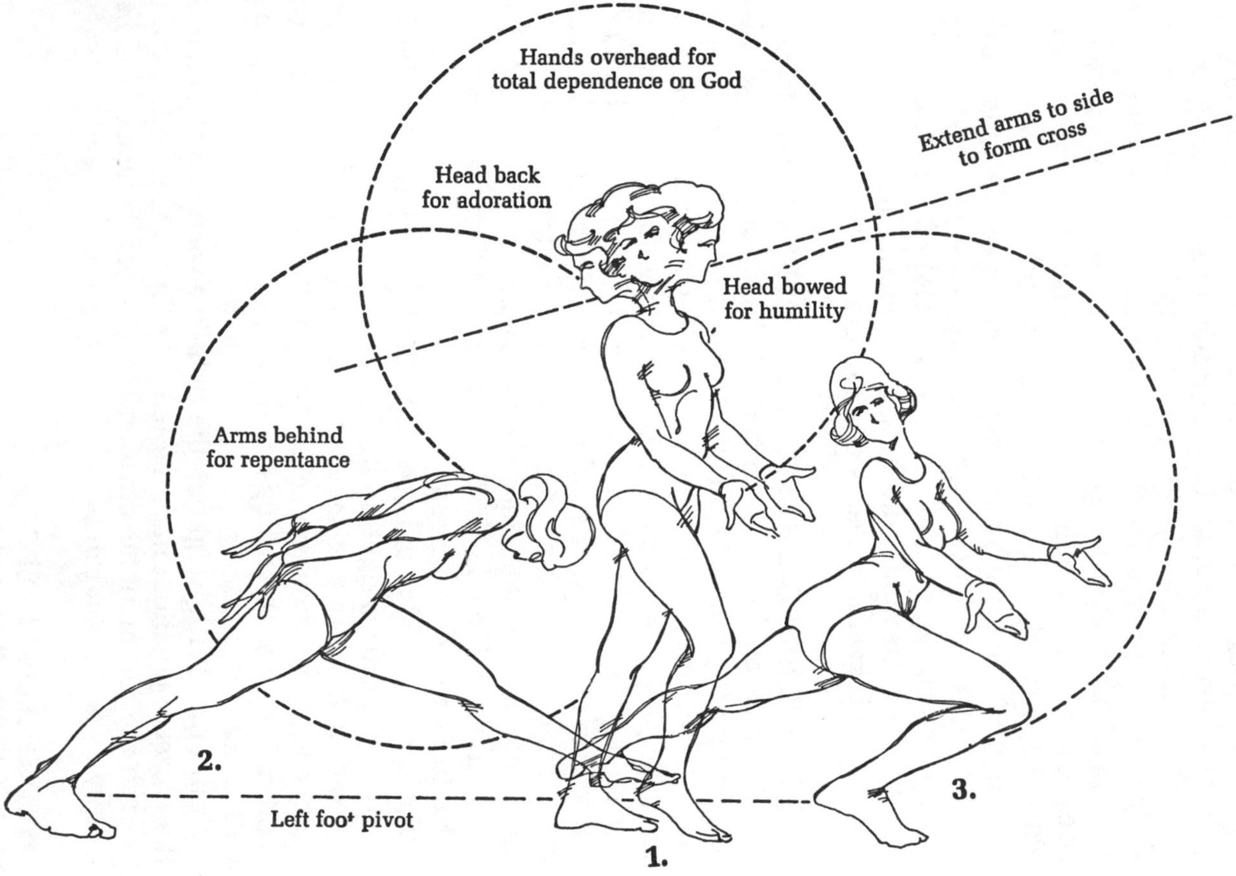

Extend arms to side
to form cross

Hands overhead for
total dependence on God

Head bowed
for humility

Head back
for adoration

Arms behind
for repentance

Left foot pivot

1.

2.

3.

vision following your hands. The twelve o'clock position shows your total dependence on God by reaching and looking up.

Position 2. The right foot moves back in its arc to the rear, while the palms of your hands turn back, your arms lower behind you, and your head bows. Now your weight is equally divided on both feet. See the left position in the diagram of the Isotonic Genuflect which expresses conviction, repentance, and humility.

Position 3. Gradually shift your weight again, leaning into your bending left knee. Repeat the arm raising, while your right foot goes slowly forward again until the bending right knee now takes the weight. Twice around with the slowly moving arms, stepping forward and backward twice, is one exercise.

BACKWARD PRAYER POSTURE TO FORM TILTED CROSS
Another more challenging exercise is to form a cross with your body (See Figure 10.) Again, begin with the original open stance with feet about a foot apart, pointing outward. Lift your arms in front as before, stepping forward on your right foot into the petition position. Remember the bread basket? Then as your weight comes back to the left foot in the Isotonic Genuflect, instead of moving your arms up, move them down in front, to the back, and up to shoulder height to form a crossbar. At the same time move your right foot back as far as you can reach. (See the first position of the Backward Prayer Postures to Form Tilted Cross.)

Position 1. Bend both knees until the left knee touches the floor gently. Rest your weight on it.

Position 2. Were you moving your arms down in front, to the back, and up to shoulder height to form the crossbar? Turn your right foot over with toes upside down so that you may lean back with control.

Position 3. With weight on the right knee and arms extended in the crossbar position, inch the left foot forward, pointing the toe to form the bottom of the cross and to give you balance. Lean back rigidly as far as you can.

LIFTING CROSS EXERCISE
Notice that the first position in this exercise (See Figure 11)) is the same as you just formed by following the Backward Prayer Postures

to Form Tilted Cross, illustrated by its third position. Now comes the sacrifice of obedient disciplined muscle.

Position 1. Lift your head and eyes and lean back, keeping your back straight.

Position 2. Bend your left knee, drawing your left heel directly in front of you. Turn your right foot forward with the toes so that you can push on the floor with both feet to lift your right knee.

Position 3. Continue to hold your back straight and rigid, and brace your thighs as you transfer half of your weight to the left foot, coming to a standing position. Knees will be straight, feet far apart and pointing outward. You'll still be tilting slightly backward, still holding the crossbar position with your arms. This will tend to balance you coming up. Now bend the left knee and lean into it, gradually shifting your weight to the left foot.

Position 4. Drag the right foot forward to the original starting position just ahead of the left foot, both feet still pointing outward for stability. Lower the arms slowly and lift vision heavenward for the Amen.

These exercises are only suggestions to get you started to worship creatively on your own. Incidentally, you will develop physical strength, endurance, and muscle tone as you worship the Lord. "Christ in you, the hope of glory." (Colossians 1:27c)

RUN AND BE NOT WEARY, WALK AND NOT FAINT

Jogging is excellent for the heart and circulatory system, using the respiratory system to replace oxygen in the blood. If you're embarrassed to jog in the street, try a school track or a bicycle trail. Early morning light and fresh air are part of the training tonic. Jogging is least tiring when you use the balls of your feet, springing with each step. It's a good idea to have good running shoes if you jog on hard pavement.

At first try to jog fifty paces, and walk fifty paces. Gradually you'll build endurance and go farther, even uphill. If you prefer to run in place in the bedroom, count your paces, increasing each day. But establish some kind of a regular exercise routine that is strenuous enough to make your heart beat faster, and cause some puffing and perspiration. Brisk walking for an hour would be a good start and would use up about 170 calories. Jogging one half hour would use

FIGURE 10.

BACKWARD PRAYER POSTURES TO FORM TILTED CROSS.

1.

Bend both knees until left knee
touches floor gently. Rest your
weight on it.

2.

Move arms down
back and up
for cross.

Turn right foot backward so
you can lean back with control.

3.

Lean back rigidly
as far as you can.

Inch left foot
forward for balance.

FIGURE 11.

LIFTING CROSS EXERCISE.

Lift head and eyes.

1.

Lean back.

2.

Turn foot forward at toes.

Push with both feet to lift right knee.

4.

Return left foot to raise cross.

Brace thighs and back.

3.

about 160 calories. (See Table 3 for calories consumed in various forms of exercise.) Skiing, swimming, tennis, and skating are enjoyable, strenuous exercises. They are all examples of the beneficial aerobic type of exercise which involves exertion of the heart and lungs. You don't have to be a Billie Jean King or a Dorothy Hamill to know the joy of exercise. But with a little discipline and encouragement you'll be surprised to notice that every day you can feel more benefits of regular exercise. You'll have more fun out of life, feel and look years younger, love people more, become more alert.

BURNING CALORIES (kJ)

At rest, the human body burns the calories (kJ) it needs for life support with remarkable efficiency. Extra calories (kJ) consumed are stored as fat. The number of calories needed to maintain an individual's basic body functions or perform any activity varies with the individual's age, weight, frame and other factors. For instance, because younger people tend to be more active, they burn more calories than older folks, and heavy people burn more calories than thin people in a given activity since it takes more energy to support their additional weight. Changeable external conditions such as extremely hot or cold temperatures also modify the rate of calorie (kJ) burning. It is surprising to learn how *few* calories (kJ) are burned in exercise. That is why exercise must be combined with a low calorie diet. The definite benefits of regular exercise are seen in toning the muscles, improving circulation and respiration, and uplifting one's mental perspective. Fifteen minutes or half an hour of daily exercise will keep you in shape, a realistic plan for a busy person to back up the diet program, including maintenance.

A glance at Table 3 will convince you that one of your best exercises is pushing back from the table. Then you may *enjoy* your regular exercise and recreation.

THE CONTINUING ENCOUNTER

Whatever kinds of exercise you begin to practice, whether isometric, isotonic, or aerobic, the application of this effort in daily life is a priceless asset in weight control. In the long run there is an accounting of caloric (kiloJoule) intake and expenditure. Therefore proper eating habits must be supported by regular exercise with

TABLE 3. CALORIE (kJ) OUTPUT CHART FOR 15 MINUTES OF ACTIVITY

To use this chart, find the weight listed closest to your actual weight. Calorie (kJ) output is listed for a 15 minute period, so divide or multiply depending on the length of time you spend on the activity.

Activity	110 lbs. (49.5 kg)		123 lbs. (55.3 kg)		150 lbs. (67.5 kg)		170 lbs. (76.5 kg)	
Lying down	16.5	(69)	18	(75)	22.5	(94)	25.5	(106)
Sitting:								
Reading	17.5	(73)	20	(83)	22.5	(94)	25	(104)
Eating	18	(75)	19.5	(81)	24	(100)	27	(113)
Driving a car	20	(83)	22.5	(94)	25	(104)	27.5	(115)
Typing: electric	21	(87)	22.5	(94)	27.	(113)	31.5	(131)
Writing	22.5	(94)	24	(100)	30	(125)	33	(138)
Typing: manual	24	(100)	25.5	(106)	31.5	(132)	36	(150)
Trumpet playing	24	(100)	25.5	(106)	31.5	(132)	36	(150)
Mild Activity:								
Meal preparation	26	(108)	30	(125)	34	(142)	37.5	(156)
Piano playing	30	(125)	33	(138)	40.5	(169)	46.5	(194)
Bowling	37.5	(157)	40	(167)	45	(188)	50	(209)
Volleyball	37.5	(157	42	(176)	51	(213)	58.5	(244)
Ironing	40	(167)	45	(188)	51	(213)	56	(234)
Bicycling: 5.5 mph (8.8 kph)	48	(200)	54	(226)	66	(276)	73.5	(307)
Heavy continuous housework	49	(205)	56	(234)	62.5	(261)	70	(292)
Dancing: contemporary	49	(205)	56	(234)	62.5	(261)	70	(292)
Drum playing	49.5	(207)	55.5	(232)	67.5	(282)	76.5	(320)
Ping Pong	51	(213)	57	(238)	69	(288)	78	(326)
Energetic Activity:								
Calisthenics	59	(246)	67.5	(282)	75	(313)	84	(351)
Walking (normal pace)	60	(251)	67.5	(282)	81	(339)	93	(389)
Golfing	64.5	(270)	72	(301)	87	(364)	97.5	(409)
Bicycling: 9.4 mph (15 kph)	75	(313)	84	(351)	102	(426)	111	(464)
Gardening	76	(318)	86	(360)	97.5	(408)	107.5	(450)
Vigorous Activity:								
Horseback riding: trot	81	(339)	92.5	(387)	104	(435)	115	(481)
Dancing: square	82.5	(345)	94	(393)	105	(439)	116	(485)
Tennis	84	(351)	95	(397)	106	(443)	117.5	(491)
Swimming (slow crawl)	96	(401)	108	(451)	130.5	(546)	148.5	(621)
Dancing: polka	106	(443)	120	(502)	135	(564)	150	(627)
Skiing: downhill	116	(485)	132.5	(554)	119	(497)	132	(552)
cross country 5 mph (8 km)	137.5	(575)	156	(652)	175	(732)	194	(811)
Jogging: 9 minute mile (14.4 km)	145.5	(606)	162	(677)	196.5	(822)	223.5	(935)
7 minute mile (11.2 km)	183	(765)	199.5	(834)	234	(979)	261	(1092)
Skiing: cross country 9 mph (14.4 kph)	196	(820)	222.5	(930)	250	(1046)	276	(1154)

which you can live joyfully. Remember, though, increased vigorous exercise may increase your appetite! Don't rationalize yourself into eating more just because you've used up some calories and feel justified in extra snacking. Keep exercising, but stick to the food portions allowed in the diet plan.

An attitude of willing exertion in every day affairs is good for you, physically. And what a witness it is to others when you willingly shovel snow, run to the mailbox, prefer stairs to elevators, go the second mile, pick up the dirty socks! You can live effectively as you take the reality of a spiritual dimension into every activity. While you rest in the Lord in spirit, you work tirelessly with the body: you plan your day, following through with an alert mind. Instead of always praying, "Dear Jesus, please find me a parking spot near my appointment," you pray, "Thank you, dear Lord, that I have time and energy to walk a block from my car, and the opportunity to use my best posture and exchange smiles with other pedestrians."

The oriental proverbs says, "Long journey begins with first step."

O Master, let me walk with Thee
In lowly paths of service free:
Tell me Thy secret; help me bear
The strain of toil, the fret of care.

Help me the slow of heart to move
By some clear, winning word of love:
Teach me the wayward feet to stay,
And guide them in the homeward way.

Teach me Thy patience; still with Thee
In closer, dearer company,
In work that keeps faith sweet and strong,
In trust that triumphs over wrong;

In hope that sends a shining ray
Far down the future's broadening way;
In peace that only Thou canst give,
With Thee, O Master, let me live.

Reverend Washington Gladden
1879

A KARATE PUNCH AT AMERICA

Closing Chapter Eleven reminds me of the business term "going Chapter Eleven", which means going bankrupt. My final plea for diet and exercise is a karate punch at America. While some Americans are taking exercise seriously, most of us are not yet realizing its importance to health. A report by Blue Cross on Food and Fitness, Volume XXLV, features a convincing article by Charles B. (Bud) Wilkinson of the football Hall of Fame, who set all-time win-loss records coaching the University of Oklahoma football team for 17 years. In the opening statement of his article entitled "We're Failing Phys Ed" he defines health as not just "freedom from disease" but adds "the ability to perform." Although our forefathers founded this beloved country on the work-faith ethic, it does seem that today a good part of the nation is "going Chapter Eleven," becoming spiritually and physically bankrupt with over-ease and dis-ease.

I felt these changing values on a recent trip to Japan when we found ourselves in a Shinto shrine at Christmas time, their New Year. Whole families of three generations came to the shrine. They were beautifully groomed, dressed in their traditional ceremonial best. There was a special blessing for the children whose ages were one, three, five, and seven. Adults tied their white paper fortunes to the trees for good luck in the new year. All over Japan the trees around the shrines looked snow laden with people's hopes and dreams. In this annual custom of the Japanese I was sure that I recognized the universal hunger for worship. Once our countries were enemies, but God has made us friends. How I longed to tell them that Jesus nailed all the world's sins to one tree—permanently. But would they know, by looking at us, that the Word was made flesh? Could we, the people of a fairly young country, convey the faith of our fathers to a people steeped in centuries of tradition, culture, and discipline? I only knew that God dearly loves this industrious, courteous people. I felt humble among them. When Japanese children stared at us I wondered if it was our strange straight eyes that fascinated them, or was it that compared to their slight, short parents, we looked large and slovenly? Did a few extra pounds betray our over-indulgent American life style? What purpose in life did we present with our careless posture? Can we ever face the hungry children in other countries of the world? Let peace begin with me, and a firmer girth on earth for all!

Almighty God, unto whom all hearts are open, all desires known, and from whom no secrets are hid, cleanse the thoughts of our hearts by the inspiration of Thy Holy Spirit, that we may perfectly love thee, and worthily magnify thy holy Name, through Christ our Lord. Amen. (The Book of Common Prayer)[22]

12
MAINTENANCE MEASURES

CONTENTMENT, RESPONSIBILITY, POWER OF CHOICE
Now that you're at goal weight, are you satisfied with the food and the results? Haven't your desires changed? Don't you realize now that gorging brings no lasting satisfaction? If you do wake up those old sweet taste buds, remember that they will be much more difficult to discipline. Substitutions tend to make us careless, and uncontrolled caloric intake will inevitably be stored as fat, sooner than you think.

Continue to stay prayerfully with the Becomers' Balanced Diet for your permanent life style. If you're thankful and satisfied, you won't need to cheat. However, if you are in touch with your Internal Instructor, you may responsibly add as much as one item a day plus exchanging one item a day in each food group for variety. It's a safe leeway, but you're still human. As a Maintainer you now have the power of choice to stay slim or add weight again, even with the controlled variety. Notice that none of the daily privileges you may choose are junk foods, but nutritionally sound, each approximating 100 calorie (kiloJoule) exchanges. Any more than one guided choice

TABLE 4. GUIDED CHOICES FOR MAINTAINERS: ONE PER DAY PLUS ONE EXCHANGEABLE ALLOWANCE* FROM EACH FOOD GROUP

(Each within 100 Calories or 418.5 kJ)

Similar Calorie (kJ) Portions:

Bread	Dairy	Fruit	Restricted Starchy "Vegies"	Meat
1 Ounce (28g) Bread =	*1 Cup (250 ml) Skim Milk =*	*1 Raw Fruit =*	*½ Cup (125 ml) Limited "Vegie" =*	*1 Ounce (28 g) Meat =*
½ Bagel	1 Ounce (28 g) Hard Cheese	½ Cup (125 ml) Regular Applesauce	¼ Cup (62 ml) Cooked Beans: Kidney, Lima, Navy, Soy	2 Slices Cold Cuts
1 2" (5 cm) Biscuit	1 Medium Egg	3 Fresh Apricots	½ Cup (125 ml) Popped Popcorn**	2 Vienna Sausages
1 2"² (5 cm²) Cornbread	1 Ounce (28 g) Roquefort Cheese	10 Cherries	½ Cup (125 ml) Corn	2 Strips of Bacon
2 Tablespoons (31 ml) Cracked Wheat (Bulgar)	2 Ounces (57 g) Cottage Cheese	3 Ripe Dates	¼ Cup (62 ml) Cooked Split or Chick Peas	
10 Small Crackers	4 Tablespoons (28 g) Parmesan Cheese	2 Dried Figs	1 Small Potato**	
½ English Muffin	½ Cup (125 ml) Ricotta Cheese	1 Small Bunch Grapes	¼ Cup (62 ml) Cooked Rice, Brown, Wild or Enriched White	
1 Regular Date or Blueberry Muffin	2 Tablespoons (31 ml) Whipped Cream	¼ Cup (62 ml) Grapejuice	¾ Cup (188 ml) Spaghetti Sauce (Replacing Tomato Juice Allowance)	
6 Small Slices Melba Thin Toast	¾ Cup (188 ml) Ice Cream = 1 day's Milk and Fruit allowances, once a week, a bonus of over 200 calories (837 kJ)	½ Mango	1 Tablespoon (15.5 ml) Sunflower or Sesame Seeds	
½ Cup (125 ml) Cooked Macaroni	2 Teaspoons (10 g) "Butter Beware!"	½ Persimmon	14 Almonds	
1 6" (15 cm) Matzo		¼ Cup (62 ml) Prune Juice	14 Cashews	
½ Cup (125 ml) Cooked Macaroni		3 Dried Prunes	10 Filberts	
2 3" (7.5 cm) Pancakes		2 Tablespoons (31 ml) Raisins	12 Pecan Halves	
½ Cup (125 ml) Cooked Spaghetti		½ Cup (125 ml) Watermelon	12 Peanuts	
1 Dinner Roll			10 Walnut Halves	
1 4" (10 cm) Waffle			3 Ounces (94 ml) Soy Nuts, Toasted	
1 Popover**				

Alcoholic beverages are not suitable exchanges for food. Also they tend to relax one off the diet.

*Deducted from commonly used diabetic exchanges, adapted and simplified.

**No butter with Popcorn, Potato, or Popover (unless accounted for in Dairy Column Choice).

Note: If you gain even 2 pounds, discontinue maintenance, reread Chapter 7, and repeat Appendix A. Then try maintenance again, having learned your own pitfalls from experience.

and one exchange in each food group a day would easily get out of hand, and the nutritional balance of the diet is quickly lost through merely counting calories.

One day at a time is easy to remember. It would be wise now to review the list of foods still to be *avoided* on pages 20 and 21. For instance, profit by my bad experience of tampering, and you won't have to start over. I tried adding Danish butter while on a short vacation in the West Indies, and learned that butter is butter, ounce for ounce; and it's not becoming or healthful to wear! Choose life, one day at a time, with guided choices. See Table 4.

MONTHLY WEIGH IN
It is absolutely necessary for a Maintainer to weigh in with another believing friend or group at least once a month. Otherwise you will give Satan a chance to chuckle as you procrastinate and rationalize. We human beings need one another, in the fellowship of the body of Christ.

ETERNAL DEPENDENCY
Never forget that self control is only won as a fruit of the Spirit. You are not now abandoned to your own unstable will power. The Internal Instructor is still with you. There is no temptation beyond His power. Remember that He resisted Satan's food proposition when He was at the point of starvation! Believe that He will never let you grow fat again. Hold fast to His hand by caring now and forever. Your life style is built on the Basic Ingredient—Jesus Christ, Lord of your body temple. Put your hand and your heart on the Table of Guided Choices For Maintainers, and pray, "Lord, feed my need, not my greed." "My God will supply all your *needs* ..." (Philippians 4:19)

PART TWO

TO THE DIET COOK:
I've loved compiling these recipes to stimulate your own creativity. They are simple enough to remember and tasty enough to be repeated often with variations. My family has lived with them contentedly for seven years. They have kept me satisfied, well, and at goal weight.

You can adapt almost any favorite recipe by using artificial sweetener for sugar, omitting fat, and accenting with herbs and spices.

Limit thickening agents to bread crumbs from your bread allowance, plain unflavored gelatine or artificially sweetened diet gelatines with fruit flavors, egg, or, for Maintainers, arrowroot or cornstarch.

Bread can be crumbled dry in the blender by first cutting it in small squares.

To speed the setting of gelatine, it is helpful to use eight ice cubes to replace one cup (250 ml) of liquid after the first cup of liquid (250 ml) has dissolved with gelatine. Plain unflavored gelatine must be softened with a small amount of liquid before dissolving with hot water.

THE DIET GOURMET

Always read the entire recipe through before starting to cook. Follow the preparatory directions mentioned in the list of ingredients to simplify the cooking procedure.

An efficient way to cook is to have the ingredients, utensils, and pans all set out before you begin. Clean up after each step. You'll be less tempted to nibble.

It's easy to be a creative gourmet cook and lose weight doing it. Go to it, Becomer! Your Internal Instructor is smiling at you, seeing you as you will become. I pray that the recipes will help teach you that obedience, discretion, and creativity can be a joyful adventure. The tools are in your hand, and you are in the Teacher's hand.

Commit your cooking to Jesus. He is the way for your peace, joy, and fulfillment. He is the Basic Ingredient of your life-style. He can make you strong and slim. Getting to know Him and trust Him, feeding on His Word, believing and following Him will give you all you need plus life eternal. Our Internal Instructor wants us to follow through in the future, and be one with Him. As we measure our lives by His, we can now learn to measure our daily food with wisdom, caution, and thanksgiving. He's offering us metric accountability. In the brief metric lesson which follows I hope that you will find that His yoke is easy and His burden is light.

Your Becomer Friend,

Barbara

Barbara C. Naylor

A MINI METRIC LESSON

I'LL TRY
I won't be petrified
By this surprise.
I can be metrified;
It's diet wise.

Here's a 7 word vocabulary for cooking with metric measurements, with obviously easy abbreviations:

gram	g
kilogram	kg
milliliter	ml
liter	1
centimeter	cm
meter	m
kiloJoule	kJ (calorie)

Metrics are uniting the world economy, and you can be one of the first to actually use metric cooking measurements while you're becoming slim. The new cup gives both the U.S. and metric markings, the old cup corresponding to 250 milliliters. The pint measure we have known corresponds to the 500 milliliter cup. Instead of a tablespoon, we are now using a 15 ml spoon, and in place of a teaspoon, a 5 ml spoon. For Becomers a pinch becomes .1 ml, and a dash .3 ml, with tiny spoons to help. Fun? Everyone likes gadgets, and a postal scale with grams is precise and indispensable for weighing proteins and bread. Everything else can be measured in milliliters for volume and liquid capacity. Figures 12 and 13 show you what to buy for metric measuring in the kitchen.

Table 5 is based on the ounce you know so well. The one ounce level is the base value from which the grams and milliliters are determined. Calculations are to the nearest gram for the mass weight column. Each of the 32 ounces is multiplied by the base gram equivalent of that one ounce, or 28.34 grams per ounce. The 2 decimals at this base level accumulate in the 32 multiplied ounces to become the 1000 gram kilogram, approximately. In the volume and liquid capacity column calculations are to the nearest milliliter. Each volume or fluid ounce is multiplied by the base level milliliter equivalent of that one fluid ounce, or 31.25 ml per ounce. Since the metric system is based on decimals, the small fluid ounce milliliter equivalent with its important decimals multiplies exactly to the 250 ml cup, the 500 ml "pint", and the 1000 ml liter. So when you see a tablespoon indicated as 16 ml, don't panic. Just use the 15 ml spoon with the grace of modern math.

For oven temperatures see Tables 6 and 7.

TABLE 5.
APPROXIMATE CONVERSION EQUIVALENTS
FOR THE U.S. AND METRIC WEIGHTS AND MEASUREMENTS
For Use With The Becomer's Balanced Diet

U.S. Cooking Measurements:		Mass or Weight Measurement .3527 ounces = 10 grams	Volume or Liquid Capacity: .338 fluid ounces = 10 milliliters
1 pinch			.1 ml
1 dash			.3 ml
⅛ teaspoon	1/48 oz.	.5 g	.6 ml
¼ teaspoon	1/24 oz.	1 g	1.2 ml
½ teaspoon	1/12 oz.	2 g	2.5 ml
1 teaspoon	1/6 oz.	5 g	5 ml
1 tablespoon	½ oz.	14 g	15.5 ml
2 tablespoons	1 oz.	28 g	31 ml
¼ cup	2 oz.	57 g	62 ml
	3 oz.	85 g	94 ml
½ cup	4 oz.	113 g	125 ml
	5 oz.	142 g	156 ml
¾ cup	6 oz.	170 g	188 ml
	7 oz.	198 g	219 ml
1 cup	8 oz.	227 g	250 ml
	9 oz.	255 g	281 ml
1¼ cups	10 oz.	283 g	313 ml
	11 oz.	312 g	344 ml
1½ cups	12 oz.	340 g	375 ml
	13 oz.	368 g	406 ml
1¾ cups	14 oz.	397 g	438 ml
	15 oz.	425 g	469 ml
2 cups	16 oz.	453 g	500 ml
	17 oz.	481 g	531 ml
2¼ cups	18 oz.	510 g	563 ml
	19 oz.	538 g	594 ml
2½ cups	20 oz.	566 g	625 ml
	21 oz.	595 g	656 ml
2¾ cups	22 oz.	623 g	688 ml
	23 oz.	653 g	719 ml
3 cups	24 oz.	680 g	750 ml
	25 oz.	709 g	781 ml
3¼ cups	26 oz.	737 g	813 ml
	27 oz.	765 g	844 ml
3½ cups	28 oz.	794 g	875 ml
	29 oz.	822 g	906 ml
3¾ cups	30 oz.	850 g	938 ml
	31 oz.	879 g	969 ml
4 cups, or	32 oz.	907 g	1000 ml
1 quart	2.2046 lbs. or 1.0567 liquid quarts	1 kilogram (kg)	1 liter (1)

FIGURE 12.

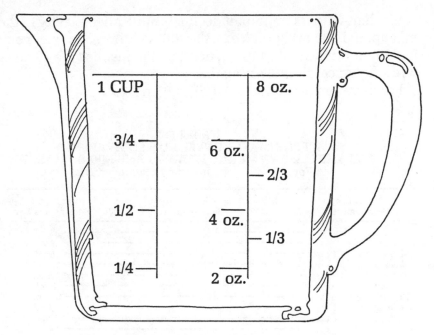

1 CUP   8 oz.

3/4 —   6 oz.

2/3

1/2 —   4 oz.

1/3

1/4 —   2 oz.

The new cup is available now. It has both measuring systems.

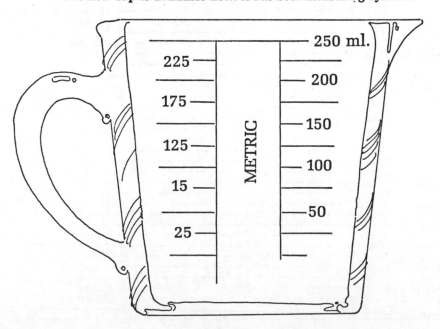

250 ml.

225 —

200

175 —

150

125 —

100

METRIC

15 —

50

25 —

My cup runneth over with metric!

FIGURE 13.

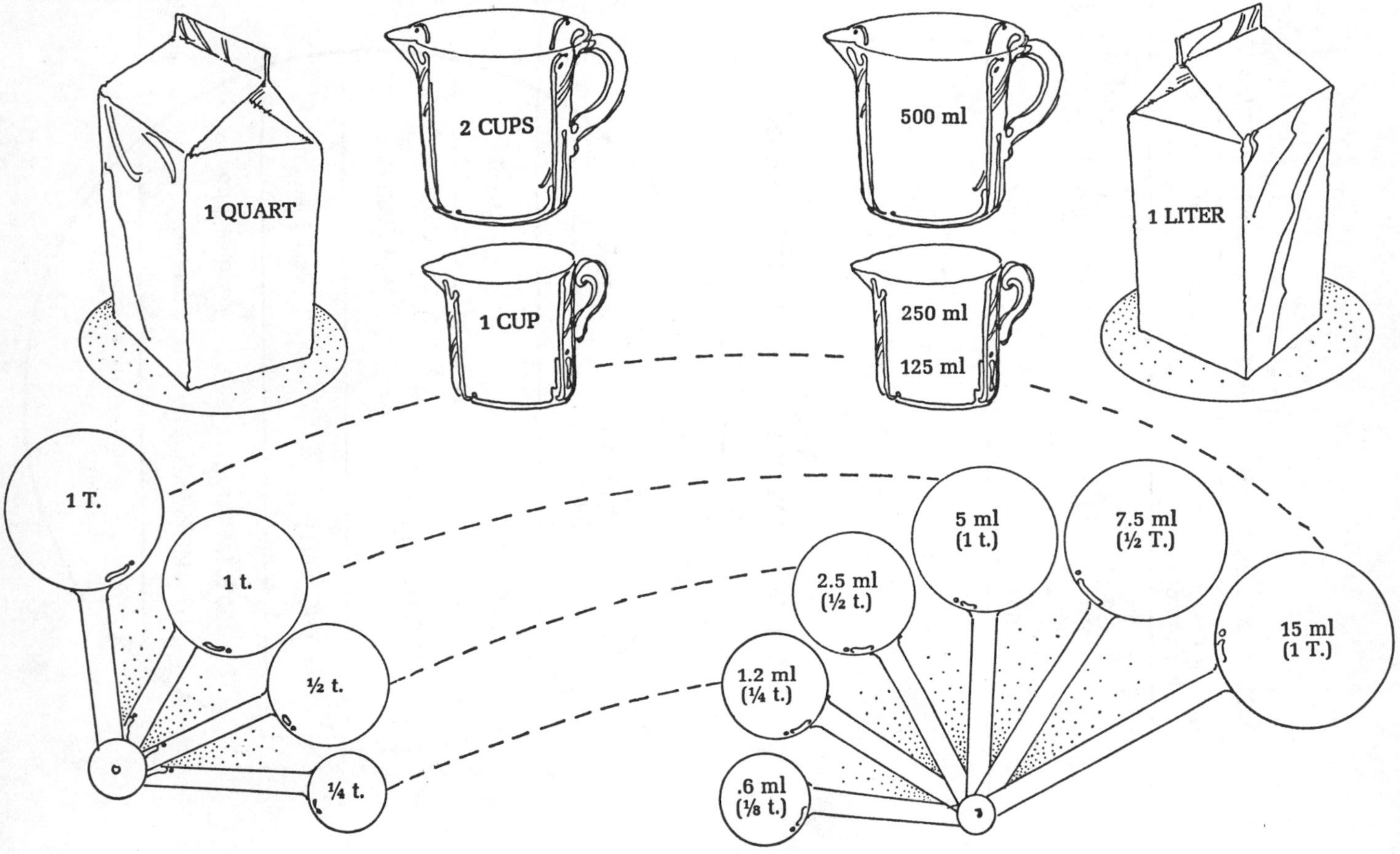

1 LITER

500 ml

250 ml
125 ml

2 CUPS

1 CUP

1 QUART

15 ml
(1 T.)

7.5 ml
(½ T.)

5 ml
(1 t.)

2.5 ml
(½ t.)

1.2 ml
(¼ t.)

.6 ml
(⅛ t.)

1 T.

1 t.

½ t.

¼ t.

TABLE 6.
OVEN TEMPERATURES: FAHRENHEIT MINUS 32 x 5/9 = CELSIUS

Baking Temperatures In Fahrenheit	Baking Temperatures In Celsius
325	162
350	176
375	190
400	204
425	218
450	232

TABLE 7.
INTERNAL MEAT TEMPERATURES, OVEN TEMPERATURE 325°F. (162°C.)

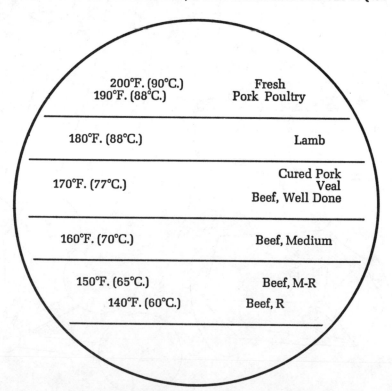

200°F. (90°C.) 190°F. (88°C.)	Fresh Pork Poultry
180°F. (88°C.)	Lamb
170°F. (77°C.)	Cured Pork Veal Beef, Well Done
160°F. (70°C.)	Beef, Medium
150°F. (65°C.)	Beef, M-R
140°F. (60°C.)	Beef, R

13
BEVERAGES

Tomato Cocktail

4 ounces (125 ml) fresh tomato
   juice
Dash (.3 ml) of soy sauce

1 slice lemon, hung on the side
   of glass

Keep a card in your wallet with the recipe so you can hand it to a
waiter or bartender. You're easily pleased, and you appreciate the
service with a tip. Three servings a day.

Becomer's V-8 Cocktail

24 ounces (750 ml) tomato juice
Sweetener to equal ½ teaspoon
   (2.5 ml) sugar
1 teaspoon (5 ml) lemon juice

Dash (.3 ml) each of celery salt,
   cloves, onion salt, thyme,
   and pepper, freshly ground

You may add vegetable juices from cooking or from the canned
vegetables, adding flavor and vitamins. You may prefer it to canned
V-8 for variable flavor and lesser cost. Drink up or share; it's best
while fresh.

Brown Cow

12 ounces (375 ml) diet root
   beer
2/3 cup (166 ml) nonfat dry
   milk

½ teaspoon (3 ml) vanilla
4-6 ice cubes

Blend and enjoy with a friend. If you drink it all, count 2 milk allowances.

Christmas Eggnog

1 cup (250 ml) buttermilk
1 cup (250 ml) pineapple juice
1 teaspoon (5 ml) vanilla
Dash (.3 ml) almond extract

Sweetener to equal ½ teaspoon
   (2.5 ml) sugar
Dash (.3 ml) of nutmeg, freshly
   ground, to garnish

This refreshing nog is without egg! You may enjoy your morning egg for breakfast, but save 2 fruit and 1 milk allowances for the happy hour. Four 4-ounce servings sipped soberly allow you to enjoy the true Christmas spirit. Count 1 milk allowance and 2 Fruit Portions.

Cranberry Punch

1 bottle low-calorie cranberry
   juice
1 can diet ginger ale
2 cans diet red apple (Shasta)
   soda

1 can diet black cherry soda
1 can diet raspberry soda
Lemon or raspberry ice milk to
   float on top

One-half cup cranberry juice is equal to 1 Fruit Portion. One-half cup of ice milk replaces 1 Fruit Portion and 1 milk allowance for the day. Use your good judgment, have a good time, and care. If you make the whole recipe, plan to invite diet friends to share the legal portion.

Diet "Wine"

1 12-ounce (375 ml) can diet
  grape soda
1 12-ounce (375 ml) can diet
  black cherry soda

12 ounces (375 ml) club soda
1/3 cup (83 ml) wine vinegar

This is a delightful facsimile for your skiing wineskin. Or put it in an
attractive wine bottle to take to a party (BYO). No one really cares
what you drink. Do you care? People are the stimulating part of a
party. Enjoy them! This drink is unlimited.

Hot Spiced Cider

1 cup (250 ml) cider
1 stick cinnamon
2 whole cloves allspice

Dash (.3 ml) of nutmeg, freshly
  ground

If this drink is served very hot, you will have to sip it slowly and
appreciate that it uses 2 Fruit Portions. Create a cozy atmosphere by
the fireplace. Let the others eat popcorn. You are safe.

Pina Colada

1 cup (250 ml) crushed pineapple with juice
Dash (.3 ml) of coconut extract
Sweetener to equal ⅛ teaspoon
  (.6 ml)

½ teaspoon (2.5 ml) rum extract
10-12 ice cubes
2/3 cup (166 ml) nonfat dry
  milk

Use your judgment on the amount of ice cubes, adding them in the
blender one at a time until the mixture is thick. It's a safe vacation
treat or a refreshing plan for after gardening on a hot day. Provides 2
Fruit Portions and 2 milk allowances.

Brandy Alexander

1 envelope nonfat dry milk

¼ cup (62 ml) evaporated skim milk

1 cup (250 ml) crushed ice

½ teaspoon (2.5 ml) brandy extract

Blend and serve immediately. Fancy glasses frosted in the freezer help a dieter feel festive at a party. Count 1½ milk allowances.

14
BREADS

Blueberry Muffins

1 cup (250 ml) nonfat dry milk
1 cup (250 ml) flour
Dry sweetener to equal 1/3 cup (83 ml) sugar
½ teaspoon (2.5 ml) salt
½ teaspoon (2.5 ml) soda
1 teaspoon (5 ml) grated orange rind

½ cup (125 ml) frozen, fresh, or canned blueberries
2 eggs
6 ounces (188 ml) yogurt or buttermilk

Toss dry ingredients together lightly. Dust blueberries with ¼ cup dry ingredients and set aside to add last. Beat eggs, add buttermilk and stir into dry ingredients briefly until batter is barely moist. Add blueberries, stirring as little as possible. Drop by heaping tablespoons into muffin tin sprayed with *Pam*. Bake at 350°F (176°C) for 15 minutes. One muffin is a bread allowance. With this quantity control, fruit and milk in the recipe are negligible.

Banana Bran Muffins

¼ cup (62 ml) nonfat dry milk
2/3 cup (166 ml) Bran Buds
½ cup (125 ml) flour
1 teaspoon (5 ml) baking
  powder
Sweetener to equal 2 teaspoons
  (10 ml) sugar
½ teaspoon (2.5 ml) cinnamon

¼ teaspoon (1.2 ml) nutmeg
½ teaspoon (2.5 ml) orange
  rind
4 ounces (125 ml) liquified
  banana (in blender)
1 teaspoon (5 ml) vanilla
1 egg

Toss dry ingredients together lightly. Combine and stir briefly until the batter is barely moistened. Bake in muffin tin sprayed with *Pam* at 350°F (176°C) for 15 minutes. Of the 6 muffins, use 3 for breakfast and/or 3 for lunch, along with protein, fruit, and beverage.

Pineapple Muffins

1 cup (250 ml) flour
1 cup (250 ml) nonfat dry milk
Dry sugar substitute to equal
  1/3 cup (83 ml) sugar
¼ teaspoon (1.2 ml) cinnamon
  and nutmeg
⅛ teaspoon (.6 ml) allspice and
  cloves

1 teaspoon (5 ml) soda
½ teaspoon (2.5 ml) salt
2 eggs
¾ cup (188 ml) crushed pineapple, pureed
1 teaspoon (5 ml) rum flavor
½ teaspoon (2.5 ml) pineapple
  extract

Toss dry ingredients together lightly. Beat egg, add pineapple, and combine with dry ingredients. Add flavorings. Stir briefly until batter is barely moistened. Bake in a muffin pan sprayed with *Pam* for 18 to 20 minutes at 350°F (176°C). One muffin represents one bread allowance. Share with the family. Serve with egg and orange juice on Sunday morning when you have time to bake with love.

Do You CARROT ALL Bread?

1 cup (250 ml) nonfat dry milk
1 cup (250 ml) flour
¾ teaspoon (3.7 ml) each all-spice, cinnamon, cloves, nutmeg
½ teaspoon (2.5 ml) soda
½ teaspoon (2.5 ml) salt
Dry sweetener to equal ¼ cup (62 ml)

1 teaspoon (5 ml) baking powder
Pinch of love
3 eggs
½ cup (125 ml) pineapple, pureed in its own juice in blender
4 ounces (125 ml) grated carrot

Toss dry ingredients together lightly. Beat the eggs, add pineapple and grated carrot. Combine and stir briefly until batter is barely moistened. Bake in loaf pan sprayed with *Pam* at 350°F (176°C) for 45 minutes. When cool, use a sharp knife to cut 15 slices. Use one slice only for breakfast or lunch as your bread allowance. That affords you the variety of your regular protein, Fruit Portion and milk allowance for beverage.

Pumpkin Bread

1 cup (250 ml) flour
1 cup (250 ml) nonfat dry milk
½ teaspoon (2.5 ml) soda
½ teaspoon (2.5 ml) salt
1 teaspoon (2.5 ml) orange rind, grated
½ teaspoon (2.5 ml) cinnamon

Dry sweetener to equal 1/3 cup (83 ml) sugar
2 eggs
½ cup (125 ml) pumpkin, cooked and pureed, or canned
½ cup (125 ml) orange juice

Toss dry ingredients together lightly. Beat egg, add pumpkin and orange juice. Mix briefly with dry ingredients until barely blended. Bake in bread pan sprayed with *Pam* at 350°F (176°C) for 35 minutes. Cut into 15 slices when cooled. Each slice equals one bread allowance. Spread with whipped "cream cheese" (cottage cheese beaten smooth, sweetened, and flavored with grated orange rind).

Cranberry Bread

1 cup (250 ml) flour
1 cup (250 ml) nonfat dry milk
2 teaspoons (10 ml) grated
  orange rind
1 teaspoon (5 ml) baking
  powder
Dry sweetener to equal ¼ cup
  (62 ml) sugar

2 eggs
6 ounces (188 ml) liquified
  banana (2 small, in blender)
½ cup (125 ml) chopped cranberries

Toss dry ingredients together lightly. Beat eggs. Add banana and cranberries. Combine and stir briefly until batter is barely moistened. Bake in bread tin sprayed with Pam at 350°F (176°C) for 35 to 40 minutes. Cut 15 slices when cooled. Count the loaf as 15 bread allowances. The fruit, milk, and egg are negligible if you limit yourself to one slice for breakfast and one for lunch.

Orange Nut Bread

1 cup (250 ml) flour
1 cup (250 ml) nonfat dry milk
Dry sugar substitute to equal
  1/3 cup (83 ml)
½ teaspoon (2.5 ml) baking
  soda
½ teaspoon (2.5 ml) baking
  powder

2 teaspoons (10 ml) orange
  rind, grated
6 ounces (188 ml) orange juice
2 eggs
1 teaspoon (5 ml) vanilla nut
  flavor
⅛ cup (31 ml) Grapenuts

Toss dry ingredients together lightly (except Grapenuts). Beat eggs, add orange juice and flavoring. Combine and stir briefly until batter is barely moist. Drop in half the Grapenuts and pour into loaf pan sprayed with Pam. Sprinkle remaining Grapenuts on top. Bake at 350°F (176°C) for 35 minutes. When cool, cut in 15 slices. One bread allowance is one slice only.

Dill Protein Bread (Two Loaves)

4½ cups flour (1.125 l)

3 teaspoons (15 ml) sugar
(helpful only in this recipe)

2 tablespoons (31 ml) dill weed

2 tablespoons (31 ml) minced
onion or raw chopped onion

2 teaspoons (10 ml) salt

1 teaspoon (5 ml) baking
powder

1 teaspoon (5 ml) soda

2 eggs

2 cups (453 g or 500 ml)
low-fat cottage cheese

2 packages yeast, softened in
½ cup (125 ml) warm water

3 tablespoons (48 ml) liquid
shortening (helpful only in
this recipe)

Add 1 teaspoon (5 ml) of the sugar to the yeast and warm water; use the other 2 teaspoons (10 ml) in the dry ingredients. Sugar helps the yeast grow. Toss dry ingredients together lightly with onion. Beat the eggs, combine with cottage cheese, oil, and softened yeast. Add half the dry ingredients to egg, cheese, oil, and yeast mixture. On a pastry cloth, spread the other half of the dry ingredients for kneading. Scrape dough onto cloth, fold cloth over dough repeatedly, pushing with the heel of your hand rhythmically against the cloth on the dough. Knead 5 to 10 minutes until all the flour is incorporated. Ignore the little loose pieces of cottage cheese—they bake in later. Let dough rise in a warm place until double, in vegetable oil sprayed bowl, covered. Punch down and shape into 2 loaves. Let rise again in bread pans sprayed with *Pam*, covered. A little moisture on top, or egg white, keeps the dough elastic for stretching. When double in size, bake at 350°F (176°C) for 35 minutes. When cool, cut into 18 thin slices per loaf. Use 2 thin slices, or 1 ounce (28 g), for breakfast or lunch, as your bread allowance. If you use this distinctive bread wisely, you can still have the regular protein on the menu.

Waffles and "Cream Cheese"

2 slices diet thin bread soaked
in: 1 egg beaten with 1/3 cup
(83 ml) skim milk and dry
sweetener to equal 2 tea-
spoons (2.5 ml) sugar

Topping:
2 ounces (57 g or 62 ml)
low-fat cottage cheese
blended with 3 teaspoons
(15 ml) pineapple juice
Pinch (.1 ml) of nutmeg
Dry sweetener to equal 2
pinches (.2 ml) sugar

Heat waffle iron sprayed with *Pam*. Place soaked bread on griddle.
Cover and bake until light goes off. Serve with "cream cheese"
topping. Orange juice and coffee complete the breakfast menu for
one.

15
CAKES AND COOKIES

Applesauce Cake

1 cup (250 ml) nonfat dry milk
½ cup (125 ml) whole wheat
  flour
½ cup (125 ml) white flour
1 teaspoon (5 ml) soda
1 teaspoon (5 ml) baking
  powder
Dry sugar substitute to equal
  1/3 cup (83 ml) sugar
1 teaspoon (5 ml) cinnamon
⅛ teaspoon (.6 ml) cloves

⅛ teaspoon (.6 ml) allspice
⅛ teaspoon (.6 ml) nutmeg
½ teaspoon (2.5 ml) salt
2 eggs
6 ounces (188 ml) applesauce
  (without sugar)
3 drops butter flavor
1 teaspoon (5 ml) vanilla nut
  flavor or 1 teaspoon (5 ml)
  maple flavor

Toss dry ingredients together lightly. Beat eggs, add applesauce and flavorings. Combine and stir briefly until batter is barely moistened. Bake at 350°F (176°C) for 30 minutes. Sprinkle additional powdered milk on top. Cut into 16 pieces. One piece must be considered a bread allowance for lunch. A Maintainer could add a piece of this cake to the dinner menu.

Banana Cake

1 cup (250 ml) flour
1 cup (250 ml) nonfat dry milk
Dry sweetener to equal ¼ cup
(62 ml) sugar
1 teaspoon (5 ml) cinnamon
½ teaspoon (2.5 ml) salt
1 teaspoon (5 ml) baking soda

1 egg
1 teaspoon (5 ml) vanilla
1 teaspoon (5 ml) butter flavor
2/3 cup (166 ml) liquified
banana (2 small, in blender)
¼ cup (62 ml) yogurt

Toss the dry ingredients together lightly. Beat the egg, and add flavoring, banana and yogurt. Combine and stir briefly until batter is barely moistened. Pour into cake pan sprayed with Pam and bake at 350°F (176°C) for 25 minutes. Cool. Cut into 16 pieces. One piece is a bread allowance, so share! You might try half a recipe, using an ice cube tray for a pan. That way you could slice it into 16 portions as a banana bread.

Chocolate Cupcakes

1 cup (250 ml) chocolate nonfat
dry milk
1 teaspoon (5 ml) baking
powder
1 cup (250 ml) flour
Dry sweetener to equal 1/3 cup
(83 ml) sugar

⅛ teaspoon (.6 ml) salt
2 eggs
6 ounces (188 ml) liquified
banana (2 small, in blender)

Toss the dry ingredients lightly. Beat eggs, add banana and stir into dry ingredients until batter is barely moistened. Spoon into cupcake liners and bake in a 12 muffin pan at 350°F (176°C) for 20 minutes. One cupcake is a bread allowance, so eat it slowly. Share or freeze the rest.

Gelatine Sponge Cake

3 envelopes of different fruit-
  flavored diet gelatines
1½ cups (375 ml) pineapple
  juice
3 cups (750 ml) boiling water

Topping:
1 cup (250 ml) low-fat
  cottage cheese
⅛ teaspoon (.6 ml) almond
  extract
1 teaspoon (5 ml) vanilla
1 teaspoon (5 ml) lemon rind
Dry sweetener to equal 1 tablespoon (16 ml) sugar

Dissolve 1 envelope of fruit-flavored diet gelatine in 1 cup boiling water. Add ½ cup (125 ml) pineapple juice. Chill until syrupy. Beat until air bubbles resemble sponge cake. Pour into 10-inch tube pan (25 x 10 cm) sprayed with Pam. Set in refrigerator while you repeat the layers. When the entire cake is fully set, tip it carefully onto a cake plate. Blend the topping ingredients together and spread gently on top of the fragile gelatine sponge cake. Sprinkle a bit of dry fruit-flavored gelatine on top for garnish. The gelatine is free, and each of 16 pieces has ½ ounce (14 g) of cottage cheese in the topping. Happy safe birthday!

Pineapple Oatmeal Cookies

¼ cup (62 ml) flour
¾ cup (188 ml) oatmeal
½ cup (125 ml) powdered milk
1 teaspoon (5 ml) baking
  powder
½ teaspoon (3 ml) cinnamon

⅛ teaspoon (.6 ml) nutmeg
Brown sugar substitute to equal
  ¼ cup (62 ml) brown sugar*
1 egg
¾ cup (188 ml) crushed pineapple, pureed in its own juice

Toss dry ingredients together lightly. Beat egg and add pureed pineapple. Bake by dropping on a cookie pan sprayed with Pam. Bake at 350°F (176°C) for 10 minutes. However many cookies you make, ⅛ is your bread portion. Are you learning control? Measure, plan, persevere.

*Brown Sugar Twin is measured by volume, but Sweet'n Low Brown Sugar substitute is measured by a tiny spoon in the package according to directions.

Sour Cream Cookies

½ cup flour
½ cup nonfat dry milk
Dry sweetener to equal ¼ cup
  sugar (5 ml)
1 teaspoon soda
½ teaspoon (2.5 ml) cinnamon

⅛ teaspoon (.6 ml) nutmeg
¼ teaspoon (1.2 ml) almond
  extract
1 egg
½ cup buttermilk (125 ml)

Toss dry ingredients together lightly. Beat the egg and add the buttermilk and extract. Combine with dry ingredients and bake at 350°F (176°C) for 10 minutes. If you make 16 small cookies, 2 would be equal to your bread allowance. If you want good cookies, you must control your portion to be safe.

16
CHEESE

Cheese Stuffed Lettuce Wedges

1 tablespoon (16 ml) un-
  flavored gelatine (1 envelope)
½ cup (125 ml) water
1 teaspoon (5 ml) vinegar
1 teaspoon (5 ml) lemon juice
1 tablespoon (16 ml) chives

1 teaspoon (5 ml) horseradish
12 ounces (340 g or 375 ml)
  low-fat cottage cheese
½ head iceberg lettuce
Garnish: paprika, pimento, or
  parsley

Sprinkle gelatine on water to soften. Heat with care to dissolve. Combine with other ingredients and mix thoroughly. Chill the mixture while you prepare the lettuce. With a small knife remove the center of the lettuce half, leaving about a ½-inch (1.3 cm) shell. Save the lettuce heart for a salad later. Line a bowl with damp paper towels, enough to hang over the edge of the bowl 6 inches (15 cm). Spoon the cheese mixture into the lettuce shell. Fold the paper towel over the top. Refrigerate until cheese sets. To serve, remove paper towels. Cut lettuce into wedges. Garnish with parsley and paprika or pimiento. This accounts for two lunch protein allowances and may be accompanied with fruit, toast triangles, and iced tea for two gardeners' lunches prepared ahead.

Cheese Ball

8 ounces (227 g) grated cheddar
   cheese, at room temperature
¼ cup (62 ml) low calorie
   Thousand Island dressing
½ roasted pepper
1 teaspoon (5 ml) horseradish
1 teaspoon (5 ml) onion flakes

Dash (.3 ml) of Tabasco sauce
1 teaspoon (5 ml) brandy
   extract
½ cup (125 ml) chopped water
   chestnuts
½ cup (125 ml) chopped
   parsley or parsley flakes

Beat together cheese, dressing, pepper, horseradish, onion flakes, Tabasco sauce and brandy extract until smooth. Shape in a ball with your hands dampened. Roll in the chopped water chestnuts and parsley. One-fourth of this is one lunch protein. Remember at cocktail hour to deduct twice as much as you eat from your dinner protein. Water chestnuts are a Restricted Starchy Vegetable, but they are only a garnish as used here. Use cheese with caution, but you don't have to be a martyr. Spread it on cucumber slices for crackers, or stuff celery as you visit. Merry Christmas!

"Macaroni" and Cheese

1 cup (250 ml) milk
2 eggs
2 ounces (57 g) white bread
   crumbled
2 ounces (57 g) cheese,
   shredded

1 tablespoon (16 ml) dried
   onion flakes
1 pound (1 liter) cauliflower,
   cooked and crumbled—or—
2 cans bean sprouts, drained
   and rinsed

Heat the milk, add beaten eggs, crumbled bread, shredded cheese, and onion flakes. Pour over cauliflower "macaroni" in a casserole dish sprayed with *Pam*. Bake at 350°F (176°C) for 40 minutes. Use half the recipe for lunch. At night you would be wise to adapt the recipe to omit bread. Puree the cauliflower for the cheese sauce, and use the bean sprouts for the "macaroni". Used at night, the recipe accounts for 8 ounces (227 g) of protein. One-fourth of it deducts 2 ounces (57 g) from your dinner meat.

Roman Cannoli

4 thin slices bread, rolled very
   flat
8 ounces (227 g or 250 ml)
   low-fat cottage cheese
Dash (.3 ml) of almond extract
Sweetener to equal 1 tablespoon (16 ml) sugar

1 tablespoon (16 ml) lemon
   juice
2 teaspoons (10 ml) lemon rind,
   grated
2 teaspoons (10 ml) orange
   rind, grated

Roll bread into cornucopias. Fasten with toothpick or wrap with foil to hold in shape. Bake at 375°F (183°C) for 10 minutes. Blend the remaining ingredients and spoon into cooled cornucopias. Each of the four portions uses 2 ounces of protein and half the bread portion for lunch. You may still have a broiled open-face cheese sandwich, gelatine dessert, vegetable soup and fruit with beverage.

Gelatine Cheesecake

1 envelope fruit flavored diet
   gelatine
1 cup (250 ml) boiling water
½ cup (250 ml) pineapple juice
4 ice cubes

½ cup (125 ml) crushed pineapple packed in juice,
   drained
6 ounces (170 g or 188 ml)
   low-fat cottage cheese

Dissolve the gelatine with boiling water. Add the pineapple juice. Put cottage cheese in the blender with the ice cubes and 2/3 of the gelatine mixture. Blend until smooth. Add crushed pineapple without blending if you like texture in your cheesecake. Pour immediately into a glass pie pan sprayed with *Pam*. While it sets firm in the refrigerator, reserve the remainder of the plain gelatine at room temperature. Spoon this third of the gelatine on top when the cake is set, for an attractive glaze. This dessert contains 1 lunch protein allowance and 2 Fruit Portions. By spacing your portions you can still enjoy a normal lunch with this dessert. One-fourth of the recipe is appropriate for either lunch or dinner.

Tropical Cheese Custard

2 beaten eggs
⅛ teaspoon (.6 ml) almond extract
½ teaspoon (2.5 ml) rum extract
⅛ teaspoon (.6 ml) coconut extract
1 teaspoon (5 ml) grated lemon rind
1 teaspoon (5 ml) grated orange rind
1½ cups (375 ml) evaporated skim milk
⅛ teaspoon (.6 ml) nutmeg
Sweetener to equal 4 tablespoons (62 ml) sugar
1 cup (250 ml) crushed pineapple in juice
12 ounces (340 g or 375 ml) cottage cheese
1 small can Mandarin orange segments, drained

Reserve Mandarin orange segments for garnish. Combine all remaining ingredients, adding pineapple and cottage cheese last. Pour into 4 custard cups sprayed with *Pam*. Set in hot water in an electric skillet. Cook covered at 250°F (126°C) for 25 minutes until custard is gently firm. When cool, garnish with 3 Mandarin orange segments in a pinwheel design on each cup. One of the four servings borrows 2½ ounces (71 g) from your dinner protein, 1 Fruit Portion, and ¾ of your milk allowance.

Apple Cheese Danish

2 ounces (57 g or 62 ml) low-fat cottage cheese
Dry sweetener to equal dash (.3 ml) of sugar
Pinch (.1 ml) of cinnamon
1 ounce (28 g) of bread (2 thin slices) toasted
¼ cup (62 ml) applesauce (without sugar)

Mix cottage cheese with sweetener and cinnamon. Spread on toast. Cover with applesauce. Broil for 2-3 minutes. Serve hot and bubbly. A delightful breakfast for one with a scant serving of orange juice and coffee.

TABLE 8. THE CHEESE WATCHERS' GUIDE

square centimeters (cm²)	milliliters (ml)	grams (g)	kiloJoules (kJ)

American Cheese:
1 inch cube (6.5 cm²) = 1 ounce (28 g) = 100 calories (418 kJ)

Blue Cheese: (Beware!)
1 inch cube (6.5 cm²) = 1 ounce (28 g) = 105 calories (439 kJ)

Low-fat Cottage Cheese:
1 cup (250 ml) = 8 ounces (448 g) = 200 calories (837 kJ)
¾ cup (188 ml) = 6 ounces (224 g) = 150 calories (628 kJ)
½ cup (125 ml) = 4 ounces (112 g) = 100 calories (418 kJ)
¼ cup (62 ml) = 2 ounces (56 g) = 50 calories (209 kJ)

*Parmesan Grated Cheese:**
4 tablespoons (62 ml) = 1 ounce (28 g) = 80 calories (334 kJ)
3 tablespoons (48 ml) = .75 ounces (21 g) = 60 calories (251 kJ)
2 tablespoons (31 ml) = .5 ounces (14 g) = 40 calories (167 kJ)
1 tablespoon (16 ml) = .25 ounces (7 g) = 20 calories (84 kJ)

*Grating doubles cheese volume, but dehydration of commercially grated cheese reduces its weight.

17
CONFECTIONS

Frozen Fruit Bonbons

1 small ripe banana, peeled, sliced, sprinkled with 2 teaspoons (10 ml) lemon juice
½ cup (125 ml) drained pineapple chunks

1/3 cup (166 ml) sugarless chocolate nonfat dry milk

Toss the fruit with the dry chocolate milk powder in a small paper bag. Freeze the bonbons separately in an ice cube tray. Cover it with tin foil to protect the flavors. This sweet and chewy fruit stretches 1 Fruit Portion and 1 milk allowance, besides quieting your devilish cravings.

Frozen Fruit Fudge

½ cup (125 ml) low-calorie fruit
salad, drained

½ cup (125 ml) crushed pineapple in juice, drained

2/3 cup (166 ml) nonfat dry
milk, white or chocolate

⅛ teaspoon (.6 ml) almond
extract

Mix fruits and powdered milk with almond flavoring. Spread in a
ice cube tray sprayed with *Pam*. Freeze until firm. Cut into small
squares. Half the recipe is equal to a Fruit Portion and a milk allowance.

Square Jelly Beans

4 envelopes unflavored
gelatine

3 envelopes diet gelatine, any
flavor

4 cups (1 liter) boiling water

1 teaspoon (5 ml) lemon juice

Combine all the gelatine in a large bowl. Add boiling water and
lemon juice. Stir until clear. Pour into 9 x 13 baking pan. Chill until
firm. Cut into squares. Mix different colored "jelly beans" for finger
nibbling, unrestricted and jolly. They bounce if you toss them, but
they won't add an ounce if you enjoy them.

18
DIPS AND DRESSINGS

Blue Cheese Dressing

1 cup (250 ml) yogurt
⅛ teaspoon (.6 ml) garlic salt
2 tablespoons (31 ml) minced
  onion
1 teaspoon (5 ml) lemon juice

⅛ teaspoon (.6 ml) pepper,
  freshly ground
1 tablespoon (16 ml)
  crumbled blue cheese

Mix ingredients together and refrigerate. This tasty dressing
amounts to 1 milk allowance.

Chilly Dilly Dressing

1 cup (250 ml) yogurt
¼ cup (62 ml) dill pickle, diced
½ teaspoon (2.5 ml) prepared
  mustard

½ teaspoon (2.5 ml) horseradish
½ teaspoon (2.5 ml) chili
  powder

Mix ingredients in a small dish and serve with fish for a special
tartar sauce. The recipe accounts for 1 cup (250 ml) of milk.

Cinchy Mayonnaise

1 cold hard boiled egg
6 ounces (170 g or 188 ml)
  low-fat cottage cheese
¼ teaspoon (1.2 ml) mustard
Sweetener to equal 3 teaspoons
  (16 ml) sugar
¼ teaspoon (1.2 ml) paprika
⅛ teaspoon (.6 ml) garlic salt

¼ teaspoon (1.2 ml) celery salt
1 teaspoon (5 ml) chopped
  chives
1 tablespoon (16 ml) vinegar
1 tablespoon (16 ml) lemon
  juice
1 tablespoon (16 ml) yogurt,
  skim milk, or buttermilk

Blend ingredients until smooth, starting and stopping the blender often. This mayonnaise holds the water packed tuna together. Use it with ham, chicken, cole slaw, in salads and sandwiches. It has body and superior flavor. It stands in peaks smoothly. The recipe yields 1 cup of 8 ounces (250 ml volume). Two ounces (62 ml) of Cinchy Mayonnaise accounts for 1 ounce (28 g) of protein.

Cole Slaw Dressing

1 hard boiled egg, chopped
¼ teaspoon (1.2 ml) prepared
  mustard
1 small onion, chopped
1 teaspoon (5 ml) vinegar

1 teaspoon (5 ml) lemon juice
Sweetener to equal 1 teaspoon
  (5 ml) sugar
½ cup (125 ml) yogurt
1 teaspoon (5 ml) celery seed

Blend the first 6 ingredients in the blender until smooth, starting and stopping often. Add the yogurt and blend only for a flash. Pour over 3 cups (750 ml) shredded cabbage, adding the celery seed whole. All that chewing and tasting satisfaction costs you only one egg and half a milk allowance. Egg adds the richness of mayonnaise. It takes only 2 minutes to care enough and prepare enough.

French Dressing

½ cup (125 ml) tomato juice
1 tablespoon (16 ml) lemon
  juice
1 tablespoon (16 ml) dill pickle
  juice
½ teaspoon (3 ml) onion salt
⅛ teaspoon (.6 ml) garlic salt
3 tablespoons (48 ml) fresh
  chives, chopped, or

1 tablespoon (16 ml) dried
  chives
Dash (.3 ml) pepper, freshly
  ground
½ cup (125 ml) yogurt or buttermilk

Mix together well. Store your French dressing in an attractive bottle. Use it liberally on lettuce. Use all you want—it's ½ cup (125 ml) tomato juice and ½ cup (125 ml) milk allowance.

Pink Pimento Dip

6 ounces (170 g or 188 ml)
  cottage cheese
½ teaspoon (3 ml) Worcestershire sauce

Dash (.3 ml) of Tabasco sauce
Dash (.3 ml) of garlic salt
1 small can pimentos

Blend until smooth. Serve with raw vegetables. Share the dip with three friends, and you deduct only one ounce of protein from dinner.

Salad Dressing

1 package plain gelatine,
  softened in:
  1 tablespoon (16 ml) lemon
    juice,
  1 tablespoon (16 ml) vinegar,
  1 ounce (31 ml or 28 g) of
    cold water
8 ounces (227 g or 250 ml)
  low-fat cottage cheese

1 egg
Sweetener to equal 2 teaspoons
  (10 ml) sugar
½ teaspoon (2.5 ml) mustard
⅛ teaspoon (.6 ml) garlic salt
¼ teaspoon (1.2 ml) onion salt
1 cup (250 ml) buttermilk or
  yogurt
¼ teaspoon (1.2 ml) paprika

Soften gelatine in a pan using the lemon juice, vinegar, and cold water. Stir constantly over low heat until dissolved. Pour into blender and add the other ingredients. Blend until smooth. Pour into pint jar, cover and refrigerate. Use this freely for ten days without worrying about calories (kiloJoules). Enough for one sandwich uses only a half ounce (14 g) of protein from your luncheon menu. Ready, Brown Bagger?

"Sour Cream" Dip

1 cup (227 g or 250 ml) low-fat
  cottage cheese
2 tablespoons (31 ml) yogurt
—or—
2 tablespoons (31 ml) lemon
  juice

¼ teaspoon (1.2 ml) onion
  powder
3 ounces (85 g) minced clams
—or—
1 tablespoon (16 ml)
  blue cheese, crumbled

This basic dip can have many variations. Clams add the least amount of calories (kiloJoules). Share the dip with four friends, and you deduct about an ounce (28 g) from your dinner menu.

19
EGGS

Chinese Egg Roll

6 slices thin white bread
  (3 ounces or 85 g)
2 eggs beaten with:
  ½ cup (125 ml) skim milk,
  Dash (.3 ml) of garlic salt
  Dash (.3 ml) of butter salt
¼ cup (62 ml) chopped green
  pepper
¼ cup (62 ml) shredded
cabbage

¼ cup (62 ml) finely chopped
  celery
1 small onion, diced
1 packet chicken or vegetable
  bouillon
Dash (.3 ml) of pepper
6 ounces (170 g) crab, tuna, or
  shrimp, finely chopped

Soak the bread briefly in the egg mixture. Fry in skillet sprayed with
Pam. After turning once, press with a spatula to make the slices firm,
thin and pliable. Cool them on a plate while you prepare the filling.
Stir fry the chopped vegetables with the bouillon, pepper and fish.
When cooled, add the remaining egg mixture to the vegetables.
Place 2 tablespoons of the mixture on each cooled "pancake". Roll
2 corners together, overlapping and fastening with a tooth pick.
Bake on a cookie sheet sprayed with Pam 2 inches (5 cm) apart at
350°F (176°C) for 10 minutes. Serve with Sweet Sour Sauce.

Sweet Sour Sauce

1 cup (250 ml) pineapple juice
Brown sugar substitute to equal
  1 teaspoon (5 ml)*
1 tablespoon (16 ml) vinegar
1 teaspoon (5 ml) soy sauce

2 teaspoons (10 ml) mustard
¼ teaspoon (1.2 ml) ginger
3 tablespoons (48 ml) arrow-
  root† or cornstarch

Reserve ¼ of the pineapple juice. Thoroughly combine and heat the first 6 ingredients. Add the thickener, preferably arrowroot,† to the reserved juice. Stir together over heat until thick. Serve in a little pitcher to pour over the finished egg rolls. The recipe provides for three ladies for lunch, allowing for a tossed salad and sherbet for dessert.

*Brown Sugar Twin
†Arrowroot has fewer calories than cornstarch, but is more expensive. The thickness will not hold over 10 minutes, nor will it reheat, but it thickens without boiling, and has no starchy taste.

Spinach Souffle

10 ounces (313 ml) chopped
  spinach, broccoli, or cauliflower
1 cup (250 ml) skim milk
2 eggs
2 ounces (57 g) bread crumbs,
  freshly crumbled in the
  blender

1 teaspoon (5 ml) lemon juice
1 teaspoon (5 ml) vinegar
2 ounces (57 g) grated Swiss
  cheese
½ teaspoon (2.5 ml) salt
¼ teaspoon (1.2 ml) paprika,
  for garnish

Cook spinach, broccoli or cauliflower. Drain very thoroughly. Beat together the skim milk, eggs and bread crumbs. Combine with lemon juice, vinegar, cheese and salt. Pour over vegetables in a straight-sided baking dish sprayed with Pam. Sprinkle the paprika on top. Bake at 350°F (176°C) for 25 to 30 minutes in the very center of your oven. The souffle serves 2 for lunch. A salad, milk allowance, and a Fruit Portion complete a satisfying menu. Eat well and live longer!

Fresh Herb Souffle

4 thin slices of bread (2 ounces or 57 g)

2 ounces (57 g) Swiss cheese

½ ounce (14 g) thin sliced boiled ham—or—

1 tablespoon (16 ml) bacon flavored bits

3 tablespoons (48 ml) fresh snipped chives

1 tablespoon (16 ml) fresh sweet marjoram, finely cut

3 tablespoons (48 ml) fresh Italian parsley, finely cut

2 eggs

1 cup (250 ml) skim milk

1 teaspoon (5 ml) prepared mustard

1 teaspoon (5 ml) Worcestershire Sauce

Prepare a bread pan with *Pam*. Arrange 2 thin slices of bread in the bottom. Place cheese and ham on each slice. Sprinkle the herbs on top. Cover with 2 more slices of bread. Beat together eggs, milk, mustard and Worcestershire sauce. Pour over all and hold at room temperature until all the milk is absorbed, at least 20 minutes. Since souffle must be served immediately, plan to start baking with a pre-heated oven at 350°F (176°C), 20 minutes before serving time. Use the center of the oven so the souffle may rise dramatically and bake evenly. The souffle serves 2 for lunch. Add a tossed salad and Fruit Portion. Planning pays off.

Deviled Eggs

6 hard boiled eggs

1 ounce (31 ml) yogurt or buttermilk

½ teaspoon (2.5 ml) prepared salad mustard

¼ teaspoon (1.2 ml) salt

¼ teaspoon (1.2 ml) paprika

Garnish: parsley flakes or chives

Cut the eggs with a zigzag line using a small paring knife around the egg lengthwise. Pull apart gently. Remove yolks and mash in a small dish. Add the other ingredients. Fill the whites and garnish with parsley flakes or chives. One egg looks like two when fancied up. It adds much to a luncheon plate even when you use only one-half. Have you had your cholesterol checked?

Glazed Hard Cooked Eggs

6 hard boiled eggs, peeled,
  halved or sliced
1 package plain gelatine,
  softened in ¼ cup (62 ml)
  cold water
1 cup (250 ml) boiling water

Sweetener to equal 3 teaspoons
  (15 ml) sugar
3 teaspoons (15 ml) lemon juice
6 ice cubes
1 teaspoon (5 ml) parsley

Peel and slice eggs as desired. Chill on flat plate. Add boiling water
to softened gelatine. Stir in sweetener and lemon juice. When the
gelatine is clear, add the ice cubes and stir until almost set, just past
the syrupy stage, but not yet solid. Spoon a teaspoon on each egg
slice. Repeat every few minutes until glaze is high and shiny.
Sprinkle parsley flakes on top. One egg is two ounces protein allowance.

Egg Salad Sandwich (for 1 lunch)

1 egg, hard boiled
3 ounces (85 g) low-fat
  cottage cheese
1 tablespoon (16 ml) each
  Onion or chives
  Parsley, chopped
  Pimentos, chopped
  Celery, finely chopped
  Dill pickle finely chopped

1 teaspoon (5 ml) lemon juice,
  yogurt, or buttermilk
⅛ teaspoon (.6 ml) paprika
⅛ teaspoon (.6 ml) pepper,
  freshly ground
Lettuce
2 thin slices of bread

(for a week's lunches for a brown-bagger)
10 slices thin bread,
  refrigerated
1 pound (453 g or 500 ml)
  low-fat cottage cheese

5 eggs, hard boiled
Optional free vegetables and
  seasonings

Mash the egg while hot with the cottage cheese. You'll never miss
the mayonnaise. Add flavor and texture with the vegies, tartness and
spreadability with the lemon juice, yogurt, or buttermilk. Garnish
with paprika, parsley, or pimento. Use mixture as a salad on lettuce
with dill pickle, or to stuff celery, as well as to make a great
sandwich.

Western Egg Sandwich

1 small onion, chopped
¼ green pepper finely diced
1 stalk celery finely diced
¼ red pepper or pimentos,
  finely diced
3 ounces (85 g) very lean,
  trimmed ham, coarsely
  chopped

1 egg, beaten
4 slices thin bread (2 ounces
  or 57 g)
Dill pickle for garnish

In a skilled sprayed with Pam, stir fry the vegetables with the ham. Pour the egg over the vegetables and ham; cook at low heat for just a minute. Turn, and cook the other side till just barely firm. Place on toasted slices of bread. Cut diagonally and serve with a dill pickle for garnish. Ham is acceptable for lunch occasionally. A little variety keeps you interested. Half of the recipe is your portion, so invite a friend to share with you.

Plain Gentle Custard

2 cups (500 ml) hot skim milk
2 beaten eggs
½ teaspoon (2.5 ml) salt
⅛ teaspoon (.6 ml) nutmeg

1 teaspoon (5 ml) vanilla
Sweetener to equal 2 tablespoons (31 ml) sugar

Combine ingredients and pour into 2 custard or coffee cups. To avoid overcooking and weeping of the custard, use an electric skillet. Set the cups in hot water in the skillet and cook at 350°F (176°C) for 20 minutes, or until the custard is gently set. It's best to leave the skillet covered, but if you peek, don't let the condensed water drip into the custard. This custard encourages you to "eat" your milk slowly with appreciation. Two servings each account for 1 milk and 1 ounce (28 g) of protein allowance from your menu. Check-up time: How many eggs have you had this week?

20
FISH AND SEAFOOD

Clams Casino

6 ounces (170 g) minced or chopped canned clams, drained

2 ounces (57 g) bread, crumbled in blender

1 tablespoon (16 ml) lemon juice

1 egg, beaten

3 tablespoons (48 ml) dried parsley

1 tablespoon (16 ml) minced onion

⅛ teaspoon (.6 ml) thyme

1 teaspoon (5 ml) Worcestershire sauce

⅛ teaspoon (.6 ml) pepper, freshly ground

¼ cup (125 ml) tomato juice

½ cup (125 ml) celery, finely chopped

⅛ teaspoon (.6 ml) paprika

Combine all ingredients except paprika and 1 tablespoon (16 ml) parsley. Toss lightly. Prepare 2 large scallop sea shells or 8 clam shells with Pam. Divide the mixture, spooning even portions into the shells. Garnish with paprika and parsley. Bake at 325°F (162°C) for 15 minutes. Serves 2 for luncheon as bread and protein allotment.

Clam Chowder with "Sour Cream"

6 ounces (170 ml) chopped or
minced canned clams with
juice

4 ounces (125 ml) canned
mushrooms with juice

1 cup (250 ml) chicken broth

1 tablespoon (16 ml) dried
onion flakes

1 cup (250 ml) yogurt

½ teaspoon (2.5 ml) dill weed

⅛ teaspoon (.6 ml) paprika

Heat clams, mushrooms and their juices with chicken broth and onion flakes. When hot, serve in 2 soup bowls. Float ½ cup (125 ml) yogurt on each serving, garnishing with dill weed and paprika. Since clams have only 90 calories (kiloJoules) for 6 ounces (170 g), enjoy this hearty low calorie (kiloJoule) protein soup for two. Add toast "crackers" for your bread allowance. Texture contrast and eye appeal satisfy.

Fish Chowder

1 pound (453 g) fresh haddock
(or any mild fish) sauteed
with:

1 onion, chopped, and

1 cup (250 ml) celery,
chopped, in

1 cup (250 ml) chicken
bouillon

4 ounces canned mushrooms
with juice

⅛ teaspoon (.6 ml) garlic salt

Dash (.3 ml) pepper, freshly
ground

1 water-packed roasted pepper,
diced

1 cup (250 ml) evaporated skim
milk

¼ teaspoon (1.2 ml) paprika

1 teaspoon (5 ml) dried parsley

Flake the cooked fish gently in the bouillon. Add the other ingredients, saving the parsley for garnish. Simmer to blend flavors. The chowder serves 4 for lunch, with toast "crackers" and fruit. The recipe uses ½ cup (125 ml) milk per serving. To use it as a dinner meal, omit the toast and add 1 cup (250 ml) of cooked carrots to serve 2.

Charlie's Dream

20 ounces (625 ml) cauliflower, cooked, drained, and mashed

12 ounces (340 g) water pack tuna, drained and flaked

4 ounces (125 ml) canned mushrooms, drained

2 ounces (57 g) Cheddar cheese, shredded

6 ounces (170 g or 188 ml) low-fat cottage cheese

1 ounce (28 g) grated Parmesan cheese (2 tablespoons or 31 ml)

Prepare a baking dish with *Pam*. Layer the ingredients, sprinkling the Parmesan cheese on top. Bake at 375°F (190°C) for 20 minutes. This recipe serves 3 for dinner or 6 for lunch, fulfilling the protein requirement for each diner.

Fish Fruit Basket

2 oranges cut in halves

2 tablespoons (31 ml) diet Italian dressing

3 tablespoons (48 ml) each chopped celery, cucumber, and green pepper

1 tablespoon (16 ml) chopped pimento

6 ounces (170 g) drained tuna, flaked

Garnish: fresh parsley

Remove the sections of the oranges carefully without disturbing the skin. Work over a wide dish to save the juice. Add juice to the salad dressing and mix it with the vegetables, tuna, and orange sections. Fill the orange cups with the mixture for a surprise picnic salad. Garnish with fresh parsley. Two persons each enjoy two fragrant orange baskets full of the proper fruit and protein allowance for lunch. Add toast to the menu like crackers, and some hot bouillon in a Thermos.

Tuna Quiche

6 ounces (170 g) tuna, water
  packed
3 ounces (85 g) shredded
  American or Swiss cheese
3 medium eggs, beaten
1 cup (250 ml) skim milk
1/3 cup (83 ml) chopped green
  pepper
1/3 cup (83 ml) chopped onion
  or 4 tablespoons (62 ml)
  onion flakes

½ teaspoon (1.2 ml) dry
  mustard
4-ounce (125 ml) can
  mushrooms
⅛ teaspoon (.6 ml) paprika or
  pimento for garnish

Mix ingredients and pour into a pie pan sprayed with Pam. Bake at 325°F (162°C) for 45 minutes. Serve hot or cold. Enjoy 1/6 for lunch or 1/3 for dinner with salad and Fruit Portion. Take it to a luncheon or dinner party. The hostess will love you because it goes with any menu, and you'll love yourself for staying on the diet.

Crabmeat Casserole

6 ounces (170 g) canned crabmeat, drained, or
6 ounces (170 g) frozen crabmeat, thawed
¼ cup (62 ml) chopped onion
1 ounce (28 g) of bread,
  crumbled

½ cup (125 ml) skim milk
2 tablespoons (28 g or 31 ml)
  Parmesan cheese
¼ teaspoon (1 ml) paprika

Combine all ingredients and bake in a dish prepared with Pam, at 350°F (176°C) for 45 minutes. This is perfect for a Maintainer's dinner or a man's menu, since there are 8 ounces of protein, counting the cheese. Two dieters could share the recipe and extend the menu with cottage cheese and pineapple salad with peas for the Restricted Starchy Vegetable.

Mackerel Cauliflower Bake

10 ounces (313 ml) cut cauliflower, cooked and drained

5 ounces (142 g) canned
mackerel, drained and
coarsely flaked, freshened
with

1 tablespoon (16 ml) lemon
juice

1½ ounces (42 g) bread (3 thin
slices) crumbled in blender
with:

1 egg and

¾ cup (188 ml) evaporated
skim milk

½ cup (125 ml) Rice Krispies
for top

Prepare a baking dish with Pam. Layer the cauliflower and lemon-freshened mackerel in the bottom. Over the top pour the mixture of bread, egg and milk. Sprinkle Rice Krispies on top. Bake for 20 minutes at 350°F (176°C). Serves 2 for lunch, ¾ cup (188 ml) milk allowance for each. Add Fruit Portion.

Mackerel Pepper Loaf

14 ounces (397 g) canned
mackerel, drained

4 ounces (125 ml) canned
mushrooms, drained

1 tablespoon (16 ml) onion
flakes

1 green pepper, seeded, diced,
and cooked briefly in a small
amount of water until bright
green

2 eggs, beaten

2 ounces (57 g) Cheddar
cheese, grated

Prepare a small loaf pan with Pam. Mix the ingredients and place in the pan. Bake at 350°F (176°C) for 25 minutes. The loaf provides 3 dinner portions of protein or 6 lunch portions.

Mackerel Marinade

1 can (340 g) mackerel drained
1 thinly sliced onion
¼ cup (62 ml) wine vinegar
Sweetener to equal 4 teaspoons
(20 ml) sugar

½ teaspoon (2.5 ml) paprika
¼ teaspoon (1.2 ml) lemon
pepper

Arrange fish opened and boned in a relish dish with other ingredients on top. Marinate several hours. Serve cold. Used as your sole protein for lunch, serves 4, or 2 for dinner. Since it is a strong, rich fish, you may want to use it as a side dish, and plan your portion accordingly. Mackerel is a very palatable variety fish. Give it a try. The price is right.

Italian Seafood

4 ounces (113 g) canned seafood (tuna, shrimp, salmon,
clams, crab, mackerel or
water-pack sardines)
⅛ teaspoon (.6 ml) celery salt
⅛ teaspoon (.6 ml) onion salt

Dash (.3 ml) of oregano
1 tablespoon (16 ml) lemon
juice
1 1-ounce (28 g) slice American
cheese
Garnish: ⅛ teaspoon (.6 ml)
paprika

Mix all the ingredients except cheese and paprika in a metal ice cube tray sprayed with *Pam*. Cover with cheese. Broil for 2 to 3 minutes. Garnish with paprika. This recipe is a fast dinner portion for 1.

Shrimp Egg Foo Young

1 cup (250 ml) bean sprouts, drained and rinsed
3 chopped scallions
¼ cup (62 ml) chopped celery
6 ounces (170 g) crumbled canned shrimp, rinsed (or use crabmeat, lobster, or tuna)

⅛ teaspoon (.6 ml) ginger
½ cup (125 ml) chicken bouillon
2 eggs, beaten with
½ teaspoon (2.5 ml) salt and
½ teaspoon (2.5 ml) pepper

Stir fry the vegetables with the shrimp, ginger and bouillon in an electric skillet until liquid is gone. Cover with egg, salt and pepper. Cook covered at 350°F (176°C) for 5 to 10 minutes. Serve with cautious use of soy sauce. This recipe provides protein for 5 breakfasts, 3 lunches, or 1½ dinners for women.

Lobster Newburg

4 slices thin bread (2 ounces or 57 g) crumbled in blender
¾ cup (188 ml) evaporated skim milk
½ teaspoon (2.5 ml) sherry extract
Dash (.3 ml) of nutmeg
⅛ teaspoon (.6 ml) paprika

1 egg yolk, beaten
6 ounces (170 g) canned lobster (or crabmeat or tuna) drained, rinsed, and broken up, or 6 ounces (170 g) cooked lobster, coarsely chopped
1 thin slice bread, toasted

Add evaporated skim milk to crumbled bread in blender. Blend until smooth. Cook this in a pan as a cream sauce, stirring constantly until thick. Add sherry flavoring, spices and egg yolk. Stir briskly, cooking only about 30 seconds. Add lobster and heat through only, while you toast bread. Serve on ½ slice of toast, diagonally cut. Serves 2 for lunch, each using ¾ cup (188 ml) milk allowance. Add a tossed salad and Fruit Portion.

Poor Man's Lobster

1 pound (453 g) haddock, fresh
   or frozen and thawed
1 cup (250 ml) water

2 tablespoons (31 ml) white
   vinegar
½ teaspoon (2.5 ml) salt

Saute the fish with the water, salt, and vinegar. Drain and cool. Use it as "lobster" cocktail with seafood sauce and lettuce. How about "lobster" Newburg using sherry extract and part of your bread allowance to thicken the sauce? Or, add "mayonnaise," onion, and celery to make a "lobster" salad. One pound (453 g) shrinks to about 12 ounces (340 g) in cooking, making 4 luncheon servings of 3 ounces (85 g) each, or 2 dinner portions, 6 ounces (170 g) each.

Smoked Trout

2 10-inch trout with heads
   on (14 ounces or 397 g)
¼ cup (62 ml) salt

1 quart (1 liter) water
Garnish: lemon and watercress

Soak the fish in a brine of the salt and water for half an hour. Drain and dry the trout. Use an old covered pan with rack for smoking. Cover the bottom lightly with hickory sawdust, or the bark or chips of hickory wood. Spray the rack with *Pam*. In the pan arrange trout in swimming position on the rack, spreading the sides of the fish wide. Cover the pan tightly with the lid. Place over high heat without any moisture for 15 minutes. The smoke is delightful even with the fan turned on! The fish skin becomes soft and dark and can be peeled off just before serving. This is a delicacy for two, enhanced by a watercress and lemon wedge garnish. Fresh peas and salad make an attractive spring dinner menu.

Florentine Fillet

1 pound (453 g) fish fillet (sole, haddock, flounder)
1 cup (250 ml) chicken bouillon
10 ounces (283 g) frozen broccoli or spinach, cooked till bright green and drained

2 cups (500 ml) thick cauliflower cream sauce (see Sauces)
1 tablespoon (7 g or 16 ml) grated Parmesan cheese
⅛ teaspoon (.6 ml) paprika

Saute the fish in a skillet with the chicken bouillon. Lift out the fish gently and drain on a paper towel. On an oven proof platter arrange the green vegetable to make a bed for the fish fillet. Spread the thick cauliflower cream sauce on top of the fish. Top with grated cheese and paprika. Bake at 375°F (190°C) for 10 minutes. Serves 2 dinners for protein. Add the Restricted Starchy Vegetable and Fruit Portion.

Gourmet Fish Fillet

1 pound (453 g) fish fillet
4 ounces (125 ml) onion, thinly sliced
½ pound (227 g) fresh mushrooms, thinly sliced
½ green pepper, chopped
2 tablespoons (31 ml) pimento, chopped

¼ cup (62 ml) chicken bouillon
1 tablespoon (16 ml) lemon juice
⅛ teaspoon (.6 ml) pepper
No salt for seafood
Garnish: lemon wedges and ⅛ teaspoon (.6 ml) of paprika

Arrange onion slices in baking dish which has been sprayed with *Pam*. Lay fish on top. Place vegetables over fish. Combine bouillon, lemon juice and pepper. Pour over fish. Bake at 350°F (176°C) for 20 to 25 minutes. Garnish with lemon wedges and paprika. Serve 2 for dinner with stewed tomatoes and tossed salad.

Buttermilk Baked Fish

⅛ teaspoon (.6 ml) celery salt
⅛ teaspoon (.6 ml) pepper,
  freshly ground
1 teaspoon (5 ml) minced onion
  flakes

½ cup (125 ml) buttermilk
8 ounces (227 g) of fish steak
1 teaspoon (5 ml) parsley for
  garnish

Mix spices with buttermilk and pour over the fish in a metal ice cube tray sprayed with Pam. Bake at 350°F (176°C) for 15 minutes till fish is barely firm and white. Garnish with parsley at serving time. Eight ounces (227 g) shrinks to 6 ounces (170 g) for one portion. The buttermilk separates into curds and whey, delicious, moist, tender and distinctive.

Tomato Topped Sole

1 small onion, chopped
1 pound (453 g) sole (or use cod
  or any other favorite or available fish) fresh, or frozen and
  thawed

1 cup (250 ml) stewed tomatoes
½ chopped green pepper
3 stalks of celery, chopped

Arrange the onion in a metal ice cube tray or shallow baking dish sprayed with Pam. Lay the fish on top. Cover with the vegetables. The tomatoes will help the raw vegetables to cook and flavor the fish. Bake at 350°F (176°C) for 20 minutes. Serve 4 for lunch or 2 for dinner. Sole is a thin fish, so if you spread it on a larger baking dish, the cooking time can be reduced to 15 minutes.

Salmon Broil

1 pound (453 g) salmon, fresh or frozen and thawed

1 tablespoon (16 ml) soy sauce

1 tablespoon (16 ml) orange juice

1 tablespoon (16 ml) tomato juice

1 tablespoon (16 ml) lemon juice

1 tablespoon (16 ml) dried parsley

⅛ teaspoon (.6 ml) garlic salt

⅛ teaspoon (.6 ml) pepper, freshly ground

Place the fish in a baking dish prepared with *Pam*. Mix the remaining ingredients and pour over the fish. Marinate for at least an hour. Broil for 10 to 15 minutes, basting frequently with the marinade. Serves 2 persons for protein allowance.

21
FRUITS

Strawberry Cream Squares

2 envelopes diet strawberry
gelatine
2 cups (500 ml) boiling water
1 cup (250 ml) juice drained
from 1 large can crushed
pineapple in juice
2 cups (500 ml) frozen strawberries without sugar
2 bananas, sliced

1 cup (227 g or 250 ml) low-fat
cottage cheese blended with:
1 teaspoon (5 ml) orange
rind, grated
1 teaspoon (5 ml) lemon
rind, grated
2 drops almond flavoring
Sweetener to equal 1 tablespoon (16 ml) sugar

Dissolve gelatine in the blender with boiling water. Add pineapple
juice and strawberries, blending briefly. Combine the gelatine mixture in a bowl with the sliced bananas and pineapple. Pour half the
mixture in a 9 x 13 (33 x 23 cm) pan treated with Pam. Refrigerate.
Blend cottage cheese with fruit rinds, almond flavor, and sweetener.
Spread this on gelatine when it is firmly set. Then pour the other half
of the gelatine mixture on top. Just before serving, cut into 12
squares. One square is a Fruit Portion plus negligible cottage cheese
protein.

Strawberry Rhubarb Pie

1 pound (453 g) diced rhubarb (4 long stalks or 2½ cups [625 ml])

12 ounces (375 ml) diet soda (strawberry, black cherry, or red apple)

Sweetener to equal 3 tablespoons (48 ml) sugar

2 envelopes strawberry diet gelatine

1 cup (227 g or 250 ml) blended cottage cheese

1 teaspoon (5 ml) lemon rind

1 teaspoon (5 ml) orange rind

Dash (.3 ml) of almond extract (optional)

Sweetener to equal 2 teaspoons (10 ml) sugar

Cook the rhubarb in the soda with the sweetener. Then stir in the strawberry gelatine. When the gelatine is dissolved, pour the mixture in a pie pan sprayed with *Pam* and chill until firm. Blend the cottage cheese with the remainder of ingredients. Spread on top of pie. One-fourth of the pie is only one ounce (28 g) of protein. Rhubarb is unrestricted, and the gelatine is free!

Cranapple Waldorf

2 cups (500 ml) low calorie cranberry juice cocktail

1 envelope diet strawberry gelatine

1 cup (250 ml) celery, chopped

1 cup (250 ml) apple, peeled and diced, with skin

½ cup (125 ml) water chestnuts, drained and chopped, for "nuts"

Heat the cranberry juice to boiling. Add gelatine and stir until dissolved. When cooled and syrupy add the celery, apple and water chestnuts. Pour into a 1-quart (1 liter) mold sprayed with *Pam*. When set, unmold on lettuce. One-fifth of the recipe is your Fruit Portion for that meal. Water chestnuts are a Restricted Starchy Vegetable, but hardly a consideration in this proportion. Enjoy all that texture!

Spring Fruit Symphony

1 small can Mandarin oranges, drained

1 apple with skin, cored and diced

1 large can chunk pineapple, in juice

1 cantaloupe halved, seeded, peeled, and diced

2 bananas, sliced

1 cup (250 ml) orange juice

1 cup (250 ml) fresh grapefruit sections (1 whole fruit)

Dash (.3 ml) coconut extract

1 cup (250 ml) fresh straw-berries, raspberries, or blue-berries

Mix the fruit and flavoring, adding fragile berries last. As a dessert, the recipe deserves your best compote glasses. Without the juices, the fruit could be a salad, accompanied by plain, fresh low-fat cottage cheese on lettuce. (Or make an attractive 3-quart [3 liter] mold using 2 packets of any fruit-flavored diet gelatine with 2 cups [500 ml] of boiling water, 8 ice cubes, and the pineapple and orange juices. When cool and syrupy, add the fruit. Pour in a mold sprayed with *Pam*.) Share and savor the 16 servings slowly with symphonic music and soft lights.

Fruit Flip

2 slices thin white bread

½ cup (125 ml) diet applesauce, peach slices, crushed pine-apple in juice, fresh rasp-berries, or sliced strawberries

1 teaspoon (5 ml) lemon juice

2 tablespoons (31 ml) water or fruit juice

Dash (.3 ml) cinnamon (or nutmeg or almond extract)

Sweetener to equal 1 table-spoon (16 ml) sugar

Trim ⅜-inch crusts off the bread and blend them into crumbs for thickening. Combine the crumbs with the fruit, juices, cinnamon and sweetener. Cook until soft and thick. Roll the thin bread slices even thinner! Moisten the edges with fruit juice. Place half the fruit mixture on each slice. Fold over diagonally, forming a triangle. Press edges together. Bake at 425°F (218°C) for 6 minutes on a pan sprayed with *Pam* until golden brown for a Sunday breakfast for 1 with 1 ounce (28 g) of hard cheese and coffee. Weekends can be easy if you know how to prepare!

Fruit Slaw

1 small head of cabbage, shredded

1 can of drained crushed pineapple

1 can drained Mandarin oranges

Sweetener to equal 1 tablespoon (16 ml) sugar

½ cup (125 ml) evaporated skim milk

1 teaspoon (5 ml) grated orange rind

Mix together and chill for an hour before serving. One-fifth of the recipe is your Fruit Portion; the milk is negligible.

Pineapple Baskets

1 ripe pineapple (tender at base) quartered lengthwise and cored

1 banana sliced, sprinkled with lemon juice

1 apple cored, diced, and sprinkled with lemon juice

¼ cantaloupe diced

¼ cup (62 ml) fresh berries

1 cup (250 ml) grapefruit sections (1 whole grapefruit)

12 ounces low-fat cottage cheese blended with:

⅛ teaspoon (.6 ml) rum extract

Dash (.3 ml) almond extract

1 teaspoon (5 ml) lemon rind and Sweetener to equal 3 tablespoons (48 ml) sugar

4 sprigs of fresh mint for garnish

Remove and dice the succulent pineapple, keeping the shell intact for baskets. Mix with the rest of the fruit, and combine gently with the cheese mixture. Spoon half of it into the 4 baskets. The other half may be used at another meal. Garnish with mint sprigs. One of the 8 servings equals 1 fruit allowance and 1½ ounces (42 g) of protein.

22
ICE CREAM
AND SHERBETS

Instant Banana Ice Cream

1 peeled banana, peach, cantaloupe or ½ cup berries
4 ounces (125 ml) evaporated
skim milk

Sweetener to equal 2 teaspoons
sugar
Dash (.3 ml) of nutmeg

Cut the banana (or other fruit) in inch-size pieces. Freeze with 3
tablespoons (48 ml) citrus juice to prevent discoloration. At serving
time, blend with milk and sweetener. Serve immediately, garnished
with nutmeg. Count 1 Fruit Portion and 1 milk allowance.

Neapolitan Ice Cream

1/3 cup (83 ml) nonfat dry milk
   mixed with
1 teaspoon (5 ml) vanilla and
1 cup yogurt
1/3 cup (83 ml) Chocolate Alba
   nonfat dry milk mixed with
1 cup (250 ml) yogurt

1/3 cup (83 ml) nonfat dry milk
   mixed with
½ cup (125 ml) strawberries,
   hulled and mashed and
1 cup (250 ml) yogurt

Beat each flavor separately. Freeze in layers in 6 individual molds which have been sprayed with *Pam*. You're ready for 6 legal treats, each containing 1 milk allowance. Fruit negligible.

Cranberry Sherbet Mold

2/3 cup (166 ml) nonfat dry
   milk
½ cup (125 ml) ice water
Sweetener to equal 3 tablespoons (48 ml) sugar
1 teaspoon (5 ml) lemon rind,
   grated
1 teaspoon (5 ml) orange rind,
   grated

1 tablespoon (16 ml) frozen
   orange juice concentrate
1 teaspoon (5 ml) lemon juice
1 cup (250 ml) yogurt, plain
1 jar low-calorie cranberry
   sauce (Ocean Spray makes it)

Whip the nonfat dry milk in ice water until stiff. Add sweetener. Mix fruit rinds, orange concentrate, and lemon juice into yogurt. Fold into whipped milk. Break up the cranberry sauce and add it last. Pour into a mold sprayed with *Pam*. Freeze until firm. Unmold and refrigerate during the main course for easy slicing at dessert time. The recipe serves 12, but you may have up to ¼ of it to provide your fruit and milk for one meal.

Flashy Fruit Sherbet

½ cup (125 ml) fruit such as
  berries, cantaloupe or
  banana, frozen—or
½ cup (125 ml) canned pineapple, apricots or peaches in
  natural juices, frozen

Sweetener to equal 1 teaspoon
  (5 ml) sugar
½ cup (125 ml) buttermilk (or
  skim milk)

It may seem strange to freeze canned fruit, but it prepares you for
instant fruit sherbet. Run hot water over the can and slide the con-
tents out after opening both ends. Divide into fourths if it is a large
can; each will be one fruit. Chop one slightly; blend with sweetener
and buttermilk. Freeze the other 3 chunks for next time. The sherbet
is like soft ice cream and must be eaten immediately. Freezing it
ahead is not satisfactory. Make what you need, 1 serving of fruit and
milk. Sit in the sun and be refreshed with your big cupful.

Orange Ice

1 envelope plain gelatine
½ cup (125 ml) cold water
1 egg, separated
Sweetener to equal ¼ cup
  (62 ml) sugar

1 12-ounce (375 ml) can
  evaporated skim milk
1 teaspoon (5 ml) vanilla
4 ounces (125 ml) frozen orange
  juice concentrate

Soften gelatine with cold water. Heat until dissolved. Beat in egg
yolk and sweetener while mixture is hot. In a large mixer bowl, beat
evaporated skim milk with the egg white until very stiff (5 to 10
minutes). Add vanilla, orange concentrate (partially thawed) and
gelatine-egg yolk mixture. Freeze in a covered plastic container.
The recipe includes 3 Fruit Portions and 3 milk allowances. The egg
is negligible. Enjoy 1/3 if you wish; one Fruit Portion and one milk
allowance accounted for.

23
MEATS

Barbecued Lamb Chops

1 pound (453 g) lean lamb
   chops, 1-inch (2.5 cm) thick
½ cup (125 ml) orange juice
3 tablespoons (48 ml) soy sauce

1 teaspoon (5 ml) horseradish
¼ teaspoon (1.2 ml) prepared
   mustard

Fire up the outdoor barbecue grill. Prepare the lamb chops in a marinade of the other ingredients. Place on sizzling hot grill. Turn and baste once, cooking about 7 minutes on each side. If you're a Maintainer, you may have a small baked potato with yogurt on it like sour cream. If you're heading toward maintenance, use the yogurt on your limited vegetable to compliment the lamb. One pound (453 g) of meat with bones and shrinkage serves 2. Remember lamb is an Alternate Choice Protein.

Beef Stuffed Peppers

2 green peppers, halved and
   seeded
1 pound (453 g) ground chuck
⅛ teaspoon (.6 ml) pepper
⅛ teaspoon (.6 ml) garlic salt
1 tablespoon (16 ml) onion
   flakes

1 teaspoon (5 ml) parsley flakes
½ cup (125 ml) chicken
   bouillon
3 tablespoons (48 ml) lemon
   juice
2 tablespoons (31 ml) tomato
   juice

Saute the peppers just until bright green. Combine the other ingredients and spoon into the 4 halves. Bake at 325°F (162°C) for 25 minutes. Adding a Restricted Starchy Vegetable, 4 people use this recipe intelligently to lose weight, providing they remember that beef is an Occasional Protein Choice. Supplement the menu with Preferred or Alternate Protein Choices.

Chili Con Carne

10 ounces (313 ml) green beans
   (or broccoli), chopped
8 ounces tomato sauce
Sweetener to equal 4 teaspoons
   (20 ml) sugar
8 ounces (227 g) ground chuck
   cooked until crumbly and
   drained on a paper towel

2 tablespoons (31 ml) chili
   powder
2 tablespoons (31 ml) minced
   onion
¼ teaspoon (1.2 ml) garlic salt
1 bay leaf

Cook the green beans in a small amount of water. Drain. Add the other ingredients and simmer on top of the stove, or bake, for 10 minutes at 325°F (162°C). Two diet portions.

Chow Mein for Maintainers

2 pounds (1 kg) of protein,
   either ground round, center
   cut chuck, in pieces, frozen
   shrimp, or raw boned chicken
   breast (4 large) in small

pieces; or you may use left
over roast beef or steak,
sliced, or canned shrimp,
drained and rinsed, or
cooked chicken breast, sliced

1 tablespoon (16 ml) each soy sauce, lemon juice, and water

1 teaspoon (5 ml) sherry flavoring

2 cups (500 ml) chicken bouillon combined with 2 tablespoons (31 ml) soy sauce and 6 tablespoons (93 ml) cornstarch or arrowroot (which has fewer calories and doesn't have to be cooked to thicken)

½ cup (125 ml) celery, cut diagonally

½ cup (125 ml) onion, chopped coarsely

3 cups (750 ml) Chinese cabbage, chopped coarsely (Bok Choy or Nappa cabbage)

2 cups (500 ml) bean sprouts, freshly sprouted or 2 cups (500 ml) canned bean sprouts, drained and rinsed

½ cup (25 ml) mushrooms, sliced

1 pound (453 g) spinach torn into pieces (1 bag)

2 cups (500 ml) cooked rice (the instant kind will take care of itself while you do your stir fry show)

A showy way to cook and serve this meal is to prepare and measure the ingredients, arrange them on a tray, and demonstrate your stir-fry skill at the table with your three dinner companions. You can do it standing or sitting down. The cooking time is necessarily brief, since the vegetables should be flavorful and crunchy. Prepare the wok or electric fry pan with Pam. Toss the protein with a marinade of soy sauce, lemon juice, water, and sherry flavoring. Stir fry, using the marinade to blend flavors until the protein is barely cooked. Push to one side. Add 1/3 cup (83 ml) of the bouillon and soy sauce mixture with the addition of each vegetable, saving the more fragile spinach until last. Dissolve cornstarch (or arrowroot) in the remaining ½ cup (125 ml) bouillon mixture. Combine this with the Chow Mein, stirring gently as it thickens. Serve over ½ cup hot, fluffy rice. Serves 4 Maintainers. The rice corresponds to your Restricted Starchy Vegetable in calories.

Crock Pot Veal Stew

1 pound (453 g) veal chunks
4 small carrots
Dash (.3 ml) lemon pepper
1 teaspoon (5 ml) dill weed

1 tablespoon (16 ml) onion
　flakes
1 packet vegetable bouillon
1 cup (250 ml) buttermilk

Combine ingredients in crock pot and set at low cooking heat. Cook all day while you play, exercise and work at "becoming." With a salad, beverage and Fruit Portion for dessert, this recipe supplies the perfect protein-carbohydrate combination for two.

Festive Ham Rolls

2 cups (500 ml) cooked winter
　squash
2 cups (500 ml) pineapple, in
　its own juice
Dash (.3 ml) cloves

12 ounces (340 ml) boiled ham,
　sliced thinly
1 green pepper, chopped and
　cooked bright green

In the blender, combine the squash with the juice from the pineapple and add the cloves. Spoon 2 tablespoons (31 ml) of squash on each slice of ham. Roll and secure with a toothpick. Arrange in a glass baking dish. Bake at 325°F (162°C) for 15 minutes until just heated through. At serving time spread pineapple and green pepper over the rolls. Tuna in a tossed salad with the ham rolls completes a safe menu for 4.

Sarma or Derivi (meaning wrapping) Greek and Armenian

1 pound (453 g) ground lamb
4 ounces (125 ml) tomato sauce
4 ounces (125 ml) lemon juice

Dash (.3 ml) of ground pepper
14 grape leaves (obtained at an
　import store in a jar)

Mix the meat and juices with the pepper. Roll 2 tablespoons (31 ml) on each grape leaf. Bake at 325°F (162°C) for 1 hour in a covered glass baking dish. Drain off fat and juice. Served as hors d'oeuvres, one represents about an ounce (28 g) of protein.

Shepherd Pie

8 ounces (227 g) ground beef
chuck
2 teaspoons (10 ml) parsley
Dash (.3 ml) of garlic salt
10 ounces (313 ml) cauliflower

1 packet chicken bouillon
½ cup (125 ml) water
1 tablespoon (7 g or 16 ml)
grated cheese
⅛ teaspoon (.6 ml) paprika

Cook the meat with the seasonings. Drain the fat off and blot with a paper towel. Spread in a pie pan. Cook the cauliflower in bouillon and water. Drain and mash. Cover the meat with the cauliflower. Sprinkle with cheese and paprika. Bake at 350°F (176°C) for 15 minutes. This yields 2 Occasional Protein Choice portions. Supplement with Preferred or Alternate Protein Choices.

Lasagna

1 pound (453 g) ground beef or
veal chuck
3 tablespoons (48 ml) minced
onion
Dash (.3 ml) each garlic salt,
pepper, and oregano
1 tablespoon (16 ml) parsley
1 teaspoon (5 ml) basil
1 cup (250 ml) tomato sauce
½ pound (227 g) fresh mushrooms, sliced

1 10-ounce (283 g) package
frozen green vegetable
thawed and drained thor-
oughly (broccoli, green
beans, or spinach)
1 cup (250 ml) low-fat cottage
cheese
3 ounces (85 g) Mozzarella or
any hard cheese, sliced.

Cook the meat with the spices until it is crumbly. Drain fat, using paper towel. Add tomato sauce and mushrooms. Layer the meat mixture, green vegetables, cottage cheese and cheese slices in a baking dish sprayed with Pam. Bake at 350°F (176°C) for 20 minutes. One-eighth is your share, so ask your Internal Instructor to take over your control. This is so hearty and delicious you'll need help. Supplement the menu with Preferred or Alternate Protein Choices.

Pepper Lasagna

10 ounces (313 ml) chopped
  green peppers
1 egg
6 ounces (170 g or 188 ml)
  low-fat cottage cheese
½ cup (125 ml) chopped onion
Dash (.3 ml) of thyme
Dash (.3 ml) of basil

Dash (.3 ml) of oregano
4 ounces (125 ml) mushrooms,
  canned or fresh
6 ounces (170 g) ground beef
  or venison chuck
8 ounces (250 ml) tomato sauce
3 tablespoons (21 g or 48 ml)
  grated cheese

Arrange the chopped peppers in a casserole dish sprayed with *Pam*.
Beat the egg and the cottage cheese together, add onion and spices
and spread over the peppers. Add a layer of mushrooms. Cook the
meat crumbly, drain off the fat, and blot with paper towelling.
Sprinkle the meat layer on next. Pour the tomato sauce on top and
sprinkle with grated cheese. Bake at 350°F (176°C) for 45 minutes.
The recipe serves 4 dieters for Occasional Protein Choice, Restricted
Starchy Vegetables and Unrestricted "Vegies." Add a gelatine, Fruit
Portion and beverage for a complete dinner menu. Supplement with
Preferred or Alternate Protein Choices.

Hot "Sausage"

3 ounces (85 g) ground beef
  chuck
½ teaspoon (3 ml) crushed
  red pepper
2 ounces (62 ml) tomato sauce
½ small onion, chopped

Small can of mushrooms
Sweetener to equal 1 teaspoon
  (5 ml) sugar
Dash (.3 ml) of garlic salt
½ teaspoon (3 ml) sage

Mix beef and pepper. Cook until done. Add remainder of ingredients and simmer 10 minutes. Serve on 1 ounce (28 g) of bread for
lunch (Occasional Protein Choice). Neither beef nor spices will
make you skinny, but used discreetly, they will keep you interested
and contented.

Fragrant Meat Loaf

1 pound (453 g) ground round
½ cup (125 ml) tomato juice
1 teaspoon (5 ml) onion flakes
Dash (.3 ml) of garlic salt
1 green pepper, chopped
1 teaspoon (5 ml) celery seed

1 can rinsed sauerkraut—or—
  French green beans, drained
1 beaten egg
1 cup (250 ml) vegetable
  bouillon

Combine ingredients and bake at 350°F (176°C) for ½ hour. One-fourth of this recipe is your portion of meat (Occasional Protein Choice) for dinner, to be supplemented with tuna in your tossed salad or a side dish of low-fat cottage cheese.

"Spaghetti" and Meat Balls

½ pound (227 g) ground beef
  chuck
1 can bean sprouts, drained
  and rinsed
1 tablespoon (7 g or 16 ml)
  chopped onion
1 tablespoon (16 ml) green
  pepper, chopped
¼ teaspoon (1.2 ml) crushed
  rosemary

Dash (.3 ml) of garlic salt
Dash (.3 ml) of oregano
Dash (.3 ml) of basil
Dash (.3 ml) of marjoram
8 ounces (250 ml) tomato sauce
1 tablespoon (16 ml) grated
  cheese for topping

Cook the meat, drain off the fat, and blot the meat with paper towelling. Add the other ingredients. Bake at 350°F (176°C) for 20 minutes. Two dinners of Occasional Protein Choice, plus tomato sauce or juice allotment for the day. Supplement with Preferred or Alternate Protein Choices.

Sloppy Joe

1 pound (453 g) ground beef
   chuck, cooked crumbly and
   drained on a paper towel
2 cups (500 ml) tomato sauce
1 teaspoon (5 ml) Worcestershire sauce

1 small green pepper, chopped
1 small onion chopped
Dash (.3 ml) of pepper, freshly
   ground

Combine and simmer ingredients together for 15 minutes. Serve on the bread allowance for lunch. This is an Occasional Protein Choice. On that day, omit all tomato juice. The recipe serves 4.

Sweet and Sour Meatballs

2 pounds (1 kg) ground beef
   or veal chuck
1 tablespoon (16 ml) dried
   parsley
¼ cup (62 ml) minced onions
1 green pepper, diced
½ teaspoon (3 ml) mustard
½ teaspoon (3 ml) cinnamon
Dash (.3 ml) red pepper sauce
2 cups (500 ml) tomato sauce
Juice from large can (250 ml)
   of pineapple chunks

1/3 cup (83 ml) lemon juice
1/3 cup (83 ml) vinegar
Sweetener to equal 1 tablespoon (16 ml) brown sugar
1 cup celery, diced
1 large can pineapple chunks,
   drained
2 cans bean sprouts* drained,
   rinsed, heated in fresh water
   and drained again

Form meatballs from chuck. Simmer in a sauce made from the remainder of the ingredients (except pineapple chunks and bean sprouts). Simmer ½ hour. Add pineapple chunks at the end. Serve on unrestricted bean sprouts. Serves 4 generous dinner portions with tea, Oriental music, and candlelight. Supplement with Preferred or Alternate Protein Choices.

*Fresh bean sprouts are very much superior in taste and texture to the canned ones. It's like the difference between fresh and canned peas. You can sprout your own from a package of mung beans available at health food stores.

Venison Patties

1 pound (453 g) ground venison, trimmed of fat
½ cup (125 ml) crushed pineapple, packed in juice
Sweetener to equal 1 teaspoon
brown sugar*

½ cup (125 ml) finely chopped
celery
1 green pepper cut in large
pieces
¼ teaspoon (1.2 ml) rosemary

Form patties, mix other ingredients and pour over patties in an
electric skillet. Cook at low heat for 20 minutes. The recipe serves
two portions for the hunter and his wife. No gamey flavor or resent-
ment here. Peas and cauliflower "mashed potatoes" add contrast
and balanced nutrition to the dinner menu.

*Brown Sugar Twin

Venison Loaf for Maintainers

1 pound (453 g) ground venison, trimmed of fat
½ pound (227 g) fresh mushrooms or 1 small can (125 ml)
drained
1 packet bouillon seasoning,
any flavor
1 tablespoon (16 ml) onion
flakes
1 teaspoon (5 ml) lemon pepper

Dash (.3 ml) of garlic salt
Dash (.3 ml) of seasoned salt
¼ cup (125 ml) lemon juice
1 teaspoon (5 ml) dill weed or
dill seed
1 egg
¼ cup (62 ml) tomato sauce
¼ cup (62 ml) oatmeal
1 green pepper sliced into rings
for garnish

Mix everything but the green pepper. Pat into a loaf pan. Arrange
pepper slices on top. Bake at 325°F (162°C) for 45 minutes. Drain and
serve on small platter. This recipe is mainly for Maintainers because
of the oatmeal. It serves 2. A dieter could use a cold slice for lunch.

24
ORGAN MEATS

Pickled Sweet Heart

4 veal hearts (about 1 pound
  [453 g])
1 bay leaf
2 teaspoons (10 ml) pickling
  spices

¼ cup (62 ml) wine vinegar
1 packet beef bouillon
Sweetener to equal 1 tablespoon (16 ml) sugar

Combine ingredients and bake in a covered dish at 325°F (162°C) for
1 hour. Cool. Remove ventricle and fat. It's easy after it's cooked.
Slice. Cool the drippings in the refrigerator to remove all fat.
Arrange sliced Sweet Heart in the fat-free broth. It's delicious hot or
cold, and it makes one more sandwich possibility. One-fourth of the
recipe is your dinner protein, ⅛ for lunch.

Sweet and Sour Chicken Livers

1 pound (453 g) chicken livers
1 cup (250 ml) chicken bouillon
1 tablespoon (16 ml) lemon
  juice
Sweetener to equal 1 teaspoon
  (5 ml) sugar
½ cup (125 ml) celery

1 green pepper, diced
1 small onion, diced
1 cup (250 ml) crushed pineapple
1 can bean sprouts, rinsed
½ teaspoon (2.5 ml) soy sauce

Cook chicken livers in the bouillon, lemon juice, and sweetener. Add celery, pepper, and onion. Saute until peppers are bright green. Add pineapple and heat through. Serve on unrestricted bean sprouts which have been heated in fresh water and drained. Use soy sauce lightly at the table. Half of the recipe is your dinner protein, or ¼ for lunch. Half is one Fruit Portion for dinner or lunch.

Sweetbreads a la King

1 pound (453 g) sweetbreads*
(pancreas, thyroid, or
thalamus glands of veal,
or lamb)
1 pint (500 ml) of ice water
1 tablespoon (16 ml) vinegar
1 tablespoon (16 ml) lemon
juice
1 teaspoon (5 ml) salt
1 cup (250 ml) chicken bouillon

1 teaspoon (5 ml) lemon juice
1 teaspoon (5 ml) vinegar
1 small can of sliced mushrooms, drained (save juice)
3 pimentos
8 slices thin bread
½ teaspoon (2.5 ml) sherry
flavoring
3 drops (1 ml) butter flavoring
Garnish: parsley or chives

Soak sweetbreads in water, vinegar, lemon juice, and salt for half an hour. Drain. Simmer in bouillon, lemon juice, and vinegar for 20 minutes. Drain and cool in ice water. Slip off the membranes bravely. Slice and combine in a pan with pimentos and mushrooms. In the blender, combine the mushroom juice with ½ cup (250 ml) chicken bouillon and 2 ounces (57 g) of bread (4 thin slices). Add the sherry and butter flavors. Cook until thick, stirring constantly. Pour over sweetbreads. Simmer until heated through. Serve on 4 pieces of toasted thin bread. Garnish with parsley or chives. One-fourth of the recipe is a royal lunch for a slim gourmet cook. Invite three friends. Serve them the fast fruit sherbet for dessert.

*Because sweetbreads are easily digested, they are frequently recommended for convalescents, but they're a gourmet treat for anyone. Don't be put off by their origin!

25
MILK

Buttermilk

1 cup (250 ml) commercially cultured buttermilk (the kind you buy in the carton)

3 cups (750 ml) warm skim milk

Mix the two thoroughly and pour into a quart (1 liter) Thermos bottle, preferably the wide-mouth type. Cover tightly and wait about 6 hours. There will be one gentle curd. Add a flick of salt and give it a little shake. Pour it into a glass quart (liter) jar. Cover and refrigerate. Buttermilk is counted just the same as milk—2 glasses a day. You can extend the buttermilk with pineapple juice for a delightful summer drink, or with hot tomato juice for a hot winter soup. Combined with chilled V8, and a dash (1 ml) of hot sauce or Worcestershire sauce, it makes a refreshingly different summer soup. Buttermilk makes magic when baked with chicken or fish (tender protein and curds and whey).

Alba

This nonfat dry milk product comes in six forms:
Chocolate Alba (3 1-quart [1 liter] envelopes in one box)
Hot Cocoa—Alba 66 (individual portions: 1/6 cup or 41 ml)
Fit'n Frosty—Alba 77: (individual portions: 1/6 cup or [41 ml]
   Chocolate
   Strawberry
   Vanilla
Alba nonfat dry milk

Evaporated Skim Milk (Pet 99)

Mix equal parts of evaporated skim milk and water to constitute regular skim milk. Use double strength, straight from the can, the evaporated skim milk may be chilled and beaten to create a "whipped cream." Just add sweetener and vanilla or other flavors of your choice. It will stand in peaks, but must be used immediately to give the "whipped cream" effect. Don't be disheartened by the odd color of the milk straight from the can. It gets lighter as air is beaten into it.

Hot Cocoa Mix

3 cups nonfat dry milk   2/3 cup (166 ml) cocoa
Dry sweetener to equal 2/3 cup   1 vanilla bean   ·
   (166 ml)

In the blender, combine the dry nonfat milk, sweetener and cocoa until it is light and fluffy. Place in a quart jar with a vanilla bean to flavor it. It costs less than the commercial mix, and the real chocolate flavor is welcome. It's safe if used with discretion. It was those whole boxes of chocolate candy and the gooey chocolate syrup with real sugar that added pounds and pimples. One-third cup of this mix equals a milk allowance.

Nonfat Dry Milk

To make one cup (250 ml):
1/3 cup (83 ml) nonfat dry milk (fortified with A and D) plus water to reconstitute 8 ounces (250 ml)

To make a quart: 1-1/3 cups nonfat dry milk plus water to reconstitute 1 quart (1 liter)

Check package directions to be certain of measurements. They may differ slightly according to brand. Mixed thoroughly and chilled, this fat-free skim milk is very acceptable. You can acquire a taste for it. It is about half the cost of bottled skim milk, and it is versatile in recipes both wet and dry. You can use it to make buttermilk and yogurt. After you've acquired a taste for skim milk, you may appreciate this fast method of mixing. Fill a large container 1/3 full of nonfat dry milk. Add water, stir or shake with cover on and refrigerate.

Milk Shakes

Chocolate:
6 ounces (188 ml) chocolate
    diet soda
1/6 cup (41 ml) chocolate non-
    fat dry milk (Alba)
4-6 ice cubes
Fruit Flavors:
6 ounces (188 ml) any fruit-
    flavored diet soda
1/3 cup (83 ml) powdered skim
    milk
4-6 ice cubes

Vanilla:
6 ounces (188 ml) club soda
1/3 cup (83 ml) nonfat dry milk
4-6 ice cubes
1 teaspoon (5 ml) vanilla

Blend ingredients until smooth and thick. Each milk shake uses 1 milk allowance.

"Whipped Cream"

½ cup (125 ml) chilled evaporated skim milk (Pet 99)
Sweetener to equal 1 tablespoon (16 ml) sugar

1 teaspoon (5 ml) vanilla
½ teaspoon (2.5 ml) unflavored
  gelatine

Whip the milk, sweetener, and vanilla with a cold beater in a cold
bowl until the volume is double. Moisten the gelatine in 2 tablespoons (31 ml) water. Heat until dissolved over low heat, stirring
constantly. Beat in the gelatine mixture when slightly cooled with
the beaten milk to stabilize the "whipped cream." The gelatine part
may be omitted if you serve it immediately. You may use double
strength nonfat dry milk in the same way (1/3 cup [83 ml] with ½ cup
[125 ml] water) instead of evaporated skim milk. Either equals 1 cup
(250 ml) of milk from your daily allowance.

Yogurt

3 tablespoons (48 ml) cultured
  yogurt, plain commercial
  brand

3¾ cups (938 ml) warm skim
  milk

Mix 3 tablespoons (48 ml) of skim milk with the yogurt. Then add
the remainder of the milk to insure even distribution of the culture.
Hold in a Thermos bottle for 6 hours. Refrigerate when thick. A
yogurt maker is a foolproof help, since the temperature is held constant. When you use skim milk, your product is fat-free, allowing
you a full cup of yogurt to replace 1 cup (250 ml) of milk.

26
PICKLES AND RELISHES

Mixed Sweet Pickles

4 medium cucumbers cut into
   fourths lengthwise
2 green peppers, seeded
2 red peppers, seeded
2 cups (500 ml) cauliflower
1 pound (453 ml) fresh green
   beans
12 small white onions, peeled

¾ cup (188 ml) salt
2 cups (500 ml) water
1 quart (1 liter) vinegar
Sweetener to equal ¾ cup (188
   ml) sugar
2 tablespoons (31 ml) pickling
   spice

Cut vegetables into 1-inch pieces. Cover with salt and water in
refrigerator overnight. Drain and rinse. Make a syrup with the
vinegar, sweetener and spices. Add vegetables and simmer until
just barely tender (about 10-15 minutes). Pack in sterile jars and seal.
Process in boiling water bath at 212°F (100°C) for 10 minutes.

Dill Pickles

12 heads of fresh dill
6 pinches (.6 ml) of alum
1 bulb garlic (about 6 cloves)
6 teaspoons (30 ml) pickling
  spices

12 medium scrubbed
  cucumbers
9 cups (2 l+250 ml) water
3 cups (750 ml) vinegar
¾ cup (188 ml) coarse salt

In each of 6 clean sterile jars place 2 heads of dill, a pinch of alum, 1 clove of garlic and 1 teaspoon (5 ml) pickling spice. Fill with whole or quartered cucumbers. Boil a brine of water, vinegar and salt. Pour over each jar and seal. Allow 3 to 4 weeks for the pickles to "ripen." The pickles are an Unrestricted "Vegie," except for your discretion with salt.

Bread and Butter Pickles

1 peck of young cucumbers
  (about 20)
8 medium onions, peeled and
  thinly sliced
4 green peppers, seeded and
  thinly sliced
½ cup (250 ml) coarse salt
1 quart (1 liter) cider vinegar
Sweetener to equal 4 cups (1
  liter) brown sugar*

1 teaspoon (5 ml) allspice
2 tablespoons (31 ml) mustard
  seed
2 teaspoons (10 ml) celery seed
½ teaspoon (2.5 ml) ground
  cloves
½ teaspoon (2.5 ml) cinnamon

Scrub cucumbers. Cover with water in a large pan and bring to a boil. Blanch for 2 minutes in cold water. Thinly slice the cucumbers; combine with the onions and peppers. Add ½ cup (125 ml) coarse salt, cover and refrigerate overnight. Rinse and drain in a colander while you boil a syrup with the remaining ingredients. Scald the vegetables gently in this syrup. Pack in 10 hot sterile pint (500 ml) jars and seal. Process in boiling water bath at 212°F (100°C) for 15 minutes.

*Brown Sugar Twin

Mustard Pickles

¾ cup (188 ml) vinegar
¼ cup (62 ml) prepared
   mustard
⅛ teaspoon (.6 ml) turmeric
⅛ teaspoon (.6 ml) celery salt
⅛ teaspoon (.6 ml) garlic salt
Sweetener to equal ½ cup
   (125 ml) sugar

2 cups (500 ml) cauliflower
   pieces, briefly cooked
2 cups (500 ml) fresh cut green
   beans, briefly cooked
1 cup (250 ml) cooked celery
   cut in pickle-size pieces
2 roasted peppers, chopped

Combine vinegar, mustard, spices and sweetener and bring to a boil. Add first 3 vegetables and simmer for 4-5 minutes. Add the peppers last since they are fragile. Chill and serve with ham.

Pickle Relish

12 green tomatoes
4 green peppers
4 red peppers
10-12 cucumbers
4 onions
6 tablespoons (93 ml) salt
1 teaspoon (5 ml) pickling
   spices

Sweetener to equal 1½ cups
   (375 ml) sugar
2½ cups (625 ml) vinegar
1 cup (250 ml) water
1 tablespoon (16 ml) mustard
   seed
2 tablespoons (31 ml) celery
   seed

Grind the vegetables and add salt to stand overnight. Drain the brine in a colander. Combine the vegetables and the other ingredients in a large pan. Simmer for half an hour. Pack in sterilized jars and seal. Process at 212°F (100°C) in boiling water bath for 5 minutes. Unrestricted "Vegie"!

Pickled Beets

1 can sliced beets with liquid
¼ cup (62 ml) vinegar
Sweetener to equal 2 tablespoons sugar

1 teaspoon (5 ml) celery seed
Dash (.3 ml) of allspice
Dash (.3 ml) of dry mustard
2 medium onions, sliced

Drain beets. Combine vinegar, sweetener and spices. Pour over beets with onions. Serve hot or cold. A Restricted Starchy Vegetable.

Orange Cranberry Relish

2 cups (500 ml) cranberries
2 navel oranges
Sweetener to equal ½ cup (125 ml) sugar

3 ounces (85 g) frozen orange juice concentrate

Use as a relish, not a fruit. The recipe accounts for 6 Fruit Portions. Care and share.

Rainbow Relish

12 radishes, sliced
1 can carrots, drained
1 can yellow beans, drained (save ½ cup [125 ml] juice)
1 can green beans, drained
2 raw Bermuda onions, sliced
2 green peppers, sliced
1 teaspoon (5 ml) caraway seeds
1 teaspoon (5 ml) horseradish

6 whole cloves
Sweetener to equal 6 tablespoons (93 ml) sugar
½ cup (125 ml) lemon juice
½ cup (125 ml) white vinegar
½ cup (125 ml) yellow bean juice
2 teaspoons (10 ml) parsley

Combine last 8 ingredients in which to marinate the first 6 in refrigerator. Serve as a Restricted Starchy Vegetable, ½ cup (125 ml) per serving.

Red Cabbage Relish

4 cups (1 liter) finely chopped red cabbage
½ cup (125 ml) green pepper
½ cup (125 ml) chopped onion
¾ cup (188 ml) wine vinegar
Sweetener to equal 3 tablespoons (48 ml) sugar

1 teaspoon (5 ml) salt
⅛ teaspoon (.6 ml) pepper
1 teaspoon (5 ml) dill weed
1 teaspoon (5 ml) celery seed

Cabbage can be chopped quickly in the blender by using water, although some vitamins are lost in draining. Sprinkle the salt on the chopped cabbage. After ½ hour, squeeze out the brine, using a colander. Add the other ingredients and serve in a 1-quart (1 liter) vegetable dish. Unrestricted "Vegie"!

Sauerkraut Relish

2 cups (500 ml) sauerkraut, drained and rinsed to reduce salt, then coarsely chopped

¾ cup (188 ml) celery, finely chopped

½ cup (125 ml) onion, finely chopped

4 ounces (125 ml) raw carrot, grated

1/3 cup wine vinegar, blended with:

2 tablespoons (31 ml) water, ½ clove garlic, and Sweetener to equal ¼ cup (62 ml) sugar

Prepare the vegetables. Marinate with the dressing made from the last 3 ingredients. Discard garlic clove before serving. The recipe is practically of Unrestricted "Vegies," the small amount of carrot being the only Restricted Starchy Vegetable.

Mincemeat for Maintainers

3 pounds (1.5 kg) green tomatoes (about 10) ground in blender with water and drained

3 pounds (1.5 kg) hard apples, cored, peeled, and finely chopped

6 ounces (188 ml) raisins

1 cup (250 ml) vinegar

Sweetener to equal 1½ cups (375 ml) brown sugar*

2 tablespoons (31 ml) salt

2 tablespoons (31 ml) cloves

3 tablespoons (48 ml) cinnamon

1 tablespoon (16 ml) allspice

1 tablespoon (16 ml) nutmeg

½ lemon, seeded and ground

Combine ingredients and simmer 1½ hours in a large kettle until thoroughly cooked and blended in flavor. Instead of using mince for pie, try ½ cup (125 ml) on cottage cheese or Banana Ice Cream as a fruit dessert. Or spread toast with cottage cheese and mince for breakfast.

*Brown Sugar Twin

Summer Relish Mold

1 envelope plain gelatine
¼ cup (62 ml) cold water
½ cup (125 ml) boiling water
1 large can crushed pineapple, in its own juice
Sweetener to equal 2 table-spoons (31 ml) sugar
¼ teaspoon (1.2 ml) salt
2 tablespoons (31 ml) vinegar

2 tablespoons (31 ml) lemon juice
½ cup (125 ml) chopped celery
¼ cup (62 ml) chopped green pepper
1 diced pimento
Garnish: endive, lettuce, or cherry tomatoes

Sprinkle gelatine on cold water. Add boiling water and stir until dissolved. Add the juice from the pineapple, sweetener, salt, vinegar and lemon juice. Cool until syrupy. Add pineapple and vegetables. Pour into mold sprayed with Pam. Chill until firm. Unmold on salad greens. Garnish with cherry tomatoes. Four Fruit Portions.

Aspic Variation (instead of pineapple and juice)
1 onion, chopped
1 cucumber with skin, diced

12 radishes, thinly sliced
1 cup tomato juice

Sprinkle gelatine on cold water. Add boiling water and stir until dissolved. Add the tomato juice, sweetener, salt, vinegar, and lemon juice. Cool until syrupy. Add onion, cucumber, radishes and vegetables. Pour into mold sprayed with Pam. Chill until firm. Unmold on salad greens. Garnish with cherry tomatoes. Four Fruit Portions.

27
PIES AND PUDDINGS

Apple Cheese Pie

2 apples, pared, cored, and cut
  into pieces
1 tablespoon (16 ml) cinnamon
1 teaspoon (5 ml) nutmeg
Sweetener to equal 1/3 cup
  (83 ml) brown sugar*
1 cup (250 ml) applesauce,
artificially sweetened

1 cup (250 ml) pineapple juice,
  unsweetened
2 ounces (57 g) cheddar cheese,
  grated
6 thin slices of bread, cut in
  half diagonally

Arrange apples in a pie pan sprayed with Pam. Add spices and
sweetener to the applesauce and spoon over the apples. Blend pineapple juice and cheese. Soak bread slices in this mixture briefly and
lift them carefully as you arrange them in a pinwheel shape on top of
the pie to form a cheesy crust! Bake at 350°F (176°C) for 20 minutes.
One-sixth of the pie is one Fruit Portion (with cheese protein negligible) plus one ounce of bread.

*Brown Sugar Twin

Pineapple Cheese Pie

1 cup (250 ml) crushed pineapple in its own juice
1 envelope diet lemon gelatine
16 ounces (453 g or 500 ml)
  low-fat cottage cheese
1 egg

Sweetener to equal 3 tablespoons (48 ml) sugar
1 teaspoon (5 ml) vanilla
  extract
1 teaspoon (5 ml) lemon juice
Dash (.3 ml) of almond extract

Heat the pineapple; add gelatine and stir until dissolved. Combine
with the rest of the ingredients in the blender and blend smooth.
Prepare a 9-inch pie pan with *Pam*. Pour the mixture into the pan.
Sprinkle with freshly ground nutmeg. Bake at 350°F (176°C) for 20
minutes. If you're in a hurry, this pie will set firm in the refrigerator
without baking. Garnish with a sprig of fresh orange mint. Five
people may share the 10 ounces of protein and 2 Fruit Portions.

Pineapple "Whipped Cream" Pie

1 20-ounce (625 ml) can
  crushed pineapple, in its
  juice
2 envelopes diet lemon gelatine
Sweetener to equal ½ cup (125
  ml) sugar
1 can evaporated skim milk,
  chilled

1 tablespoon (16 ml) lemon
  juice
1 teaspoon (5 ml) orange rind,
  grated
Dash (.3 ml) of nutmeg, freshly
  ground

Heat the pineapple in a saucepan. Add the gelatine and sweetener.
Refrigerate until thickened. Beat together the evaporated skim milk
and lemon juice until stiff peaks form. Fold gelatine mixture and
the "whipped cream" together and spoon into a pie dish sprayed
with *Pam*. Garnish with orange rind and nutmeg. Refrigerate for
several hours before serving. The recipe contains 5 Fruit Portions
and 3 milk allowances. One-fifth is a large serving!

Blender Pumpkin Pie

1 envelope plain gelatine
½ cup (125 ml) cold water
½ cup (125 ml) boiling water
Sweetener to equal ½ cup (125 ml) brown sugar*
1 cup (227 g or 250 ml) low-fat cottage cheese
1 teaspoon (5 ml) cinnamon
⅛ teaspoon (.6 ml) salt
¾ teaspoon (3.6 ml) nutmeg
¼ teaspoon (1.2 ml) ginger
2 cups (250 ml) pumpkin
1 cup (250 ml) evaporated skim milk
1 egg

In the blender, sprinkle gelatine over cold water. Add boiling water and blend until gelatine dissolves. Then blend in other ingredients. Pour into pie plate sprayed with Pam and chill until firmly set. Plan your portion from the entire recipe which includes 2 milks, 4 limited vegetables, and 10 ounces of protein. One-sixth of the pie is appropriate for dinner dessert if you deduct 2 ounces of protein from your main course.

*Brown Sugar Twin

Pie Crust

3 drops butter flavoring
1 cup (250 ml) skim milk
Sweetener to equal 1 table-spoon (16 ml) sugar
½ teaspoon (2.5 ml) salt
6 thin slices white bread, cut diagonally

Combine the butter flavoring, milk, sweetener and salt in a shallow dish. Prepare the pie pan with Pam. Roll the thin bread with a rolling pin to make it formable. Dip each piece into the milk mixture briefly. Arrange pieces in the pie pan with corners extending up the sides for fluting. Bake at 350°F (176°C) for 15 minutes. Cool. If this seems fussy, remember, it's not as messy as pie crust made with shortening, and it uses only 3 bread allowances. If you must have a crust, it's more acceptable than a meringue or cereal crust.

Lemon Pie

1 cup (250 ml) boiling water
2 envelopes diet lemon gelatine
3 cups (750 ml) yogurt
Sweetener to equal ½ cup (125 ml) sugar

1 drop yellow food color (too much looks artificial)
1 egg

Add boiling water to gelatine. Cool until syrupy and stir into the yogurt with sweetener and food color. Lastly beat in raw egg. Pour into a pie pan sprayed with *Pam*. When it sets solid you can lift it with a spatula onto a diet style pie crust. Or use a sprayed Tupperware mold for easy showmanship, without a crust. Decorate the pie with "meringue." (Recipe below)

"Meringue"

¾ cup (170 g or 188 ml) low-fat cottage cheese
Sweetener to equal 2 tablespoons (31 ml) sugar

1 teaspoon (5 ml) vanilla
¼ teaspoon (1.2 ml) grated lemon rind

Blend and spread on the firm pie. Count 3 milk allowances, 1 egg and 6 ounces (170 g or 188 ml) cottage cheese (without using crust).

Banana Pudding

1 envelope plain unflavored gelatine
½ cup (125 ml) cold water
½ cup (125 ml) boiling water
8 ice cubes
2 envelopes Alba 77 Fit 'n Frosty (Chocolate or Vanilla)

1 teaspoon (5 ml) vanilla extract
1 raw egg
Dash (.3 ml) of nutmeg for garnish
2 small bananas, sliced

Soften gelatine in cold water. Dissolve in boiling water. Cool, stirring in ice cubes to hasten thickening. Blend with Alba 77, vanilla and egg. Pour over sliced bananas in 6 dessert glasses. Garnish with freshly ground nutmeg. Enjoy up to 3 servings a day of this low calorie (kilojoule) pudding. The entire recipe uses 2 milk allowances and 2 Fruit Portions.

28
POULTRY

Breaded Buttermilk Chicken

4 chicken breasts boned and
   skinned
1 cup (250 ml) buttermilk
1 teaspoon (5 ml) paprika
Dash (.3 ml) of pepper

Dash (.3 ml) of garlic salt
2 teaspoons (10 ml) onion
   flakes
4 thin slices white bread,
   crumbed in blender

Prepare a casserole dish with *Pam*. Arrange the chicken in the bottom. Mix buttermilk with the spices and onion flakes. Pour over the chicken. Top with bread crumbs. Bake covered at 325°F (162°C) for 30 minutes covered; 15 minutes uncovered. This serves 4 for lunch with a salad and tomato juice plus 4 toast "crackers" per serving (1 thin slice of bread cut diagonally both ways and toasted). For dinner the recipe serves two with a salad and a Restricted Starchy Vegetable.

Chicken Cacciatori

4 chicken breasts, boned and
skinned
Dash (.3 ml) of garlic salt
Dash (.3 ml) of butter salt
2 green peppers, chopped
1 medium onion, chopped
12 ounces (375 ml) tomato juice

2 tablespoons (31 ml) parsley
flakes
1 teaspoon (5 ml) oregano
2 teaspoons (10 ml) fresh basil,
chopped
1 bay leaf
½ teaspoon (2.5 ml) cinnamon

Simmer all the ingredients for 1 hour. You'll love the fragrance all
through the house! Serve 4 for lunch or 2 for dinner. Choose raw
Unrestricted "Vegies" such as celery sticks and cucumber slices to
contrast with the tomato flavor, and add a Restricted Starchy Vegetable to complete the menu. How many limited vegetables can you
choose from for dinner? Two ounces of tomato sauce could be one
choice.

Chicken Cheese Loaf

1 envelope unflavored gelatine
1 cup (250 ml) cold chicken
broth
½ cup (125 ml) buttermilk
3 teaspoons (16 ml) lemon juice
3 ounces (85 g or 94 ml)
low-fat cottage cheese
½ teaspoon (2.5 ml) grated
lemon rind

½ teaspoon (2.5 ml) salt
6 ounces (170 g) diced chicken
½ cup (125 ml) chopped celery
1 tablespoon (16 ml) chopped
parsley
½ teaspoon (2.5 ml) dill weed
Lettuce or curly endive

Soften the gelatine with the cold chicken broth. Heat to dissolve.
Cool and add buttermilk, lemon juice, cottage cheese, rind and salt.
Blend. Chill until syrupy. Add chicken, celery, parsley and dill
weed. Pour into loaf pan or mold sprayed with Pam. Serve on lettuce
or curly endive. Serves 3 for lunch or 3 supplemental portions to go
with Occasional Protein Portions for dinner.

Chicken Mushroom Bake

1 pound (453 g) fresh
   mushrooms
¼ cup (62 ml) chopped parsley
2 tablespoons (31 ml) chopped
   chives
4 chicken breasts, skinned and
   boned

½ cup (125 ml) lemon juice
1 teaspoon (5 ml) onion salt
1 teaspoon (5 ml) paprika
½ teaspoon (2.5 ml) poultry
   seasoning

Prepare a low casserole dish with *Pam*. Arrange mushrooms, parsley and chives in the bottom, with the chicken on top. Pour lemon juice over the chicken, and sprinkle with seasonings. Bake at 325°F (162°C) for 35-45 minutes. With this main dish, you and your dinner partner may enjoy a tomato aspic and peas plus fresh fruit in season.

Chicken Teriyaki

4 chicken breasts, boned and
   skinned
¼ cup (62 ml) soy sauce
¼ cup (62 ml) white wine
1 clove garlic

Sweetener to equal 3 tablespoons (48 ml) sugar
½ tablespoon (7.5 ml) ginger
1 cup (250 ml) crushed pineapple in its own juice

Marinate the chicken in the other ingredients for several hours. Bake at 325° for 45 minutes. Baste with marinade while cooking. Discard garlic clove. Serve 4 for lunch or 2 for dinner. How about a green bean salad and beets?

Cheese Dressing

1 pound (453 g or 250 ml)
   low-fat cottage cheese
½ cup (125 ml) lemon juice
½ teaspoon (2.5 ml) garlic salt
Sweetener to equal 2 teaspoons
   (10 ml) sugar

1 teaspoon (5 ml) Frito green
   onion dip in packet
⅛ teaspoon (.6 ml) pepper,
   freshly ground

Combine until smooth in blender. Store in pint (500 ml) jar.

Creamy Chicken Salad

6 ounces (170 g) diced cooked chicken breast

¼ cup (62 ml) diced Spanish onion

1 green pepper, chopped

1 cup (250 ml) celery, diced

1 cucumber, unpeeled, diced

1 pint (500 ml) cheese dressing (below)

3 radishes

1 teaspoon (5 ml) dill weed

3 hard boiled eggs

½ teaspoon (2.5 ml) paprika

Toss first 5 ingredients. Mix in cheese dressing and garnish with last four ingredients. Serve two for dinner with carrot strips, or four for lunch with toast "crackers."

Cutting and Boning Chicken

The ultimate in boning chicken is the "galantine" for experts only. It is a boned chicken with stuffing, sewn together. Just appreciate it if you see one at a party. Start by learning to cut up a whole chicken. Save yourself at least 5¢ a pound (kilogram)! Choose broiler/fryers (3-3½ pounds or 1.36-1.59 kg) for more meat and less bone. Roasters are too fat for us. With a sharp narrow boning knife sever the legs and wings at the joints. Find this spot by extending and working the joints. Remove the skin and the "Pope's nose" (the tail). Break the back by bending it backward and freeing it with the knife. Spread the breast, bone side down. Split it with a strong butcher knife, for barbecuing or boning.

Boning is no magic trick. The chicken flesh is so fragile you can do it with your fingers, or use a boning knife. You won't be an expert the first time, but the bones won't be wasted if you don't get all the meat off. You will be stewing the gizzard, heart, and liver with the neck and back bones. Just toss your mistakes in the pot. Practice makes perfect. Boning chicken has several advantages. The weight of portions is more accurately determined. (Allow one ounce [28 g] of shrinkage for four ounces of the chicken breast, usually one side.) The meat is more versatile boned. You can slice, dice, or make salad strips. Without the skin, a dieter is much safer, not having to pass up that temptation if it is cooked. Boned chicken is better able to absorb the sauces and flavors, it cooks faster, and is easier to serve and eat. It's not too expensive if you learn to bone and skin it yourself. At least bone the breasts for diet fare. It's your best protein buy.

Hurry Curried Chicken

½ cup (125 ml) lemon juice
2 tablespoons (31 ml) vinegar
¼ cup (62 ml) water
¼ cup (62 ml) soy sauce
Sweetener to equal ¼ cup (62 ml) sugar

1 teaspoon (5 ml) ginger
1 teaspoon (5 ml) onion flakes
2 teaspoons (10 ml) curry powder
4 chicken breasts, boned and skinned

Combine the marinade ingredients and pour over the chicken for a day in the refrigerator, turning once. For a hurried supper, broil the chicken 7 minutes on each side while you toss your salad and open a can of carrots. If your dinner partner doesn't show up, you'll have two tasty lunches of chicken to eat with pineapple and whole wheat bread tomorrow. Leftover chicken breast can be sliced, diced, and tossed in a julienne salad.

Turkey Stroganoff

1 cup (250 ml) fresh mushrooms, sliced
1 teaspoon (5 ml) celery salt
1/3 cup (76 g or 83 ml) low-fat cottage cheese
2 teaspoons (10 ml) onion flakes

1 teaspoon (5 ml) lemon juice
2 ounces (57 g) cooked turkey breast, diced
½ teaspoon (2.5 ml) sherry flavoring

Arrange the mushrooms in a baking dish sprayed with *Pam*. Sprinkle with celery salt. Combine the cheese, onion flakes, lemon juice, turkey, and sherry flavoring. Spoon over mushrooms. Bake at 325°F (162°C) for 20 minutes. Love yourself a little with this special Alternate Protein. Toast "crackers" furnish the crunch and the bread allowance. Topped off with a Fruit Portion, the menu should serve your body, mind and spirit.

Turkey Stuffing

1 onion, diced
1 apple, cored and diced
½ cup (125 ml) celery, finely
  chopped
½ cup (125 ml) fresh parsley or
  3 tablespoons (48 ml) dried
  parsley
4 ounces (125 ml) mushrooms
  with juice
8 ounces (227 g) bread crumbs
  (or 8 thick slices)

½ teaspoon (2.5 ml) thyme,
  dried, or 1½ teaspoons (7.5
  ml) fresh
2 tablespoons (31 ml) lemon
  juice
1 cup (250 ml) vegetable
  bouillon
1 cup (250 ml) diet apricots,
  drained and chopped

Mix and toss all ingredients together. Heat in a baking dish sprayed with *Pam* the last few minutes before serving. The turkey cooks more quickly and there is less chance of salmonella poisoning with the stuffing cooked separately. Also you skip the fat drippings. Your family will like your diet stuffing. Use it discreetly; ⅛ of the recipe is a bread allowance.

29
SALADS

Tomato Tarragon Marinade

3 tomatoes, sliced

1 cucumber scored lengthwise with a fork, and thinly sliced, skin on

1 green pepper, seeded and sliced

½ cup (125 ml) onion, finely chopped

½ cup (125 ml) tarragon vinegar

¼ cup (62 ml) lemon juice

¼ cup (62 ml) water

Dash (.3 ml) of celery salt

Dash (.3 ml) of garlic salt

Sweetener to equal ¼ cup (62 ml) sugar

Dash (.3 ml) of pepper, freshly ground

1 tablespoon (16 ml) fresh Italian parsley, finely chopped, or 1 teaspoon (5 ml) dried parsley

Combine ingredients and marinate for at least an hour. Drain before serving. Since a tomato can be a Restricted Starchy Vegetable or a fruit, the recipe allows you all you wish up to a third of the marinade. At noon count it as a Fruit Portion, at night a vegetable.

Easy Aspic

1 envelope diet lemon gelatine
1 cup (250 ml) boiling water
1 cup (250 ml) tomato sauce
2 tablespoons (31 ml) wine
vinegar
½ teaspoon (2.5 ml) seasoned
salt

¾ cup (188 ml) celery, finely
chopped
¼ cup (62 ml) green pepper,
finely chopped
¼ cup (62 ml) sweet onion,
finely chopped
1 teaspoon (5 ml) horseradish

Combine the gelatine and boiling water, stirring until the gelatine dissolves. Add tomato sauce, vinegar, seasoned salt, and horseradish. When partially set, add the finely chopped vegetables. Use a mold or cake pan sprayed with *Pam.* The aspic is of Unrestricted "Vegies," but omit tomato juice from your menu for the day, and count it as your Restricted Starchy Vegetable for dinner.

Pickled Tomato Aspic

16 ounces (500 ml) tomato
juice
1 envelope unflavored gelatine
1 tablespoon (16 ml) mixed
pickling spices
1 tablespoon (16 ml) dill pickle
juice

Dash (.3 ml) of pepper
½ cup (125 ml) dill pickles,
chopped
½ cup (125 ml) sweet onion,
chopped

Soften the gelatine in the tomato juice. Stir in the pickling spices, dill juice and pepper. Simmer briefly to blend flavors; then strain out the spices. Refrigerate to cool quickly. When syrupy, add pickles and onion. Pour into a mold sprayed with *Pam.* This clever use of free tomato juice goes well with low-fat cottage cheese, hard boiled eggs, fish or chicken. You may use up to ¾ of the aspic in one day.

Herbal Aspic

2 envelopes plain gelatine
½ cup (125 ml) cold water
1 bay leaf, broken
½ tablespoon (7.5 ml) parsley, dried
½ teaspoon (2.5 ml) dill weed, dried
⅛ teaspoon (.6 ml) sweet basil, dried
⅛ teaspoon (.6 ml) ground allspice
⅛ teaspoon (.6 ml) ground cloves
⅛ teaspoon (.6 ml) oregano, dried
⅛ teaspoon (.6 ml) rosemary, dried
⅛ teaspoon (.6 ml) thyme, dried
⅛ teaspoon (.6 ml) tarragon, dried
1 cup (250 ml) hot tomato juice
1½ cups (375 ml) cold tomato juice
1 teaspoon (5 ml) vinegar
2 teaspoons (10 ml) lemon juice
Sweetener to equal 1 tablespoon (16 ml) sugar
Lettuce

Soften the gelatine in the cold water. Add the herbs and spices to the hot tomato juice and simmer for 10 minutes. Remove the bay leaf. Dissolve the gelatine with the hot tomato juice. Add cold tomato juice, vinegar, lemon juice and sweetener. Pour into a small mold or cake pan sprayed with Pam. Serve on lettuce when firm. If you have an herb garden, use your fresh herbs three times as heavily as the dried. Tomato aspic is a natural showcase for herbs. It's a tantalizing, colorful contrast on your plate, a creative way to use your tomato juice.

Limed Cucumber Ring Mold

1 package diet lime gelatine
1 cup (250 ml) boiling water
1 tablespoon (16 ml) vinegar
1 teaspoon (5 ml) onion juice
6 ounces (188 ml) yogurt
1 large cucumber, diced
Lettuce

Dissolve gelatine in boiling water. Add vinegar and onion juice. Chill until syrupy. Mix in the yogurt and cucumber. Pour into 4-cup (1 liter) ring mold sprayed with Pam. Unmold on lettuce when set. A safe, attractive salad of Unrestricted "Vegies"!

Green Garden Salad

2 envelopes diet lime gelatine
2 cups (500 ml) boiling water
14 ice cubes
3 tablespoons (48 ml) vinegar
1 teaspoon (5 ml) horseradish
Sweetener to equal 3 tablespoons (48 ml) sugar

2 cups (500 ml) cabbage, finely
   chopped
½ raw onion, finely chopped
½ cup (125 ml) raw carrot,
   finely shredded

Dissolve the gelatine with boiling water. Cool quickly by adding ice cubes and stirring. Add vinegar and horseradish with sweetener. When almost set, add the vegetables. Pour into a 4-cup (1 liter) mold which has been prepared with Pam. The salad is practically un-limited, with the small amount of carrot being the only Restricted Starchy Vegetable. It's a tangy, refreshing salad for a hot day.

Tangy Beet Mold

2 envelopes unflavored
gelatine
1 cup (250 ml) cold water
1 cup (250 ml) boiling water
12 ice cubes
Sweetener to equal 2 tbsp. sugar
¼ teaspoon (1 ml) salt
¼ cup (62 ml) vinegar
1 can shoestring or diced beets
   with juice

2 teaspoons (10 ml) horseradish
¼ cup (62 ml) green pepper,
   diced
¼ cup (62 ml) onion, diced
½ cup (125 ml) cabbage, finely
   chopped

Moisten gelatine with cold water. Dissolve with boiling water and cool with ice cubes, stirring until syrupy. Add sweetener, salt, vinegar, beet juice and horseradish. When partly set, add the vege-tables. Fill a 6-cup (1.5 liter) mold which has been prepared with Pam. The colorful mold includes 4 Restricted Starchy Vegetables. One-eighth of it saves room for peas, or enjoy a fourth of it for dinner.

Cold Creamed Beets

¾ cup (188 ml) yogurt
1 tablespoon (16 ml) wine
   vinegar
1 teaspoon (5 ml) horseradish

Sweetener to equal 1 tablespoon (16 ml) sugar
2 cups (500 ml) sliced, diced,
   or julienne beets, drained

Mix first four ingredients and toss with beets. One-fourth of the recipe fulfills your Restricted Starchy Vegetable for dinner. Eat it slowly; savor the old world flavor!

Cabbage Carrot Slaw

½ head of cabbage
4 carrots
½ lemon with rind, seeds
   removed

1 cup (250 ml) crushed pineapple in its own juice
Sweetener to equal 3 tablespoons (48 ml) sugar

Chop the cabbage, carrots and lemon in the blender with water. Drain. Add crushed pineapple and sweetener. A fast and easy salad to go with dinner. Count 4 servings of Restricted Starchy Vegetables, 2 Fruit Portions. Your share is one-fourth.

Bean Salad

1 can French green beans
1 can French yellow beans
4 ounces (125 ml) canned
   mushrooms
½ cup (125 ml) onion, chopped
¼ cup (62 ml) water
¼ cup (62 ml) wine vinegar
¼ cup (62 ml) lemon or lime
   juice

Sweetener to equal ¼ cup
   (62 ml) sugar
⅛ teaspoon (.6 ml) garlic salt
1 green pepper, chopped
1-2 pimentos, chopped
1 tablespoon (16 ml) dried
   parsley flakes

Drain the vegetables. Prepare the dressing. Toss and marinate. This is an unlimited salad to make meals filling, or to have ready for safe snacks. It's tireless.

"Potato" Salad

1 large head of cauliflower, or 2 10-ounce (283 g) packages frozen cauliflower, cooked and drained
½ teaspoon (2.5 ml) salt
2 teaspoons (10 ml) lemon juice
1 green pepper, chopped
6-8 radishes, sliced
½ cup (125 ml) celery, chopped
½ cup (125 ml) onion, chopped

1 cup (250 ml) Cinchy Mayonnaise (See Dips and Dressings)
3 hard boiled eggs, chopped
3 teaspoons (15 ml) fresh parsley, chopped, or 1 teaspoon (5 ml) dried parsley
½ teaspoon (2.5 ml) paprika for garnish

Reduce the cooked cauliflower to small pieces with a spoon or knife. Add salt and lemon juice while hot. Cool before adding the other ingredients. Reserve some egg and parsley for garnish with the paprika. To figure protein, count 4 ounces (113 g) in the Cinchy Mayonnaise and 6 ounces (170 g) for the hard boiled eggs, totalling 10 ounces (283 g). One whole cupful of "Potato" Salad costs you 2½ ounces of protein. The salad makes 4 cups.

Cucumbers and "Sour Cream"

2 medium cucumbers, thinly sliced
3 ounces (85 g or 94 ml) low-fat cottage cheese
1 tablespoon (16 ml) prepared diet Italian salad dressing
Sweetener to equal 1 tablespoon (16 ml) sugar

1 teaspoon (5 ml) celery seed
Dash (.3 ml) of pepper
2 tablespoons (31 ml) wine vinegar
2 tablespoons (31 ml) lemon juice
1 teaspoon (5 ml) parsley for garnish

The "sour cream" is made by blending the cottage cheese with the succeeding ingredients, saving the parsley for garnish. Celery seed adds a contrasting texture and flavor. The entire recipe uses half your lunch protein. One-fourth of it will please you and leave you free to enjoy poultry, cheese, ham, or beef, according to plan.

Raw Spinach Salad

1 bag fresh spinach, torn in
large pieces
¾ cup (188 ml) Bermuda onion
sliced and separated

1 cup (250 ml) Mandarin
oranges, drained
¾ cup (188 ml) prepared diet
Italian dressing

Toss ingredients together. Count two fruits for the whole salad.

Marinated Mushrooms

2 8-ounce (250 ml) cans mushrooms, stems and pieces,
drained

1 teaspoon (5 ml) fresh basil
½ cup (125 ml) diet Italian
dressing

Mix and chill the recipe. It's an Unrestricted "Vegie", except for the
dressing. Just don't lick the dish.

Creamy Tuna Salad Mold

2 envelopes unflavored
gelatine
1 cup (250 ml) cold water
1 cup (250 ml) boiling water
8 ice cubes
1½ cups (375 ml) Cinchy
Mayonnaise (See Dips and
Dressings)
2 tablespoons (31 ml) lemon
juice
1 teaspoon (5 ml) prepared
mustard

1 teaspoon (5 ml) horseradish
⅛ teaspoon (.6 ml) salt
6 ounces (170 g) water pack
tuna, drained and flaked
1 cup (250 ml) celery, finely
chopped
¼ cup (62 ml) green onion,
thinly sliced
2 pimentos, chopped
¼ cup (62 ml) green pepper,
finely chopped
Curly endive

Soften the gelatine in cold water, then add boiling water to dissolve.
Cool with ice cubes by stirring until syrupy. Blend in mayonnaise,
lemon juice, mustard, horseradish and salt. Add the remaining
ingredients except for endive. Pour into a 6-cup salad mold sprayed
with Pam. When firmly set, unmold on curly endive. The recipe
serves 4 or 6 people for lunch and you could have with it a toasted
cheese sandwich and/or a deviled egg, or cold turkey or ham. How
easy to achieve variety in color, texture and flavor!

Pink Crab Salad Mold

2 envelopes plain gelatine
½ cup (125 ml) cold water
1 bay leaf, broken
¼ teaspoon (1.2 ml) celery salt
½ cup (125 ml) hot water
1 cup (250 ml) tomato juice
1 cup (250 ml) yogurt
1 cup (250 ml) buttermilk

¾ cup (188 ml) celery, chopped
½ cup (125 ml) onion, chopped
¼ cup (62 ml) parsley, chopped
6 ounces (170 g) crabmeat,
    drained, and freshened with
    3 tablespoons (48 ml) lemon
    juice

Soften the gelatine with cold water. Simmer the bay leaf and celery salt with the hot water. Remove the bay leaf, and dissolve the gelatine with the hot water. Cool. Add tomato juice, yogurt and buttermilk, mixing thoroughly. When partially set add the chopped vegetables and crabmeat and pour into a 6-cup mold (1.5 liter) sprayed with *Pam*. Fish is beautiful. The recipe uses 2 milk allowances and 2 lunch proteins, or 1 dinner protein. However, a 6-cup (1.5 liter) mold serves 6-8 people. These normal servings allow you variety in other foods, or in this case, a second helping.

Hawaiian Clam Salad

½ cup (125 ml) crushed pine-
    apple in its own juice
3 ounces (85 g or 94 ml)
    low-fat cottage cheese
1 green pepper, diced

3 ounces (85 g) chopped clams,
    drained
Lettuce
1 small slice pimento for
    garnish

Combine first 4 ingredients. Serve on lettuce with pimento on top. The contrasting textures and flavors of this salad make one very satisfying lunch, combined with toast "crackers." One and a half ounces (42 g) of clams would be the correct protein with 3 ounces (85 g) cottage cheese, but clams are only 90 calories (377 kJ) for 6 ounces (170 g), so if you enjoy clams, live it up safely with the 3 ounces (85 g). Anything canned is slightly salty, so the texture and flavor are almost nutty.

"Little Shrimp" Molds

1 envelope unflavored gelatine
½ cup (125 ml) cold pineapple juice (drained from large can)
½ cup (125 ml) pineapple juice heated to boiling
6 ounces (170 g or 188 ml) low-fat cottage cheese
Sweetener to equal 1 tablespoon (16 ml) sugar
3 ounces (85 g) canned shrimp, rinsed, and freshened with 2 tablespoons (31 ml) lemon juice

1 cup (250 ml) crushed pineapple, in its own juice, drained
½ cup (125 ml) celery, finely chopped
Lettuce

Soften gelatine with cold pineapple juice. Dissolve with hot pineapple juice. Combine gelatine mixture in the blender with cottage cheese and sweetener. Stir in, without blending, the shrimp, lemon juice, crushed pineapple and celery, saving 4 shrimp for garnishes. Prepare 4 small molds with *Pam*. Divide the mixture evenly into the molds and set. Unmold on lettuce on individual salad plates. Garnish with shrimp. Each serving contains 1 Fruit Portion and ½ the lunch protein.

Oriental Turkey Salad

1 tablespoon (15 ml) soy sauce
½ cup (125 ml) crushed pineapple, in its own juice
1 small can Mandarin oranges, drained
6 ounces (170 g) cooked turkey, diced

1 can bean sprouts, drained and rinsed
½ cup (125 ml) carrot, grated
½ cup (125 ml) celery, chopped
½ cup (125 ml) onion, chopped
½ cup (125 ml) green pepper, chopped

Add the soy sauce to the pineapple. Combine with the rest of the ingredients. What a huge lunch for two, with toast "crackers!" Your own fresh bean sprouts taste much better than the canned. Obtain the mung beans at a health food store and do it yourself!

Waldorf Valentine

1 head cabbage, finely chopped
1 apple, cored and diced with
skin on
1 can Mandarin oranges,
drained
1 cup (250 ml) pineapple
chunks, packed in own juice

1 cup (227 g or 250 ml) low-fat
cottage cheese blended with:
1 tablespoon (16 ml) frozen
orange juice, 1 teaspoon (5
ml) fresh lemon juice, ½ teaspoon (2.5 ml) fresh lemon
rind

Slice one side of the apple off before coring and dicing. Carve a heart with the red skin showing. Mix the ingredients, saving 3 table-spoons (48 ml) of the blended cheese for a center top setting for the apple heart garnish. Love is your Internal Instructor, and you are the apple of His eye. He's watching, so count 1/6 of the recipe your fruit portion. The cheese is negligible.

Honey, Dew-Right Ring Mold

1 envelope lime diet gelatine
1 cup (250 ml) boiling water
½ cup (125 ml) lime juice
½ cup (125 ml) yogurt
Sweetener to equal 1/3 cup (83
ml) sugar

⅛ teaspoon (.6 ml) salt
2 cups (250 ml) honeydew,
diced
6 ounces (170 g or 188 ml)
low-fat cottage cheese
Lettuce

Dissolve the gelatine with the boiling water. Cool. Add lime juice, yogurt, sweetener and salt. When partly set, add melon. Fill a 4-cup (1 liter) ring mold which has been prepared with Pam. Unmold at meal time on lettuce. Fill the ring with cottage cheese. Green is beautiful. One-fourth of the recipe is 1 Fruit Portion. One-fourth of the cottage cheese allows you to enjoy a deviled egg and chicken or tuna sandwich.

Cranberry Gelatine Salad

2 envelopes diet strawberry
  gelatine
2 cups (500 ml) boiling water
1 can low calorie cranberry
  sauce (Ocean Spray makes it)
1½ cups (375 ml) cold water

¾ cup (188 ml) celery, finely
  chopped
1 cup (250 ml) crushed pineapple in its own juice
1 apple, diced
Lettuce

Dissolve the gelatine in the boiling water. Add cranberry sauce, stirring well. Add the cold water. When syrupy, add celery, pineapple and apple. Let the salad set in a 6-cup mold or glass cake pan that's been sprayed with *Pam*. Serve on lettuce. Count one-sixth as a Fruit Portion.

Amazing Grace's Pineapple Cheese Salad

1 envelope diet lemon gelatine
1 cup (250 ml) boiling water
16 ounces (500 ml) crushed
  pineapple in its own juice
2 tablespoons (31 ml) lemon
  juice

¾ cup (188 ml) carrots, finely
  grated
12 ounces (340 g or 375 ml)
  low-fat cottage cheese

Dissolve the gelatine with the boiling water. Add the other ingredients after it cools. Pour into a 4-cup (1 liter) ring mold which has been prepared with *Pam*. Grace and peace to you. One-fourth of the recipe equals 1 fruit allowance and half a lunch protein. The carrots, although restricted, are negligible in proportion. They're there to add color and texture and a vitamin A bonus.

Orange Cheese Mold

1 envelope diet orange gelatine
1 cup (250 ml) boiling water
8 ice cubes
1 cup (250 ml) Mandarin
   oranges, drained

1 teaspoon (5 ml) orange rind
6 ounces (170 g or 188 ml)
   low-fat cottage cheese
¾ cup (188 ml) celery, finely
   chopped

Dissolve the gelatine with the boiling water. Add ice cubes, stirring to thicken. When partly set, add remaining ingredients. Pour into a 4-cup (1 liter) mold prepared with *Pam*. One-fourth of the recipe borrows 1½ ounces (42 g) of protein from your lunch allowance, and accounts for ½ of one Fruit Portion. Use the mold as a salad or dessert.

30
SANDWICH SPREADS

Creamed Cheese Spread

3 ounces (85 g or 94 ml)
    low-fat cottage cheese
2 drops almond extract
Sweetener to equal 2 teaspoons
    (10 ml) sugar

2 teaspoons (10 ml) lemon juice
1 teaspoon (5 ml) lemon rind
1 teaspoon (5 ml) orange rind

Blend the ingredients, turning the blender on and off patiently until the mixture is thick and smooth. Spread on thin bread with crusts removed, cut into 4 diagonal hors d'oeuvre type sandwiches, open-faced. You may decorate them with colorful designs using pimento, green pepper slivers, Mandarin oranges, or crushed pineapple, drained. The spread also makes a good celery stuffing. This spread, if shared, need not be counted. If you use it all with crushed pineapple on whole wheat bread, count it as half your lunch protein.

Busy Day Egg Salad Spread (Fast Version)

1 hard boiled egg, mashed
  while hot
3 ounces (85 g or 94 ml)
  low-fat cottage cheese

1 teaspoon (5 ml) dried chives
  or 1 tablespoon (16 ml) fresh
  chives

Mix and be happy without mayonnaise. Spread two thin slices of bread. Arrange lettuce between and fold together for a tasty egg salad sandwich. The simple recipe provides one lunch. Succeed one day at a time!

Hot Seafood Spread

½ cup (250 ml) onion, finely
  chopped
¼ cup (125 ml) green pepper,
  finely chopped
3 tablespoons (48 ml) tomato
  juice

6 ounces (170 g) crabmeat or
  shrimp, frozen or canned and
  drained, and flaked
1 teaspoon (5 ml) soy sauce
2 ounces (57 g) mozzarella
  cheese, crumbled

Cook the onion and green pepper in the tomato juice, stirring constantly. Add the other ingredients and spread on toast. The spread will cover 6 pieces of thin toast, serving 3 persons. If you are alone, use only 1/3; save the rest for two other lunches.

Liver Pate

1 pound (453 g) chicken livers
1 cup (250 ml) chicken bouillon
1 small onion, finely chopped
¼ teaspoon (1.2 ml) ground
  pepper

Dash (.3 ml) of garlic salt
1 hard boiled egg, mashed
6 ounces (170 g or 188 ml)
  low-fat cottage cheese

Cook the chicken livers in the bouillon. Remove them and chop very finely. Combine onion, seasonings, egg and cottage cheese. The pate can be a sandwich spread, stuffing for celery, or topping for cucumber slices. The pate contains 16 ounces (453 g) of protein. Can you judge one ounce at the cocktail hour? Subtract it from your dinner menu. Three ounces (85 g) is a welcome change for lunch meat spread. You're on the "weigh" with liver pate.

Giblet Cocktail Spread

3 ounces (85 g) chicken or turkey gizzards

2 cups (500 ml) water

1 packet vegetable bouillon powder

1 tablespoon (16 ml) chives, freshly snipped (1 teaspoon [5 ml] dried)

1 tablespoon (16 ml) fresh parsley (1 teaspoon [5 ml] dried)

1 teaspoon (5 ml) Tabasco Sauce

1 dill pickle, finely chopped (½ cup [125 ml])

1 tablespoon (16 ml) minced onion flakes

3 ounces (85 g or 94 ml) low-fat cottage cheese

1 hard boiled egg, mashed

Cook the gizzards until tender (about 1½ hours) in the bouillon powder and water. Drain and chop finely. Add remaining ingredients. Spread on toast points. The spread serves 2 for lunch. Use it to stuff celery bites for a party—a safe hors d'oeuvre.

Tuna Salad Spread

6 ounces (170 g or 188 ml) cottage cheese

3 ounces (85 g) water pack tuna, drained and flaked (or try shrimp, salmon, mackerel, crab, even sardines)

1 teaspoon (5 ml) lemon juice

1 teaspoon (5 ml) horseradish

1 teaspoon (5 ml) Worcestershire sauce or soy sauce

2 ounces (57 g) bread (4 thin slices)

½ medium onion, thinly sliced

6 dill pickle slices

2-4 lettuce leaves

Mix cheese, fish, lemon juice, horseradish, and Worcestershire sauce. Spread on each slice of bread. Place onion, pickles, and lettuce on top, and fold over. The spread provides 2 protein servings for lunch. It's fun to be a brown bagger if you're thinking thin and succeeding. A little preparation makes a good first step, provides satisfaction and security, and eventually changes the lifetime habits.

Orange Marmalade

1 envelope unflavored gelatine
½ cup (125 ml) cold water
1 cup (250 ml) boiling water
1 6-ounce (188 ml) can frozen
    orange juice concentrate

1 teaspoon (5 ml) orange rind
1 teaspoon (5 ml) lemon rind

In the blender, soften the gelatine with cold water. Pour in the boiling water and blend to dissolve. Blend in the other ingredients and pour into a small jam jar. When set, it spreads like jam. One sixth is a Fruit Portion. Use it on low-fat cottage cheese on toast, or use it as a spread for a cheese or ham sandwich.

Apricot or Pineapple Jam

1 envelope unflavored gelatine
1 large can crushed pineapple
    in its own juice or

1 large can low calorie diet
    apricots

Soften the gelatine in ½ cup (125 ml) liquid from the can of fruit. Heat to dissolve. Combine with the fruit in the blender. Keep the blending brief to retain some texture. Pour into a pint (500 ml) jar and store in the refrigerator. The jam counts for 4 Fruit Portions.

Very Berry Jam (Strawberry, Red Raspberry, Blackberry or Blueberry)

1 quart (1 liter) fresh ripe
    berries, or 1 quart (1 liter)
    frozen without sugar, and
    thawed
1 cup water

1 envelope appropriate berry-
    flavored diet gelatine
Sweetener to equal ¼ cup (62
    ml) sugar
1 teaspoon (5 ml) lemon juice

Simmer the berries in the water. Add the gelatine, sweetener and lemon juice, stirring until the gelatine is completely dissolved. Pour into a pint (500 ml) jar (the berries cook down). Refrigerate. One-eighth is a Fruit Portion, tastes like concentrated summer glory!

31
SAUCES, GRAVY AND TOPPINGS

Country Chili Sauce

1 large can of tomatoes
1 green pepper, seeded and chopped
⅛ teaspoon (.6 ml) red hot pepper
Sweetener to equal ½ cup (125 ml) brown sugar*
¼ cup (63 ml) vinegar
½ teaspoon (2.5 ml) salt
⅛ teaspoon (.6 ml) black pepper

⅛ teaspoon (.6 ml) allspice
⅛ teaspoon (.6 ml) cloves
⅛ teaspoon (.6 ml) ginger
⅛ teaspoon (.6 ml) nutmeg
½ teaspoon (2.5 ml) celery seed
½ teaspoon (2.5 ml) dry mustard
½ cup (125 ml) onion, chopped
1 cup (250 ml) applesauce, unsweetened
½ teaspoon (2.5 ml) cinnamon

Simmer all the ingredients until thick, stirring frequently. It makes 2-2/3 cups (666 ml). Four Restricted Starchy Vegetables and 2 Fruit Portions are in the recipe. Use 1/3 of it with green beans for a family dish, and you won't have to count it. Or count 1 cup as a Fruit Portion and a Restricted Starchy Vegetable.

*Brown Sugar Twin

Spaghetti Sauce

1 cup (250 ml) tomato sauce
Sweetener to equal 1 teaspoon (5 ml) sugar
½ cup (125 ml) mushrooms, chopped
¼ cup (62 ml) green pepper, chopped
¼ cup (62 ml) onion, finely chopped or 3 tablespoons (48 ml) minced onion

1 bay leaf, broken
⅛ teaspoon (.6 ml) garlic salt
½ teaspoon (2.5 ml) dried rosemary, crushed
¼ teaspoon (1.2 ml) dried basil or 2 leaves fresh basil
⅛ teaspoon (.6 ml) dried oregano or 2 leaves fresh oregano
½ packet beef bouillon powder

Mix and simmer 15 minutes. If desired, add 6 ounces (170 g) cooked and crumbled beef chuck to serve over 1 can of bean sprouts, drained, rinsed, heated in fresh water and drained again. I like plain spaghetti sauce on top of low-fat cottage cheese. Try it. One cup furnishes the Restricted Starchy Vegetable and your day's tomato juice.

Zingy Barbecue Baste

1 8-ounce (250 ml) can tomato sauce
Sweetener to equal 1 teaspoon brown sugar*
1 tablespoon (16 ml) dried onion flakes or 1 ounce onion, chopped
Dash (.3 ml) of cloves
Dash (.3 ml) of allspice
⅛ teaspoon (.6 ml) cinnamon

⅛ teaspoon (.6 ml) dry mustard
Dash (.3 ml) of garlic salt
2 tablespoons (31 ml) vinegar
¼ cup (62 ml) green pepper, chopped
1 tablespoon (16 ml) liquid smoke, or 1 tablespoon (16 ml) Worcestershire sauce, or 1 tablespoon (16 ml) soy sauce

Mix together and simmer 10 minutes. Use on fish, poultry or a toasted cheese sandwich. Two ounces (62 ml) is a Restricted Starchy Vegetable, but if you haven't had your tomato juice today, use all you wish, up to 1 cup (250 ml)!

*Brown Sugar Twin

Sweet and Sassy Barbecue Sauce

1 cup (250 ml) crushed pineapple, in its own juice
1 teaspoon (5 ml) mustard
Dash (.3 ml) of cloves

¼ teaspoon (1.2 ml) ginger
Sweetener to equal 1 teaspoon
  (5 ml) brown sugar*

Mix and simmer 15 minutes. Use on beef, ham, pork, chicken or turkey. Baste with it when you're cooking out, or serve it at the table. Two Fruit Portions for basting a whole family's meat course should be divided accordingly. Just enjoy it and eat slowly.

*Brown Sugar Twin

Basting Sauce

½ cup (125 ml) crushed pineapple, in its own juice
¼ cup (62 ml) wine vinegar
1 tablespoon (16 ml) fresh
  parsley, chopped, or 1 teaspoon dried parsley
Sweetener to equal 1 teaspoon
  (5 ml) brown sugar

1 teaspoon (5 ml) soy sauce or
  liquid smoke flavor
⅛ teaspoon (.6 ml) garlic salt
½ teaspoon (2.5 ml) prepared
  mustard

The sauce only counts one Fruit Portion.

Cheese Sauce

2 slices thin white bread or
  1 slice regular white bread
½ cup (125 ml) skim milk

1 ounce (28 g) of your favorite
  hard cheese

Blend the three ingredients in the blender. Cook on low heat, stirring constantly on top of the stove, using a small pan. Add 1½ ounces (42 g) of tuna or crabmeat to make a full lunch protein, or use it for "macaroni" and cheese, with rinsed bean sprouts or cauliflower for the "macaroni." A rich sauce enhances any vegetable, but it limits the portion size.

"Hollandaise" Sauce

1 cup (227 g or 250 ml)
  low-fat cottage cheese
3 tablespoons (41 ml) lemon
  juice
1 egg

½ teaspoon (2.5 ml) prepared
  mustard
⅛ teaspoon (.6 ml) seasoned
  salt
⅛ teaspoon (.6 ml) salt

Here's a gourmet sauce that doesn't even have to be cooked. Blend it smooth and pour over hot cauliflower or broccoli. It amounts to 6 ounces (170 g) of protein when served at dinner. For a family of 6, just deduct one ounce of protein from your meat allowance. You'll love your "vegies" this way. If you want more than one helping, deduct accordingly from your meat protein.

Seafood Cocktail Sauce

8 ounces (250 ml) tomato sauce
1 tablespoon (16 ml)
  horseradish
1 tablespoon (16 ml) lemon
  juice

Sweetener to equal 1 tablespoon (16 ml) sugar

Mix the ingredients and serve over shrimp, crabmeat or lobster in a lettuce-lined low glass. This serves 2, and each dieter may count it as replacing 8 ounces (250 ml) of tomato juice. Then you may still have your Restricted Starchy Vegetable with the meat course.

Tartar Sauce

1 cup (250 ml) evaporated
  skim milk
2 tablespoons (31 ml) vinegar
2 tablespoons (31 ml) lemon
  juice
Sweetener to equal 1 tablespoon (16 ml) sugar

1 teaspoon (5 ml) dill weed
1 teaspoon (5 ml) prepared
  mustard
1 tablespoon (16 ml) onion
  flakes

Blend together until light and thick. Count 2 cups (500 ml) of milk. Your portion may be ¼ of the recipe, or ½ a milk allowance.

Cauliflower Cream Sauce

1 10-ounce (283 ml) package
  frozen cauliflower or ½ head
  fresh cauliflower
1 packet chicken bouillon
  powder
1 cup (250 ml) water

1 tablespoon (16 ml) onion
  flakes
½ cup (125 ml) evaporated
  skim milk for thin cream
  sauce or 2/3 cup (83 ml) nonfat dry milk for thick sauce

Cook the cauliflower until soft with the bouillon, water and onion
flakes. Puree them together in the blender, adding the milk. This
cream sauce may be the basis of your own favorite soup. For instance, just add mushrooms. Or pour it over fish before baking to
keep the fish moist. Try adding cheese and/or crabmeat! The sauce
itself accounts for 1 milk allowance.

Good Gravy!

2 slices thin white bread or
  1 slice regular white bread
½ cup (125 ml) chicken or
  turkey or beef broth,
  skimmed of fat*

1 teaspoon (5 ml) appropriate
  bouillon powder (beef,
  chicken, vegetable, onion,
  tomato)
Dash (.3 ml) of pepper

Combine all ingredients in the blender. Cook in a small pan on top
of the stove at low heat, stirring constantly. Count 1 bread allowance. Use half and you still may use a thin slice of toast.

*The only way to remove all the fat from drippings or broth is to refrigerate it so you can
remove the solid fat entirely.

Wild Blackberry Fruit Sauce

1 quart (1 liter) long blackberries, frozen in late July
  and early August, thawed out
  of season

Sweetener to equal 3 tablespoons (48 ml) sugar
1 cup (250 ml) unsweetened
  pineapple juice

Enhance the thawed berries with the sweetener and pineapple juice.
One-half cup costs you 1 Fruit Portion but used economically,
they're free. You're the child of a King, and cared for like a Princess!

Fruit Topping for Low-fat Cottage Cheese or Yogurt

1 cup (250 ml) crushed pineapple, in its own juice
1 cup (250 ml) red raspberries,
   strawberries, or blueberries
1 small banana, sliced
Sweetener to equal 3 tablespoons (48 ml) sugar

1 teaspoon (5 ml) rum or
   almond extract
½ teaspoon (2.5 ml) orange
   rind, grated

Mix the fruits very lightly with the sweetener, flavoring and orange rind. Your portion is still ½ cup (125 ml) of fruit, but look at the variety and class it lends to cottage cheese and yogurt!

Whipped Cheese Topping

1 cup (227 g or 250 ml)
   low-fat cottage cheese
Sweetener to equal 2 tablespoons (31 ml) sugar
2 tablespoons (31 ml) pineapple juice

1 teaspoon (5 ml) lemon rind
⅛ teaspoon (.6 ml) nutmeg
2 tablespoons (31 ml) lemon
   juice

This topping is formed by turning the blender on and off patiently until the mixture is smooth and stands in peaks. It's a perfect topping for fruit and gelatine desserts; appropriate for sparkling parfaits, puddings, cream pies and cake frosting. The recipe equals 4 ounces (113 g) of protein, ⅛ of it is harmless.

32
SNACKS

Cauliflower "Popcorn"

1 tablespoon (16 ml) vinegar
1 tablespoon (16 ml) lemon
   juice
2 tablespoons (31 ml) water

Sweetener to equal 1 tablespoon (16 ml) sugar
1 head cauliflower broken into
   florets

Combine the vinegar, lemon juice, water, and sweetener . Sprinkle over the uncooked florets. It's pleasant and crunchy. Double the pleasure as you succeed. Cauliflower is an Unrestricted "Vegie."

Cucumber "Cookies"

2 cucumbers
Score the cucumbers with the tines of a fork. Slice the thickness of cookies. Enjoy freely, with more crunch to the bunch than the best cookies you remember. These leave you with a fresh mouth and no depression or guilt.

Frothy Fruit Gelatine

1 envelope any flavor diet
  gelatine
1 cup (250 ml) boiling water
1 teaspoon (5 ml) grated lemon
  rind

1 cup (250 ml) buttermilk
Sweetener to equal 1 teaspoon
  (5 ml) sugar

Dissolve the gelatine with the boiling water. Cool until syrupy. Beat in 1 cup buttermilk with sweetener until frothy. Refrigerate. Count only 1 cup of milk from your daily allowance.

Heavenly Fluff

1 envelope any flavor diet
  gelatine
1 cup (250 ml) hot water
Sweetener to equal 1 tablespoon sugar
3 tablespoons (41 ml) lemon
  juice

1 cup (250 ml) evaporated skim
  milk, chilled or 2/3 cup (166
  ml) dry milk whipped with
  ½ cup (125 ml) water
1 teaspoon (5 ml) vanilla
1 teaspoon (5 ml) lemon rind

Combine first 4 ingredients. Stir until the gelatine dissolves. Refrigerate for 20 minutes. Beat the milk until it stands in peaks like whipped cream. Add vanilla, cooled gelatine mixture and lemon rind, beating until smooth and fluffy. The recipe contains 2 milk allowances, but it makes a huge bowlful. Snack on the whole thing, considering it as your day's milk.

33
SOUPS

New England Clam Chowder

10 ounces (283 g) frozen cauliflower or half a head of fresh
cauliflower, diced to re-
semble potato
½ cup (125 ml) onion, chopped
1 stalk celery, chopped
1½ cups (375 ml) water
1-1/3 cups (333 ml) nonfat
dry milk

Dash (.3 ml) of ground cloves
Dash (.3 ml) of cayenne pepper
1 teaspoon (5 ml) dill weed
6 ounces (170 g) minced or
chopped clams, canned, including liquid
4 ounces (125 ml) mushrooms,
canned, including liquid

Cook cauliflower, onion, and celery in water until tender. Drain
liquid, which is rich in vitamins, into blender. Add nonfat dry milk
and seasonings. Blend. Combine liquid, cauliflower, clams and
mushrooms in the original saucepan, and heat until steaming. Do
not boil. You may have 2 (500 ml) of the 4 cups (1 liter) of chowder,
providing half your lunch protein, and 2 milk allowances.

Manhattan Clam Chowder

1 10-ounce (283 g) package
   frozen cauliflower, or half a
   head fresh cauliflower, diced
   to resemble potato
½ cup (125 ml) onion, chopped
2 cups (500 ml) tomato juice
1 ounce (28 g) white bread,
   crumbled
6 ounces (170 g) minced or
   chopped clams, canned, including liquid

1 pimento, canned with water,
   chopped
Dash (.3 ml) of garlic salt
⅛ teaspoon (.6 ml) celery salt
1 tablespoon (16 ml) parsley,
   dried, for garnish

Cook the cauliflower and onion in the tomato juice until tender. Drain the hot tomato juice into the blender. Add crumbled bread and blend to thicken the chowder. Combine the tomato juice, clams, vegetables and seasonings in the original saucepan. Simmer 5 minutes, and serve 4 cups, garnished with parsley. Two cups supply ½ your lunch protein, ¼ the bread allowance, and 8 ounces of tomato juice.

Cold Seafood Soup

6 ounces (170 g) crabmeat,
   shrimp, lobster, or clams,
   canned, including liquid
2 cups (500 ml) buttermilk
Dash (.3 ml) of garlic salt
½ cup (125 ml) green pepper,
   seeded and diced

½ cup (125 ml) Spanish onion,
   chopped
1 teaspoon (5 ml) dill weed
1 cucumber with skin, diced
½ cup (125 ml) tomatoes, diced

Combine all the ingredients and serve chilled. Of the 4 cups (1 liter), 2 supply ½ your lunch protein and 1 milk allowance, an outstanding marriage of flavors and textures.

Gazpacho

3 tomatoes, unpeeled and diced
1 cucumber, unpeeled and
 diced
1 green pepper, seeded and
 diced
1 small onion, diced
1 stalk celery, chopped
1 cup (250 ml) tomato juice
1 tablespoon (16 ml) lemon
 juice
2 tablespoons (31 ml) vinegar
1 egg
⅛ teaspoon (.6 ml) cayenne
 pepper
⅛ teaspoon (.6 ml) basil
Dash (.3 ml) of oregano
1 tablespoon (16 ml) fresh
 parsley
Dash (.3 ml) of garlic powder

Did you know that this is a liquid salad originating in Spain? To save time, you may chop the vegetables in the blender by turning it on and off briefly once or twice, using the tomato juice for liquid. Serve chilled on a hot day. Except for the egg, everything in the recipe is Unrestricted "Vegies"! Consider the 3 tomatoes part of your daily tomato juice.

Tomato Soup

8 ounces (250 ml) tomato juice
⅛ teaspoon (.6 ml) oregano
¼ teaspoon (1.2 ml) garlic salt
¼ teaspoon (1.2 ml) onion salt
1 tablespoon (16 ml) chives,
 dried
1 tablespoon (16 ml) parsley,
 dried
Sweetener to equal 1 tablespoon (16 ml) sugar
8 ounces (250 ml) buttermilk

Heat the tomato juice with the spices, herbs, and sweetener. Add buttermilk, heating only one minute longer to prevent curdling. There is no hidden starchy thickener in this soup. It's easy to account for your 1 glass of milk and 8 ounces of tomato juice. Two cups (500 ml) will surely fill your cravings and empty spaces! Toast "crackers" are a fine accompaniment, or try an open-faced cheese sandwich, broiled.

Broccoli Cheese Soup

1 10-ounce (283 g) package
frozen broccoli or 1 small
head of fresh broccoli
1 packet chicken bouillon
powder with
2 cups (500 ml) water
1 ounce white bread, torn in
pieces

1/3 cup (83 ml) nonfat dry milk
1 tablespoon (16 ml) lemon
juice
2 ounces (57 g) Cheddar cheese
⅛ teaspoon (.6 ml) onion salt
¼ of a red roasted pepper

Cook the broccoli in the chicken bouillon until bright green. Combine in the blender with the other ingredients, except for the red pepper. Slice it and float it for a garnish on top as you serve in your best soup bowls. The recipe serves 2, providing each with 1 ounce (28 g) of cheese and half a milk allowance.

Cheese Bouillon

1 packet bouillon powder of
your choice: chicken, beef,
vegetable, tomato or onion
(cubes are acceptable)

1½ cups (375 ml) boiling
water
6 ounces (170 g or 188 ml)
cottage cheese

Package directions for the bouillon suggest using 1 cup (250 ml) of water to dissolve 1 packet, but the solution is too salty for dieters. You may be satisfied to dilute it by using 1½ cups (375 ml) water per packet as indicated in this simple recipe. Serve 2 cups, each ¾ (188 ml) full. Drop 3 ounces (85 g or 94 ml) of low-fat cottage cheese in each. You will be delighted with contrast in color, temperature, texture and flavor; a quick and hearty protein soup. It's so filling and delicious, you may need to be reminded to eat your "vegies." You may have 2 cups for lunch!

Pretend Pea Soup

1 large can French green beans,
  or 1 pound fresh green beans,
  cooked, including liquid
1 large can asparagus, or 1
  pound fresh asparagus,
  cooked, including liquid
1 small carrot, chopped
1 green pepper, seeded and
  diced

¼ teaspoon (1.2 ml) basil
¼ teaspoon (1.2 ml) thyme
Dash (.3 ml) of garlic salt
3 peppercorns
3 whole cloves
¼ teaspoon (1.2 ml) celery salt
1 bay leaf, broken
1 ham bone, trimmed of fat

Puree the asparagus and French green beans in the blender with their liquid. Simmer with the other vegetables, seasonings, and ham bone for 2 hours. Makes an amazing facsimile of pea soup! The 4 cups (1 liter) are Unrestricted "Vegies", the small carrot being negligible.

Vichyssoise

10 ounces (283 g) frozen cauliflower or ½ head of fresh
  cauliflower
1 cup (250 ml) water
1 packet chicken bouillon
  powder
1/3 cup (83 ml) nonfat dry milk
3 tablespoons (48 ml) onion
  flakes

1 teaspoon (5 ml) salt
1 tablespoon (16 ml) parsley,
  dried
3 tablespoons (48 ml) chives,
  dried
½ teaspoon (2.5 ml) paprika for
  garnish

Cook the cauliflower with the water and bouillon until tender. Puree with the cooking liquid in the blender. Add powdered skim milk, onion flakes and salt. Blend until smooth. Add parsley and chives without blending. Chill. Serve cold, garnished with more chives and paprika. You won't believe this is a facsimile.

Bicentennial Zucchini Soup

4 cups (1 liter) cooked zucchini
   squash, drained
8 ounces (250 ml) tomato sauce
½ teaspoon (2.5 ml) basil
½ teaspoon (2.5 ml) garlic salt

½ teaspoon (2.5 ml) oregano
½ teaspoon (2.5 ml) onion salt
1 tablespoon (7 g or 16 ml)
   grated cheese

Blend all the ingredients in the blender. Serve this rosy-red soup hot or cold in blue soup mugs, using white napkins to complete the effect. This soup may be frozen. Leave about an inch of space at the top of the jar for expansion. Blend again when thawed. The entire recipe includes one day's tomato juice and 1 ounce (7 grams) of hard cheese. (Grated cheese is dehydrated.)

Rescue Soup

Unlimited vegetables, fresh,
   frozen or canned, finely cut
   (cabbage, celery, green
   beans, mushrooms, peppers,
   cauliflower, broccoli, asparagus, yellow beans)

12 ounces (375 ml) tomato juice
2 cups (500 ml) water
1 bouillon cube, any flavor
1 onion, chopped
1 carrot, sliced

Simmer the cut vegetables with the tomato juice, water, bouillon cube, onion, and carrot until they are soft and the flavors blend, about 1½ hours. Enjoy this safe, filling soup freely. The Restricted Starchy Vegetables are negligible in 2 quarts (2 liters) of soup.

Cock-a-Doodle Sunshine Soup

2 small summer squashes, diced, or 1 pound yellow beans

1 cup (250 ml) water

1 packet chicken bouillon powder

2 tablespoons (31 ml) lemon juice

⅛ teaspoon (.6 ml) salt

1 tablespoon (16 ml) fresh parsley

Cook the squash in the water and bouillon. Blend to a coarse texture together in the blender. When cooled, add lemon juice and salt. Chill. Serve with parsley garnish. This bright soup is an adventure in taste and temperature, as well as color. An Unrestricted "Vegie"!

34
VEGIES

Mixed Vegetables with Pea Pods

10 ounces (283 g) frozen pearl onions

1 packet chicken bouillon powder

1 cup (250 ml) water

10 ounces (283 g) frozen peas

1 cup (250 ml) celery, diced

8 ounces (250 ml) fresh pea pods

1 can sliced carrots, drained

First, drop the onions in the bouillon and water. When partly cooked, add peas, then celery, then pea pods. Last, add the carrots to heat through. Break the vegetable monotony with contrasting colors, textures, and flavors. The combination will serve 8 whole cup (250 ml) portions, including both Restricted Starchy Vegetables and Unrestricted "Vegies." If you don't need that many servings for your family, it will be ready for tomorrow night.

Hungarian Cauliflower

10 ounces (283 g) frozen
  cauliflower
1 teaspoon (5 ml) onion salt
1 teaspoon (5 ml) parsley flakes

½ cup (125 ml) plain yogurt
1 ounce (28 g) bread, crumbled
  in blender
1 teaspoon (5 ml) paprika

Cook the cauliflower and drain it. Prepare a shallow baking dish
with *Pam*. Put the cooked cauliflower in the baking dish. Add the
onion salt and parsley flakes to the yogurt, and spread over the
cauliflower. Sprinkle bread crumbs and paprika on top. Bake at
400°F (204°C) for 10 minutes. The recipe is unrestricted except for
1 bread allowance and ½ cup (125 ml) of milk. This is a good recipe
for a hungry day alone at home. Add protein for the beautiful
balance.

Cauliflower "Mashed Potatoes"

1 large head cauliflower (or
  2 10-ounce (283 g) packages
  frozen cauliflower) cut to
  cook efficiently
2 cups (500 ml) water
1 packet chicken bouillon
  powder

2/3 cup (166 ml) nonfat dry
  milk
1 tablespoon (16 ml) fresh
  parsley, chopped and ½ teaspoon (2.5 ml) paprika for
  garnish

Cook the cauliflower in the bouillon and water until soft. Puree it
in the blender, using as little liquid as possible. Start and stop the
blender, urging the cauliflower into the blades only in the "off"
position. Add nonfat dry milk, blending until smooth and white
like mashed potatoes. Serve with parsley and paprika for garnish.
The "potatoes" are unlimited, except that the entire recipe includes
2 milk allowances. They are versatile, laced with crabmeat or tuna.

Spaghetti Squash

1 ripe spaghetti squash
16 ounces (500 ml) tomato
  sauce
Sweetener to equal 1/3 cup (83
  ml) sugar
1 teaspoon (5 ml) garlic salt
1 teaspoon (5 ml) oregano

1 teaspoon (5 ml) basil
1 teaspoon (5 ml) fennel seed
1 teaspoon (5 ml) crushed
  rosemary
8 ounces (227 g) ground beef
  round or chuck, cooked
  crumbly and drained of fat

Spaghetti squash is a newly developed hybrid with characteristic spaghetti-like strands. It may be boiled whole or baked, after puncturing, so that it won't explode in the oven. Bake at 350°F (176°C) for 45 minutes until soft. The seeds may be eaten or discarded. Let it cool for easier handling. Scrape the strands away from the skin. Add tomato sauce and remaining ingredients. It's fantastic hot or cold. Use up to 1/3 as a Restricted Starchy Vegetable plus tomato juice allowance for the day. That portion borrows half your dinner protein.

"Sweet Potato" Squash

1 package frozen winter squash
1 tablespoon (16 ml) frozen
  orange juice concentrate
1 tablespoon (16 ml) frozen
  pineapple juice concentrate
⅛ teaspoon (.6 ml) salt

Dash (.3 ml) of black pepper,
  freshly ground
¼ teaspoon (1.2 ml) cinnamon
Dash (.3 ml) of nutmeg
½ navel orange, thinly sliced

Thaw the frozen ingredients to mix thoroughly. Add the spices and place in a small baking dish prepared with Pam. Garnish with orange slices. Bake at 325°F (162°C) for 25 minutes. One-half cup is a Restricted Starchy Vegetable.

Mexican Summer Squash

1 medium summer squash, diced (about 10 ounces [313 ml])
1 cup (250 ml) chicken bouillon
1 tablespoon (16 ml) green pepper, chopped
1 tablespoon (16 ml) water packed red roasted peppers, chopped
½ teaspoon (2.5 ml) chili powder

Cook the squash in the bouillon until almost soft. Add the green pepper, cooking only until it turns bright green. Lastly, add the red peppers and chili powder. This tasty dish is of Unrestricted "Vegies."

Eggplant Lasagna

1 medium eggplant, peeled and sliced (about 3 cups [750 ml] raw, 2 cups [500 ml] cooked)
2 cups (500 ml) water
1 bay leaf
1 medium zucchini, sliced
2 green peppers, seeded and chopped
1 can water-packed roasted peppers, drained and sliced
2 cups (500 ml) tomato sauce enhanced with:
Dash (.3 ml) of oregano
Dash (.3 ml) of garlic salt
1/3 cup (83 ml) fresh parsley, chopped finely, and
1 medium onion, finely chopped
8 ounces (227 g) Muenster cheese

Cook the eggplant in the water with bay leaf until soft. Drain. Discard the bay leaf. Cook zucchini and green peppers in 1 cup (250 ml) of water. Drain. Prepare a lasagna pan with *Pam*. Layer the eggplant, zucchini, red and green peppers and cheese, spreading tomato sauce on each layer. Bake at 350°F (176°C) for 20 minutes. One-eighth of the recipe accounts for your Restricted Starchy Vegetable. Deduct 2 ounces (57 g) from your protein portion. Let the family enjoy this with you. Eat your portion slowly and be careful—no seconds.

Chumbut (Italian Vegetable Stew)

1 medium eggplant, diced with skin
1 medium zucchini, diced with seeds and skin
1 clove garlic
2 medium onions, diced
2 green peppers, diced

24 ounces (750 ml) tomato sauce
1 teaspoon (5 ml) oregano
3 sprigs fresh Italian parsley, finely chopped, or
1 teaspoon (5 ml) dried parsley

Cook the fresh vegetables together until soft and transparent. Drain. Add tomato sauce, oregano and parsley. Simmer for ½ hour to blend flavors. Discard garlic clove. Serve hot or cold, using 1 full cup (250 ml) to furnish the Restricted Starchy Vegetable portion, instead of the usual ½ cup allowance. You may add cheese or ground chuck or veal for meat allowance at night.

Tomato Zucchini Stew

6 ripe tomatoes, peeled and quartered (Have you discovered how easy it is to peel tomatoes after running boiling water over them?)
1 medium zucchini squash, cubed
2 medium onions, chopped

1 cup (250 ml) celery, chopped
2 green peppers, seeded and diced
1 cup (250 ml) tomato juice
1 teaspoon (5 ml) salt
Dash (.3 ml) of garlic salt
Dash (.3 ml) of oregano

Mix and simmer together long and slowly in a crock pot. Serve hot or cold. Count 6 fruits and 1 Restricted Starchy Vegetable, or 8 Restricted Starchy Vegetable portions. The choice is because the tomato may be used either as a fruit or a vegetable.

Stuffed Celery

1 cup (250 ml) diet sandwich
   spread of your choice:
   cream cheese, egg salad, tuna
   salad (or shrimp, salmon,
   mackerel, crab, or sardine)
   liver pate
   giblet cocktail spread

1 bunch of crisp celery, washed
   and cut in 6-inch (15 cm)
   pieces

Stuff the celery. Cut into smaller bite-sized pieces. The celery is un-limited, but deduct from your protein allowance for the sandwich spread stuffing, according to your own good judgment.

Cheddar Peppers

4 green peppers
½ cup (125 ml) water
2 ounces (57 g) bread, crumbled
1 8-ounce (250 ml) can mushrooms, drained and sliced
4 ounces (113 g) cheddar
   cheese, cubed or shredded

1 teaspoon (5 ml) minced onion
   flakes
Dash (.3 ml) of garlic salt
1 cup (250 ml) tomato juice

Saute the peppers until bright green in water. Drain and stuff with a mixture of the remaining ingredients. Bake at 350°F (176°C) for 25 minutes. The recipe serves 2 for lunch.

Red Cabbage Casserole (German)

1 small head red cabbage, chopped finely in 4 cups (62 ml) water in the blender, (half at a time)
¼ cup (62 ml) onion flakes
1/3 cup (83 ml) vinegar
Sweetener to equal 1/3 cup brown sugar*
1 tablespoon (16 ml) bacon flavoring

1 cup (250 ml) applesauce without sugar
½ teaspoon (2.5 ml) cinnamon
Dash (.3 ml) of cloves
Dash (.3 ml) of nutmeg
4 ounces (125 ml) water chestnuts, chopped

Cook the cabbage in the water in which cabbage was chopped. Drain. Add remaining ingredients except water chestnuts. Simmer to blend flavors, about 15 minutes. Add water chestnuts. Serve hot. The recipe contains 2 Fruit Portions and 2 Restricted Starchy Vegetable servings. You can afford seconds of up to half of the recipe!

*Brown Sugar Twin

Country Cabbage

1 small head of cabbage
2 teaspoons (10 ml) seasoned salt
3 cups (750 ml) water

8 ounces (227 g) cheddar cheese
¼ cup (62 ml) skim milk

Cook the cabbage in the salt and water in a large pan for about 20 minutes until the cabbage is chewy. Meanwhile, melt the cheese in a double boiler with the milk. Drain cabbage and place in a 1-quart casserole dish sprayed with Pam. Pour the cheese and milk over the cabbage and bake at 325°F (162°C) for 45 minutes, until cabbage is tender. The recipe serves four for lunch. If you use it for dinner protein, deduct 1 ounce (28 g) from your regular allowance, using ¼ of the recipe.

Swiss Chard

1 grocery bag full of fresh cut Swiss chard, thoroughly washed
1 cup (250 ml) water
1/3 cup (83 ml) vinegar
Sweetener to equal 1/3 cup (83 ml) sugar
½ teaspoon (2.5 ml) salt
Dash (.3 ml) of pepper
Dash (.3 ml) of garlic salt

Cut the chard coarsely. Cook with the water until it wilts down to one-fourth the size of the raw leaves. Add the other ingredients. Serve hot or cold. Another way is to use Good Seasons Diet Italian Dressing on drained cooked chard. This is a delightful unlimited vegetable, excellent to prepare ahead for quick meals. When you cut it in the garden, without pulling out the roots, it grows back again to please you. It is milder tasting than spinach, and a little lighter in color. Italian restaurants often include Swiss chard in their luncheon salad bar.

Parsleyed Turnips

4 young turnips, peeled and sliced (2 cups [500 ml])
1 envelope chicken bouillon powder
1 cup (250 ml) water
3 drops butter flavoring in ½ cup (125 ml) evaporated skim milk
1/3 cup (83 ml) dried parsley
½ teaspoon (2.5 ml) paprika

Drop the turnips in the bouillon and water. Cook until soft, about 20 minutes. Drain. Add butter flavored milk and parsley. Garnish with paprika. One-fourth accounts for a Restricted Starchy Vegetable serving; milk is negligible.

Baby Beets with Greens

8 young beets with greens
2 cups (500 ml) water
1/3 cup (83 ml) vinegar
Sweetener to equal 1/3 cup
   (83 ml) sugar

¼ teaspoon (1.2 ml) salt
Dash (.3 ml) of pepper

Cut the beets from the greens. Scrub them and boil until tender in 1 cup (250 ml) water. Wash the greens, dousing thoroughly in a full sink of water. Drain and chop coarsely. Cook until brightly colored and soft in 1 cup (250 ml) water. When the beets are cooled, slip the skins off, discarding with the liquid. Slice and add to the greens with vinegar and sweetener. Add salt and pepper last. Toss and serve hot or cold. Both the beets and greens are a Restricted Starchy Vegetable. The three cups furnish 6 portions, so be discreet.

Cucumber Roll-Ups

½ cup (125 ml) diet sandwich
   spread of your choice:
   cream cheese, egg salad, tuna
   salad (or shrimp, salmon,
   mackerel, crab, or sardine)
   liver pate

giblet cocktail spread
1 medium cucumber, sliced
   lengthwise thinly

Spread the cucumber slices with the desired filling. Roll up from end to end. Fasten each cucumber roll with a toothpick. An easier approach is to spoon the filling on round slices of cucumber. It's still a fancy hors d'oeuvre. The cucumber is an Unrestricted "Vegie," but the filling is part of your protein allowance. Rely on your built-in calculator, the Internal Instructor.

Herbed Artichokes

10 ounces (313 ml) water
  packed or frozen (283 g) arti-
  choke hearts
Dash (.3 ml) of garlic salt
2 teaspoons (10 ml) chives,
  freshly snipped
1 teaspoon (5 ml) fresh sweet
  marjoram

1 teaspoon (5 ml) fresh orange
  mint, chopped finely
1 teaspoon (5 ml) fresh
  tarragon, finely cut
½ cup (125 ml) yogurt

Drain the artichokes, or cook the frozen ones, drain and cool. Stir
the herbs into the yogurt and marinate the artichokes. Serve cold.
The recipe includes 3 servings of a Restricted Starchy Vegetable.
The milk allowance is negligible.

As you can see from our creative, low-calorie recipes, dieters need
not be "disadvantaged!" In fact, when your life includes the Basic
Ingredient, the love of Jesus, you will be richer and healthier in
body, soul and spirit than you've ever been before!

Becomers, unite! Maintainers, stand firm!

APPENDIX A.
SEEING = BELIEVING = BECOMING

Dotted line: My potential for losing twenty pounds in ten weeks
Solid line: My actual progress in becoming

Lbs.	Starting Weight	Weekly Losses	1	2	3	4	5	6	7	8	9	10
1												
2												
3												
4												
5												
6												
7												
8												
9												
10												
11												
12												
13												
14												
15												
16												
17												
18												
19												
20												

In this column make comments about your attitudes and feelings as you lose weight.

Record your starting weight at the head of the first column. Then fill in the 20 pounds by counting backward. See, believe, become!

APPENDIX B.
CALORIE COUNT FOR A TYPICAL MENU
OF THE BECOMER'S BALANCED DIET FOR WEIGHT LOSS*

Breakfast:	*Calories*
4 ounces grapefruit juice, unsweetened	50
1 egg, soft boiled or poached	80
1 ounce whole grain or enriched bread	80
coffee, no milk or cream	00

Lunch:	
3 ounces light meat tuna, oil pack, drained (water pack would be even less, but more costly)	170
1 ounce whole grain or enriched bread	80
1 cup Unrestricted "Vegies" in tossed salad: lettuce, cucumber, radishes, pepper	30
Medium apple, raw	70
8 ounce glass of skim milk reconstituted from non fat dry milk	80

Dinner:	
6 ounces light meat chicken without skin	250
4 ounces winter squash (Restricted Vegetable)	43
1 cup Unrestricted "Vegies": asparagus	35
½ grapefruit, pink, fully ripe and sweet enough	55
8 ounces skim milk reconstituted from non fat dry milk	80
TOTAL	**1103 Calories**

*The Family Guide To Better Food And Better Health by Ronald M. Deutsch
  "The most acceptable, comprehensive and readable book on food and health for the layman."–Dr. Philip L. White, A.M.A.

NOTES

1. Norman Jolliffe, M.D., *Reduce and Stay Reduced on the Prudent Diet* (New York: Simon and Schuster, an Essandess paperback, 1964).

2. Theodore Berland and the Editors of *Consumer Guide, Rating the Diets*, Vol. 53 (Printed in the U.S.A.: April, 1974), p. 347.

3. Morton B. Glenn, M.D., *How to Get Thinner Once and for All* (New York: E. P. Dutton & Co., Inc., 1965; Greenwich, Conn.: Fawcett Crest Book Co., 1970).

4. Morton B. Glenn, M.D., *But I Don't Eat That Much*, (New York: E. P. Dutton & Co., Inc., 1974).

5. Order from: Slide Chart Corporation, Westchester, Pa. 19380.

6. Ogden Nash, "I Do, I Will, I Have," *Versus* (Boston: Little, Brown & Company, 1949).

7. Jean Mayer, M.D., *Human Nutrition*, (Springfield, Illinois: Charles C. Thomas, 1972).

8. In this passage from Luke (King James Version), note the word "surfeiting." Webster defines it as, "excess, crime, to take advantage, to overdo, superfluity, overabundant supply, intemperate or immoderate indulgence, as in food or drink, any morbid condition arising from excess in eating or drinking, disgust caused by excess, satiety." The King James Version here is bold, beautiful, and authoritative.

9. Lawrence Galton, *The Truth About Fiber in Your Food*, (New York: Crown, 1975).

10. Order from: Church and Dwight, Inc., Two Pennsylvania Plaza, New York, New York 10001.

11. David Reuben, M.D., *The Save Your Life Diet* (New York: Random House, 1975).

12. Galton, *The Truth About Fiber in Your Food*.

13. From "America the Beautiful" by Katherine Lee Bates and Samuel A. Ward.

14. Glenn, *But I Don't Eat That Much*, p. 194.

15. Neil Solomon, M.D., and Sally Sheppard, *The Truth About Weight Control* (New York: Dell Publishing Co., 1971) p. 61.

16. Glenn, *But I Don't Eat That Much*, p. 174.

17. Karl Menninger, M.D., *Whatever Became of Sin?* (New York: Hawthorn Books, Inc., 1973) p. 91.

18. Theodore Isaac Rubin, M.D., *Forever Thin* (New York: Bernard Geis Associates, 1970) p. 105.

19. Leslie Weatherhead, M.D., *The Resurrection of Christ* (Nashville: Abingdon, 1959).

20. Maltbie Davenport Babcock, "Give Us This Day Our Daily Bread," *Familiar Quotations*, John Bartlett Eleventh Edition Revised and Enlarged (Boston: Little, Brown, and Co., 1940) p. 731.

21. *Graded Rounds and Catches*, Curwen Edition 6079 (J. Curwen & Son, Ltd.) A round used by the Girl Scouts and Girl Guides throughout the world.

22. *The Book of Common Prayer*. Collect for Purity used by the Protestant Episcopal Church in America.

BIBLIOGRAPHY

Berland, Theodore, and the Editors of *Consumer Guide. Rating the Diets*, Vol. 53 (Printed in the U.S.A.: Publications International, Ltd., 1974).

Bennett, Iva, and Simon, Martha. *The Prudent Diet*. New York: David White, 1973.

Butterick, George A. *So We Believe So We Pray*. New York and Nashville: Abingdon Press, 1950.

Clark, Glen. *How to Find Health Through Prayer*. New York: Harper & Brothers, 1940.

Cooper, Kenneth H. *Aerobics*. New York: M. Evans and Company, Inc., 1968.

Deutsch, Ronald M. *The Family Guide to Better Food and Better Health*. Toronto, New York, and London: Bantam 1971. *The Nuts Among The Berries*. New York: Ballantine Books, 1968. A casual commentary on misunderstandings of food faddists; recommended by the American Medical Association; foreword by Frederick J. Stare, M.D., Department of Nutrition, Harvard School of Public Health, Boston, Massachusetts.

Food and Fitness, A Report by Blue Cross, Vol. XXLV, No. 1, "Blue Print for Health". Blue Cross Association. Chicago, 1973.

Galton, Lawrence. *The Truth About Fiber In Your Food*. New York: Crown, 1975.

Glenn, Morton B., M.D. *How To Get Thinner Once And For All*. New York: E. P. Dutton & Co., Inc., 1965.

Graded Rounds and Catches, Curwen Edition 6079. J. Curwen & Son., Ltd.

Gwinup, Grant. *energetics: Your Key to Weight Control*. Los Angeles: Sherbourne Press, 1970.

Jolliffe, Norman, M.D. *Reduce And Stay Reduced on the Prudent Diet*. New York: Simon and Schuster, an Essandes paperback, 1964. Report of a seven-year study of men who used the Prudent Diet with consistent success.

Jones, Jeanne. *The Calculating Cook*. San Francisco: 101 Productions, 1972. A gourmet cookbook for diabetics and dieters.

Kelsey, Morton. *Healing And Christianity*. New York, Evanston, San Francisco; and London: Harper & Row, 1973.

Lindauer, Lois L. *It's In To Be Thin*. New York: Award Books, 1970.

Menninger, Karl, M.D. *Whatever Became Of Sin?* New York: Hawthorn Books, Inc., 1973.

Morehouse, Laurence, and Gross, Leonard. *Total Fitness in 30 Minutes A Week*. New York: Simon and Schuster, 1975.

Royal Canadian Air Force Exercise Plans for Physical Fitness. New York: Pocket Books Inc., 1976.

Rubin, Theodore Isaac, M.D. *Forever Thin*. New York: Bernard Geis Associates, 1970.

Reuben, David, M.D. *The Save Your Life Diet*. New York: Random House, 1975.

Selected Nutrition References., Massachusetts Department of Public Health, Nutrition Program, 600 Washington St., Boston, Massachusetts 02111, 1972.

Solomon, Neil, M.D., and Sheppard, Sally. *The Truth About Weight Control*. New York: Dell Publishing Co., 1971.

Sebrell, W. H., Jr., M.D., and J. J. Haggerty, and Editors of LIFE. *Food And Nutrition.* Chicago: Time Life Books, 1967. Why man needs food, the miracle of digestion, under and over nutrition, fads and frauds, food preservers by fire, spice and ice, and the race to beat famine; illustrated with colored picture essays, charts and tables.

The Book of Common Prayer. Charles Mortimer Guilbert, Custodian of the *Standard Book of Common Prayer.*

Tournier, Paul, M.D. *The Healing Of Persons.* New York, Evanston, and London: Harper & Row, 1965.

U. S., Congress, Senate, Select Committee on Nutrition and Human Needs. *Dietary Goals for the United States.* Report to 95th Cong., 1st sess., 1971.

Weatherhead, Leslie, M.D. *Psychology, Religion and Healing.* New York: Abingdon-Cokesbury Press, 1951.

—————. *The Resurrection Of Christ.* Nashville: Abingdon, 1959.